NORTHERN
HARVEST

NORTHERN HARVEST

TWENTY MICHIGAN WOMEN
IN FOOD AND FARMING

Emita Brady Hill

A PAINTED TURTLE BOOK
DETROIT, MICHIGAN

ISBN 978-0-8143-4713-3 (paperback)
ISBN 978-0-8143-4714-0 (e-book)

Library of Congress Control Number: 2019954075

Wayne State University Press
Leonard N. Simons Building
4809 Woodward Avenue
Detroit, Michigan 48201-1309

Visit us online at wsupress.wayne.edu

This book is dedicated to women in the food business:
farmers, fruit growers, chefs, bakers, cheese makers,
all the women working as prep and wait staff in all the kitchens,
and to the mothers and grandmothers who inspired them.

And to Madeleine Hill Vedel,
without whom this book would not have existed.

V

WRITERS AND TEACHERS

The Joy of Sharing

VI

TWO HOMESTEADS

Preserve the Past and Celebrate the Future

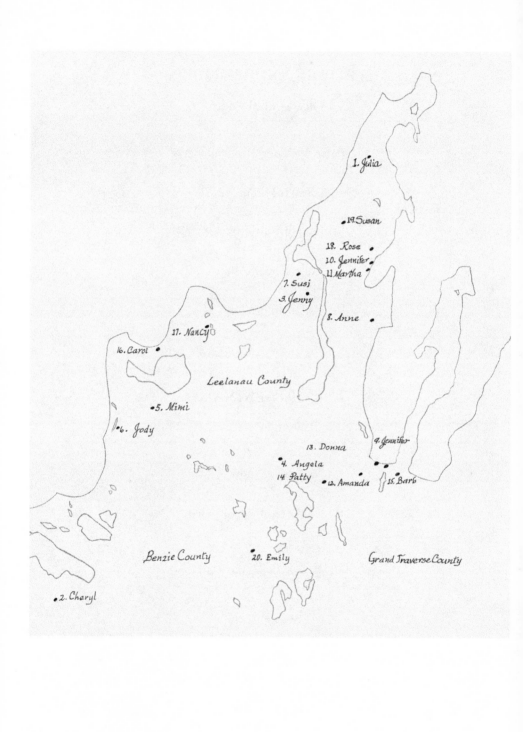

1. Julia

19. Susan

18. Rose
10. Jennifer
11. Martha

7. Susi

3. Jenny

8. Anne

17. Nancy

16. Carol

Leelanau County

5. Mimi

6. Jody

13. Donna

4. Jennifer

4. Angela

14. Patty

12. Amanda

15. Barb

Benzie County

20. Emily

Grand Traverse County

2. Cheryl

List of Enterprises

Introduction

Traverse City, Michigan, and the surrounding region today boast top-notch restaurants, diverse ethnic foods, a growing number of flourishing wineries, breweries, and cideries, and multiple farmers markets. It's a far remove from the so-called culinary wasteland of decades past. As recently as February 2019, the website of the Rowe Inn, opened in 1972, referenced that wasteland. Laurel Westhoven told me that they have since revised their website, but the memory remains.

When I first came to Traverse City as a child in the 1940s we never ate out. I remember as a highlight getting a fried egg sandwich at a drugstore. Even three decades later in the 1970s and '80s there were only a few outlier restaurants: Tapawingo and the Rowe Inn opened in Ellsworth in 1972; La Bécasse in Maple City, Leelanau County, in 1986. These excellent, ambitious restaurants served haute cuisine to a small, select clientele, but none of them was closer than an hour's drive from Traverse City, though well worth the drive. *Vaut le détour* and even *le voyage.*

Almost half a century has passed since Tapawingo, now closed, and the Rowe Inn opened their doors and three-quarters of a century since I enjoyed that egg sandwich. The transformation of this region into a culinary and agricultural Eden was a labor of love and an act of faith. This book presents the oral histories as told to me by twenty women whose dreams and hard work were central to that renaissance. While almost none were born in northern Michigan, many grew up in the southern part of the state, often in a suburb of Detroit. Some knew the northern region from vacationing with a parent or grandparent; others discovered it when they married into a family with roots there. In their stories they, too, testify to the culinary poverty of earlier decades.

Nancy Krcek Allen told me, "In 1976 when I first moved up here there was nothing. I mean, you could get potatoes and beets and cabbage locally." In 1989, more than a decade later, when Rose Hollander moved to Suttons Bay, she was "appalled" by the scarcity of ethnic foods, especially Asian foods that she had encountered while living in Asia and Northern California. Rose went downstate in search of ingredients so that she could create for herself and share with others this cuisine that she loved.

In 1972 when Donna Folgarelli moved up north from Detroit, quality Italian products such as prosciutto, Parmigiano-Reggiano, homemade pastas, and much more were unknown. Her parents sent up truckloads from downstate until she and they opened the store that has now celebrated more than forty years. "Not everyone has the accessibility to go to Europe; so we bring Europe to them."

Northern Michigan was always farm country in the pre-industrial, pre-mega-farm era when Percheron horses pulled the plows and the mechanization of farming with the million-dollar equipment from John Deere and Caterpillar was still in the future. Most of the food in my childhood was in fact locally grown and produced, but no one talked about it or used that vocabulary. Small subsistence farming was widespread, and homesteaded farms were passed down from generation to generation. Anne-Marie Oomen's memoirs and short stories, such as her *Pulling Down the Barn*, document life on one such farm.

Several forces intervened to shutter many of these farms. But, as the decades passed, cherry growers persevered, wineries began to emerge with ever better wine, and chefs in new restaurants began to source their ingredients from local farms. Today the farm-to-table movement is taken for granted. Nonexistent in the 1970s, farmers markets now abound in the region. Oryana, the food co-op that opened in 1975, counts almost seven thousand loyal members who appreciate organic produce and ingredients.

Why only women? Why not also include the histories of some remarkable male farmers, bakers, and restaurateurs in this region? When I began this project in 2015 what stood out, what needed documenting and celebrating, were the stories of women, many of whom would tell me—as do women in other areas of our society, including my sisters and me—"I was the first to . . ." "My orchard was the first to . . ." And it was true. What they accomplished at great cost over many years was inevitably the first of its kind in this region.

Julia Brabenec and her husband planted each of their 1,100 fruit trees by themselves and at the same time built their home stone by stone—an "off the grid" home, long before that term entered the language. In the 1980s they were the first organic growers of table fruit: apples and peaches. Julia wonders now, "How on earth did we ever do that?"

Cheryl Kobernik first heard of organic farming in 1999 and exclaimed, "Let's do this." It took three years to transition their cherry orchard, but by 2002 they had completed the transition, and the fame of North Star Organics cherries spread rapidly.

When Anne Hoyt and her husband started Leelanau Cheese in 1995, "We were the only cheese maker in this part of Michigan."

Angela Macke's tea farm, started in 1996, was the only certified organic and biodynamic tea farm in the entire country—unexpected in these northern climes, not your typical environment for cultivating tea plants.

Grocer's Daughter Chocolate in Empire, started by Mimi Wheeler in 2004 and continued by Jody Dotson Hayden since 2012, introduced fair trade chocolate from Ecuador to this region and coupled it with local organic products like North Star cherries to make their signature truffles.

Finally, why this region in northern Michigan, Traverse City and its surrounds, Leelanau County? That's easy. Because I was here. Because my mother was here before me; she came as a child with her family to Forest Lodge on Long Lake before 1900. Unlike the women whose stories I celebrate here, I am only a summer resident, but the roots go deep. I can count almost eighty summers. During the 1940s my older sisters picked cherries and also worked in the canning factory. My son spent several summers in the 1980s picking cherries on the peninsula, and one of my grandsons has now spent four summers harvesting cherries in Northport.

For me, it's here and it's now. History is evanescent unless it is carefully preserved, and the women who have entrusted me with their histories are here, most of them still active in raising, crafting, marketing, and promoting food that is locally and organically grown, artisanally produced, and sold at farmers markets or directly to restaurants or schools.

Several of these women worked with a single product: cherries, chocolate, or cheese. Others navigated through different culinary scenes, including working in restaurants, before focusing on one particular skill like baking. Several own restaurants, and here, too, their paths differ, with some of them born into restaurant families and knowing early on that this would be their career, and others launching their own restaurant only after stages in restaurants or bakeries owned by other people.

There are many points of contact in the stories. It's no surprise in a fairly circumscribed region that most of these women know one another. Some worked together earlier in their careers in a food establishment like Stone House Bread, or a hospitality business like Carol Worsley's Thyme Inn, or in another field altogether like social work.

Some found their culinary inspiration in Europe and subsequently attended famous cooking schools in France, Ireland, or Switzerland. Several are authors. Patty LaNoue Stearns has published three books about food and food preparation in northern Michigan. Nancy Allen's magnum opus, *Discovering Global Cuisines: A Culinary Textbook*, published in 2014, literally covers the globe and twenty diverse cuisines. Barb Tholin's quarterly publication, *Edible Grande Traverse*, already celebrating more than fifty issues, presents articles that highlight local artisans.

The primary influence for almost all the women in this book was a mother or grandmother. The cultural and culinary heritage from parents or grandparents included Danish, Polish, French, German, Lebanese, Finnish, Italian, Czech, Lithuanian, and Ukrainian. In these stories the Lebanese or German or Italian grandmother often holds center stage. Donna Folgarelli remembered that "every Sunday morning we were at Grandma's house by 10:30 in the basement learning to roll gnocchi and making the homemade sauce." Emily Umbarger's grandmother, now a great-grandmother, looms large as "the coolest person I know."

Two women in the twentieth century transformed the way American chefs and home cooks sourced and prepared food in their kitchens: Julia Child in the 1950s and Alice Waters in the 1970s. For both of them, France, French vegetables, and French cooking were a revelation. Julia's first encounter with French food took place in an era—now happily forgotten—when most American home cooks relied on canned and prepared foods.

Alice's encounter came later, but her influence on our expectations for the food we grow and consume has been huge. When her restaurant, Chez Panisse, opened in 1971, she led the way to farm-to-table for many other restaurateurs. Alice's influence stretches beyond restaurants into how we feed our children. Her Edible Schoolyard project, initiated in 1995 at the Martin Luther King Jr. Middle School in Berkeley, has expanded to schools in many other cities and provides one of the inspirations for the Traverse City–based Groundwork Center for Resilient Communities.

This region is fortunate to have close ties with both women. Carol Worsley traveled, cooked, and taught with Julia and Simca (Simone Beck). Alice Waters's sister Ellen lives in Traverse City, and with her late husband, Bob Pisor, started Stone House Bread in Leland in 1995.

Local restaurants play an important role in a community when they source directly from farms and wineries. The different artisans also support one another. Mimi Wheeler commented that "we bought from each other." Anne Hoyt remembered that Leelanau Cheese and Stone House Bread started in the same year, and since "cheese and bread go together, we did a lot together from the beginning." As a community, the storytellers recognize the positive environment in the region. In Jody Hayden's words, "Traverse City likes to support food entrepreneurs, and people here care where their food comes from."

Woven into each story is the desire to share and to educate, to share food and knowledge about food. Rose Hollander said, "The giving and sharing of food was a big part of my life." Barb Tholin realized that "a lot of people didn't know where their food came from." Of the people who come to Hillside Homestead, Susan Odom said, "They had a connection [to the land], but it's gone, and they want it back."

Emily Umbarger with Hearth and Harvest Homestead in Interlochen said, "I can't just pretend that I don't know about genetically modified foods or pesticides or fungicides or herbicides that are really harmful." She added, "I believe we can all be teachers and mentors to each other and build a community of learners."

Each woman tells a different story in a different voice, but they come together as a choral group in a contrapuntal work of music.

Thanks to their labors and their vision, the "culinary wasteland" of the first three-quarters of the twentieth century has borne fruit that is rich and various.

The women's stories lead naturally into larger issues such as climate change and the increasingly unpredictable seasons, the role of GMOs for good or ill, and the challenges in eschewing chemicals and choosing to farm organically.

While this book is not a cookbook, nonetheless, many of the story-tellers have contributed recipes coming from their family or their restaurant, covering the full gamut from cocktails to desserts. I hope readers, while relishing the stories, will also savor these recipes.

Many more stories are still untold. My hope is that these twenty stories will serve to quicken the interest and appreciation not only for the women in this book but also for all the pioneering women—and men—in the region, and to celebrate the agricultural and culinary flowering of the past fifty years.

These are personal stories. I have edited them lightly, primarily for clarification or to avoid repetition. My commitment was to respect and preserve these memories as they were told to me. If you would like to read the full transcripts or listen to the individual voices, the Traverse Area District Library on Woodmere has committed to archiving and preserving all the recordings and transcripts of the oral histories in this book and others that may be added in the future.

A Note on Oral History

Neither fact nor fiction, neither literature nor strictly speaking history, oral history captures and preserves the memories of individuals. These stories come from my narrators' memories, from their hearts. If dates are off, if events happened slightly differently or at different times, this has no consequence. If the narrators have been selective and deliberately omitted some portions of their personal stories, that is their choice and their privilege. What matters, what is precious, is the immediacy and integrity of what they remember, what they have chosen to share, and the words and images in which they chose to share it.

I

TWO ORCHARDS AND A CSA

Becoming Organic

Photo by Madeleine Hill Vedel

1

Julia Brabenec

When I first met Julia, she was eighty-nine years old, beautiful and vibrant, a fruit grower, home builder, poet, and singer. Born in the state of Michigan, it took decades and some seminomadic travels in the canonical white van of the hippie 1960s before she and her husband found their way to Leelanau County and called it home. They explored Colorado and fell in love with the mountains. During the Vietnam War era they also explored Canada, but soon returned to the United States. Everything they built, everything they planted and cultivated was with their own hands, true labors of love and of commitment to local and organic agriculture before those terms came into our everyday parlance.

Julia Brabenec, b. December 12, 1926
Interview: August 26, 2016
Engles Road, Northport

We did everything ourselves, as well as planting the trees.

Where shall I begin? At the very beginning. I was born in Dearborn, Michigan, when it was still all a very rural place. I was the sixth child of my parents who emigrated from Czechoslovakia. When I was about six months old my dad decided that we needed to be on a farm, and so he bought fifty acres—I think it was fifty acres, but it may have been one hundred—out in Saint Clair County, near Richmond, Michigan, and we moved there when I was under one year old. My grandmother had come from Europe before I was born to live with us because my mother needed some help with her children. I was the sixth child, and there would be two more following me. My only brother, born first, was followed by seven sisters. I think my parents kept hoping for another boy.

So we all moved out to this farm together. It was a beautiful old stone house with a big barn, and that's where I grew up. But my dad worked in the city as a tool and die maker—he came from Europe with that skill and was able to get a good job—and so he commuted on weekends. It was my mother who really raised us and managed the farm—a much bigger job than she was ever cut out to do—but we were all her helpers. In the little house in Dearborn where they had started out they had planted some climbing roses that were called Seven Sisters, and then my mother always referred to us as her roses.

I went to a one-room schoolhouse for eight years and went to high school in Richmond. By that time my mother was getting to a point where she was unhappy to be alone for weeks at a time, just seeing my dad on weekends. When he came home he was more interested in the farm things, all new for him, the tools that he would accumulate, and the new challenges. It was not a really happy life for her. Finally, after shouldering many years of hard work, she said, "We need to go back to Detroit," so they bought a little house on the west side of Detroit. I think I was fifteen when I moved back. I finished my high school in Detroit, at MacKenzie High. I pretty much stayed there. They kept the farm for a while, and my younger sister who was loath to leave stayed there with my grandmother and went to school in Richmond.

My plans to go off to college didn't materialize at the time. I worked at various things. My earliest job was probably at Hudson's as a contingent in children's shoes. After graduating in 1944 I got a war job working for the Army, Office Chief of Ordnance at the Union Guardian Building in downtown Detroit. Then after the war I got a job in National Advertising at the *Detroit News*. My boss, Reg Brophy, was a Canadian, and when he found out that I was one of eight children, he hired me, because, he said, "Anyone who grew up in a family like that knows how to work."

It was there that I met my husband, John. He was also working in advertising. We started to date and, of course, fell in love. He had been raised in the city, but he had always dreamed of being out in the country and having a raspberry patch. So I said, well, I was a country girl, and I knew how to garden. When we got married we bought a little acre out near Mount Clemens, and we had a huge garden. There we started our family, and then in about ten years we bought five acres up near Richmond, almost within sight of our old farm. There we had gardens, raspberries, and fruit trees, and our children all learned to garden. We lived there for about ten years.

We went out to Colorado on a bike trip, and we fell in love with the mountains. We had friends there, too, so we ended up buying some property near Boulder, and we built a little house. By the way, we built all the homes we lived in. The little home we built in Chesterfield near Mount Clemens was just a small home that we ended up adding onto, and when we moved to Richmond we built another larger home. Then when we moved to Colorado we built a home up in the mountains near Boulder. The kids fell in love with that, so it was hard to come back here, although we traveled back and forth a lot.

From there we decided during the Vietnam War—which we protested—that we weren't going to allow our kids to be involved. We actually immigrated to Canada and we bought fifty acres near Goderich, a small town on Lake Huron. It was beautiful and we loved it, but the kids still wanted to be in Boulder and finish high school and possibly go to the University of Colorado, so we were kind of back and forth again.

At that time I think maybe we were considered to be hippies. We drove a white Volkswagen van. My husband had a beard and I had long hair, just typical—so I think we were not really welcome there. It was a country location, and the people were pretty conservative. We just had the feeling like, "No, this is not really the place for us." And border crossings were horrible. They were very embarrassing sometimes.

We ended up selling that property in Canada. That was about the time we decided to come up and investigate Leelanau County. The reason we came here was that we had been here on our honeymoon and fell in love with it, of course. We always knew that we would come back eventually.

By this time I was bordering on fifty, and my husband was a couple of years younger than I. We bought our property here and immediately started to garden and located where all the places were that we could haul any goat manure or horse manure and start to build up the soil, which was sandy, typical Leelanau County sand. Our gardens just kept building up. Our land here was about one-third of a mile off the highway, with no electricity available, and it would have been very expensive to bring it in, so we just thought, "No, we don't need it."

We lived pretty primitively for a while with kerosene lanterns. We had a well where we pumped our water for all the water needs. We lived that way for about six years and finally got interested in some alternative energy. John started to look into it and found a company, a young couple out in Idaho that had a new business and were working toward alternative energy, so we bought solar panels from them.

First of all we bought a little wind generator and attached it on the roof of our house. We built this little house as a temporary home until we decided where we were going to build our permanent home. That's another story, but anyway, this little house that we built, we attached a wind generator at the top, and we had some batteries which we bought used from the telephone company, and now we made our own power. When my husband wired our home he wired it for both AC and DC so that eventually when we had more power we'd be able to use the other.

During the next twenty years or so we gardened extensively. During that time the land next to us became available. We thought it would be a good idea to buy a little extra land, so we did. And then we thought, "What are we going to do with it?" It was hilly. We didn't want to put it into more gardens, so we planted an orchard, shovels in hand. It took two or three years to plant the eleven hundred trees that we ended up with, of peaches and apples, quite a variety of interesting apples. That became our main income eventually, although we sold a lot of produce locally to the food co-op in Traverse City, Oryana. This was in the '80s. We were still doing this in the '90s.

When our orchard became very productive that pretty much took our time. We did everything ourselves, as well as planting the trees. We pruned, and we thinned the fruit, and we harvested, and we marketed. We never had any help except once in a while when the kids were around. None of them lived really close, but when they came to visit they always helped. My two youngest grandkids who would sometimes help us in the orchard would always tell people (they called me Bubby), "Bubby is the boss of the gardens, but Grampa is the boss of the orchards." And he was. He managed it.

We decided that we needed to be organic. We already were with our gardens. So we did the whole three-year trial period and ended up with certified fruit. I think we were the first organic fruit growers of table fruit. There were probably other organic orchards in the state, but they mostly went into cider. Ours was beautiful fruit. We used to enjoy going to market with it because people at various markets in mid-Michigan weren't used to all this gorgeous, beautiful, succulent, tree-ripened fruit.

It began to be a lot of work. We were beginning to wonder whether we would be able to hold out. We worked very hard, but we were both in really good health. But then my husband developed Parkinson's, so that kind of slowed things down. We began to think that we really needed to sell the orchard, which was very difficult for us to do. The people who bought it were not much interested in keeping it up. That was hard because it was like losing a child and seeing it not cared for.

At that time we had started this home that I'm living in now. We had started building it early in the '80s but never had time to work on it because we were too busy farming. We decided that we would like to have a stone house. We could have been considered back-to-the-landers then as we were very caught up with the lives of Scott and Helen Nearing—the gurus of many young folk at the time. We loved their stone homes and decided we needed to have a stone house. For all these years we had collected piles of stones, and then, eventually, we got around to starting the stonework, and that took quite a few years to accomplish. We started the foundation in 1983 and finally moved into this larger house, our permanent house, in 2005. We'd built the house to a point, but there was a lot of finishing to be done, like the drywall and all that, and my husband, John, was not anymore able to do all this. So my daughter and her husband and their two kids, they just came, and within a very short time they had it all finished and we moved in.

I had three children, two daughters, Rebeca and Elisa, and a son, Jeff, and my son worked with his dad from the time he was twelve or thirteen. They built the house together in Colorado. My kids decided somewhere along the line that Michigan winters were just not what they liked. They are all scattered now. Rebeca is in Bellingham, Washington. Jeff is in Colorado, and Elisa is currently near Nashville. They are all in other places, but we are a really close family, and we get together several times a year. When I can, I travel to visit them.

When the farm market in Traverse City was just beginning we were the only organic peach orchard here, apples also, but there was so much fruit here that we thought we wouldn't be able to do that well locally. We did sell to Oryana. They took our fruit and our garden produce, but the peaches and the apples needed to go somewhere where they would be more cherished. We began to go to the Midland market, and to the Bay City market, to Saginaw and that area, and eventually we contacted Whole Foods. We went to Lansing markets sometimes. When Whole Foods was beginning to take our apples, we would have to cart them down to Ann Arbor. That was always something that we thought was the biggest fault of our business, having to go so far, but we just got accustomed to doing it.

We didn't take our peaches to Ann Arbor because we felt that peaches have to be tree-ripened. They are too perishable to go very far, and since we picked them when they were at the stage where they were just on the verge of softening, we couldn't take them all the way to Ann Arbor. Even taking them to the markets mid-state was risky, but if some of them got a little bruised, we would sell them as seconds, and people would use them for canning. People just absolutely waited for us to bring them down there because a lot of them had never before tasted a ripe peach.

This was our life, and we loved it. We worked very hard, and in later years when we would think back and talk about all that we did, we would say, "How on earth did we ever do that?" I think a lot of people when they reach a point where they are not working hard anymore really wonder how their bodies ever managed to hold up under the strain. Being young is the secret.

When we planted the eleven hundred trees we could have had an augur come in, but what we did—and we did it very methodically—we dug all the topsoil where the hole was going to be and placed it aside, and dug out the sandy part and placed that on the other side of the hole, and then planted the tree with the topsoil around the roots, and then some of the sand would go on top. So that's what we did. It took probably about three years to plant the whole orchard. We would only plant perhaps two or three rows in one year, rarely more than that. In a day, I think there were probably times when we would get a whole row done. I can't tell you exactly how many there were in a row. I'm not very good at math. I don't even want to try to figure it out. It was about seven acres of orchard. The orchard pretty much spanned the whole width of the property. The apples were in the lower part, and as the hill rose it was a really good site for the peaches, because the peaches needed a little more air and less chance of frost.

In the center of the orchard there was a little pine tree growing, and we left it there. Now it's huge. But it was pretty much the center of the orchard. The apples were below it, and the peaches were above it. Also starting to grow was a little forest. There were a lot of little maple trees there. We hated to pull them out. We had to pull some of them, but some we left. There was a man who was a supervisor of a group of orchard workers that managed the orchard beyond us here where the winery is now located. He was from the island of Grenada and was a sweet man. He would stop by and talk to me about my garden. He knew what everything was, and he'd sample a bit here and there. He knew that we had planted an orchard. He said, "John, Julia, are you planning to have an orchard or are you planning to have a woods?" He said, "You know, you have to pull the trees out. You cannot have an orchard with all those trees." So we took his wise advice and methodically started to dig them out. A few people were interested in transplanting some. We gave some away to people. But, reluctantly, we pulled them all out, and then we had a true orchard.

Within about four to five years the small trees had fruit on them. I actually have some photos sitting under a tiny little fruit tree that looks like I'm wearing a huge hat full of apples. Early on we didn't allow them to hold too much fruit, but as they grew there was more fruit, and more work every year. As the orchard grew we began to realize what we were getting into because it was a huge job for both of us. We were pretty independent and liked doing things our own way, and I guess we just felt that no one would handle our trees the way we did. It was a lot of TLC. We pruned the apple trees not in a pine tree pyramid shape, the way orchards were being pruned, but we pruned them to be flat-topped so that the sun could get into the fruit. We never had to have ladders to pick our fruit. Our fruit was beautiful because it was all exposed to the sun. The apples got beautifully colored. We pruned the peaches pretty heavily, but they'd still grow huge, and that was more of a problem. We did have to get a ladder out, because the trees were a lot taller. We had to thin off a lot of fruit because, if we didn't, the branches would break. The trees would overbear. That was always hard because it's difficult to thin off beautiful fruit. You just have to make up your mind. Only one here, another in eight inches, then another eight inches, and so on.

A big problem for the apples was being attacked by rose chafers, which are very prevalent here. They burrow into the ground to winter in the hayfields, and we have a lot of unused land around us, so it's a haven for them. They destroy a lot of fruit. There was no organic way we could control them, so we thought, "Well, maybe we should just let them do their job, and when they are finished, in about two weeks, we'll thin off all of the bad fruit." And fortunately there was always more than enough left that they hadn't touched. So we decided to let them help us do our thinning.

The peaches had the problem of brown rot, a virus that hits stone fruit. My husband did the spraying. I think it was sulfur that he used with the brown rot. There was also a peach tree curl that wouldn't hurt the fruit, but it would weaken the trees, so that had to be handled too. We learned a lot about what we could use, and what were organic-accepted sprays. There was a loss because we couldn't control every-thing, but we always ended up with enough fruit to market. And the less than perfect fruit ended up in our (and other people's) canning shelves. I did a lot of canning from the garden and from the orchard. I canned a lot of peaches, and lots of applesauce.

We had a small "home" orchard right here in our yard that included apricot trees. We had some wonderful apricots. I have never tasted an apricot as good. It was a variety that is not grown commercially because it's too perishable. Most commercial apricots are grown for their ability to be shipped and held for a while, with their flavor sacri-ficed for serviceability.

We once had three or four gardens scattered about. Now my garden is very small. I planted garlic—I always have to do that—and onions, and squash, and tomatoes and beans. I have some pole beans, too, and I actually have one tomatillo plant. This morning I went out and it was top heavy; a couple of branches had cracked. I had to tie it up so hopefully it will survive. I also have a little broccoli. I don't need much because I don't really want to can anymore, and my freezer doesn't have a lot of room. So I just have enough for my own use and to share with others, too, a little here and there.

Our road here is not a county road, so we have to hire someone to plow the snow, and the same guy who plows the road comes back and plows our individual driveways. We have to manage that ourselves, but, as neighbors, we share the cost of the road. It's all taken care of, and I seldom get snowed in. Unless the weather is really bad I can usually get out whenever I need to or feel the desire.

I like to sing, and I write poetry, and that's my outlet for creativity. For the Traverse City Poets' Night Out, I entered some poetry, and about a year ago one of my poems was chosen. I got a special prize, and the *Edible Grande Traverse* printed one of my poems with a little article. I wrote an "Ode to the Odious (autumn) Olive" (an invasive species). They printed that with a little bit of an essay and also a picture of the jam I make. My philosophy is, "If you can't lick 'em, eat 'em." So every year I gather several pails full of them and make jam. It's wonderful on toast and also can be used as a condiment with meat. I make a lot of it and then give it away as gifts. I wait until the berries are really, really ripe, just before they freeze when the heavy frost comes, because that's when they are the most flavorful.

We have a pretty active arts community here and lots of things to keep active in. Share/Care—which is an organization, you can become a member of it and it does a lot to help seniors stay in their homes—last year sponsored a Follies in Leland at the Old Art Building. I was involved with that. I sing in church and sing with the Village Voices in Northport. I sing whenever I can. My friends say, "How can you still sing? You are almost ninety." I don't know. I tell them, "My mother had a beautiful voice." I don't feel that I could ever sing as beautifully as she did, but I've got to think she left a little bit of it with me. So as long as I can, I'll keep on singing.

Autumn Olive Jam

RECIPE BY JULIA BRABENEC

Gather a small bucketful when they are at the peak of ripeness (an important note).

Wash them thoroughly, removing all the chaff that comes along in the picking (don't worry about stems).

Crush them in a large cooking pan, add a little water (maybe a cup), cook them down, and strain the juice.

I like to use the old-fashioned cone strainer, but a food mill should work as well. The single seeds are large, so it takes some elbow grease to strain off as much pulp as you can.

Measure 4 cups of the juice into a large saucepan, stir into it 3 table-spoons of No/low sugar pectin (I use the Ball brand), and bring to a rolling boil.

Add 1½ cups sugar, bring back to a rolling boil, and then time for at least 2 minutes, stirring constantly.

Test to see if the juice has reached the "jelling stage"—where it slides off the spoon, rather than falling in easy drops.

When this happens, turn heat down very low and fill jelly jars. Have the jars sterilized, hot, and ready. Fill and seal jars immediately.

Photo courtesy of Cheryl Kobernik

2

Cheryl Kobernik

I interviewed Cheryl late on a working day, not a day working in the orchard but in her day job as a social worker. Key to her story were the fruit trees in her German parents' urban backyard and her father's frequent escapes to northern Michigan where she and her husband met, bought a farm, and over time committed to organic ways of farming with their cherry orchard. Always in her thoughts and decisions was that German heritage of hard work as she and her husband committed to the three-year-long transition from traditional growing using chemical sprays to organic and biodynamic methods renewing the soil and waiting for the cherries to ripen more slowly and naturally.

Summer 2019 as this book goes to press, Cheryl tells me that for the first time they have had to abandon the majority of this year's tart cherries. The combination of pests, disease, and blight—including a cool June and July—was too much to have a high-quality product for their customers. The farm celebrated its annual U Pick but that was all. We hope that by summer 2020 when this book is in print that Mother Nature will be less angry and will have returned to her nurturing self and that this great organic cherry farm will be flourishing again.

Cheryl Kobernik, b. May 14, 1957
Interview: August 29, 2017
North Star Organics, 1139 Forrester Road, Frankfort

Not growing up in agriculture it's an honor to be accepted
into that.... I have never met people with such integrity.

Once upon a time. A little bit of what informs where I am now—I'm not going to go into longitudinal thinking—my parents are both immigrants from Germany, so I am first generation in this country. They didn't come together—that doesn't matter. My dad in particular suffered the consequences of World War I: poverty and lack of food. My mom was here during the depression. They both were. Food gathering and canning—not so much freezing—was always critical. Even though I grew up in a suburb of Detroit, a very urban setting, our backyard was full of fruit trees and Concord grapes and a vegetable garden alongside of the garage. It was a nice heavy clay soil that just produced amazingly. My dad was an engineer, but also always a frustrated farmer. We had grafted trees in the backyard. One side was an apple; one side was a pear.

They also owned ninety acres of woods in Boyne City, northern Michigan. That was my dad's place of solace. We spent a lot of time up there. The other thing about me, my parents had a sixteen-, a fifteen-, and a thirteen-year-old, and then I was born. So I was your typical menopause baby. My mom was forty-five, and my dad was fifty, and there I was. So they started all over again. My parents had gray hair by the time I was in kindergarten. My dad took early retirement at sixty, I think, so I was like ten years old. Even prior to that, probably every fourth or sixth weekend throughout the year, we were traveling up north. And in the summertime, certainly, "vacation time." It was literally a cabin, for a long time with just an outhouse. After my dad retired I would travel with him up north a lot.

On that property he had a hay field, and they had big gardens and more grapes and more fruit trees. I learned to drive a tractor. I learned to operate a chain saw. I should have been a boy, but since I was a girl he just kind of ignored that. I was just Cherry, and whatever he did, I did.

It was a natural world. Even though I was a "city girl," I had a strong tie to—I don't know whether at that time I would have called it agriculture—but the ethnicity of boiled potatoes almost every night for dinner, with the German background, and getting fresh herring and cutting off their heads and making herring and sour cream and onions. Some of the things that I grew up with were even more old school than should have been for a child born in 1957. Ranch dressing was new, and microwaves, but I'm excited because I've got herring. It's a little weird. So there's a difference in my background from that of my friends.

Jumping all the way ahead I did a year at Eastern, thinking I was going to be a nurse. I couldn't afford to stay on campus so I transferred to Wayne State. I grew up hearing, "You are going to college." They weren't going to help me pay for it but, "You are going to go to college." They were good German parents, which are not the most kid-friendly all the time.

I transferred to Wayne State, still in nursing. Took microbiology. Got a C. Loved it. Took it all over again. Got a C the second time and decided, "This may not be where I belong, getting a registered nurse degree." Because at that time you were a nurse or a stewardess or a teacher. So I said, "That's not going to work." I was getting As in all my sociology classes. I had no idea why I chose them in the beginning, but there must have been something. So I ended up getting an undergrad degree in sociology at Wayne.

I still wanted to be in a hospital setting so I worked really hard. I was working on a master's degree in counseling at Wayne State at the same time as I was working on a master's in pastoral ministry at Mary Grove College, which is a Catholic college. They were nuns from Honduras. The experience that I had there shaped a lot of my life as well as the master's in counseling. I got the master's in counseling and before I finished the master's in divinity I left and moved north to the cabin in Boyne City. My childhood years had me still drawn to the north.

I was a sexual assault counselor for a while, and I was the director of a hospice. That's thirty-three years ago. Hospice was pretty new back then, so that was an interesting challenge. I did that for a number of years, and then I met Alan. Ten miles from where I live right now. At his uncle's farm. His uncle happened to be a German professor during the winter at Grand Valley College. They had bought this cherry farm on a fluke. Alan used to spend the summers up here. He lived downstate, Saugatuck. He would come up for long weekends. They were like his second parents. He was an only child, and he spent a great deal of time up here.

Long story. My dad knew something about the farm. I ended up there. And just noticed this guy. His aunt—she died a few years ago—and the best word is that she was a comet that just came through my life. My girlfriend and I were traveling around the state and stopped by, and she wouldn't let us leave. She was an amazing hostess. So we were there for probably four or five days, and then I was only a couple of hours away, so Joni would call and say, "Why don't you come? We're going to have a good dinner," or something, "in a couple of weeks." And so I would come for the weekend. Well, she timed it all the time so that she could call Alan and say, "Hey, Alan, why don't you come?" She wouldn't tell either one of us that she had told us. So, by chance, we were always ending up at the farm together.

She always needed something when I would get there. "Alan, I don't have any butter. Why don't you take the motorcycle? Why don't you take the bike and go get me some butter? And Cheryl, why don't you go with him?" So, on and on and on. Eventually we told her, "We don't both have to go get the butter. And I know you have three pounds of it in your refrigerator." It was a great day for her when we announced that we were going to be married. We were going to get engaged.

Alan had a lot of experience from spending his summers as a child and later his weekends as an adult on a cherry farm. I had grown up in the north, and we were getting married in 1985, and I was kind of burned out from the hospice, and he didn't want to stay down in Saugatuck anymore, so we spent our courting, so to speak, the weekends before we got married, up here looking for a farm. We decided, "Let's do this." And we looked all over northern Michigan.

I kept explaining to real estate agents that we wanted a farm. We didn't care what the house looked like—Alan is an amazing builder—but we needed an existing orchard of some kind. We didn't care if it was cherries, apples, pears, a combination thereof, but orchard. They would show us a beautiful house on five acres with three cherry trees in the yard. And I was like, "This isn't working." We saw many of those.

And then we just started driving around. That was our weekends. And we came here and saw a farm down the road from us. It was mostly an apple farm and it was being leased out. So who was leasing it? His name was Don Nugent. We said, "Maybe we should go talk to him and see what the production is like, and soil and everything." Potential. Things like that. The acreage. It was right next door to us where we are right now.

We went up there in the winter. We couldn't see this place because it was deep in snow. We went up to his place, we're next door to it now ... and asked him about that farm. It was called the Franklin Farm. He said, "I don't know. But the wife and I were talking about selling." The farm that they had here. "Why don't you just come look at it?" It was a heavy snow winter. He had a Saint Bernard. We walked from up the hill down the hill with the Saint Bernard making the path, and we came and looked at this place.

And yes, the house was exactly what we were asking for. It was deplorable. It had been rented out and used as migrant housing. Nothing against migrants by any means, but it had been rented out for four or five years. And so nothing had been done. The furnace wasn't working right, and the house was black with smoke. So it was perfect. It was perfect. Exactly what we were looking for. There were raccoons living in the back porch, and you could just tell that it was: "Yes!"

It was forty acres, which is rather unusual. We bought this in 1985. Most farms way back in the late 1800s or the early 1900s would start out with forty acres, but then they would grow. They would become eighty acres. They would find another parcel, or they would grow to 240 acres, or something like that. Maybe not that big up here with farming and fruit growing, not like flatland farmers, but it would be bigger than forty acres. This was unusual. It was kind of an anomaly that it's always stayed forty acres. But for us it was perfect. It had existing sweet cherries and tart cherries. It had a few pears and a few apples. We had found our home.

We bought it, got married in February, and moved here in April. Alan was still working downstate. I was unemployed at that point. I found a job at Gwen Frostic, an artist's shop that does a lot of creative things. It's just down around the corner. It wasn't quite full time as I recall. We needed money, so Alan was working with his dad's construction firm downstate. He would leave Monday mornings at 4:00 a.m. and head downstate to work, and then he would come up Friday nights.

Then it was April and spring was coming, and we had a farm. So we hurried up, and, fortuitously at the time, we found a tractor for $500. We found a sprayer for $500. And we found a mower for $500. It was just a weird karma. We were looking at junk in the weeds. They were only worth $500. We didn't get a $10,000 tractor for $500. It was a $500 tractor and needing help. Alan would work on them when he was here on the weekends, and then he would leave. But spraying had to be done, and mowing and things like that during the week, too. So I had a crash course in operating and figuring out spraying schedules, and amounts, and all kinds of things. Just, okay. It was before cell phones, so we had a lot of long distance phone calls. Usually when Cheryl was in a panic. But we made it work.

I can just picture, sitting here looking out in the driveway—I don't know why I had them up here all the time, I don't remember. But the tractor and the sprayer . . . I could get the tractor running or—the sprayer had its own engine—I could get the sprayer running, but darn if I couldn't get them both running at the same time. I could get the sprayer running and I'd hop on the tractor and that was like . . . What?! Alan's uncle, by the way, who was still just ten miles away, he was pretty geeked that we got the farm. He just "happened" to be in the neighborhood Monday through Friday a lot. He just "happened" to be in the neighborhood. And God bless him. I can still see me sitting there probably with the air blue with smoke, the sprayer running and not the tractor, and he would walk down the driveway and say, "Just happened to be in the neighborhood." I wouldn't say it. "Really? How fortuitous, because I'm in trouble." He could see that. So, yeah, Lord knows, there were some exciting adventures back then.

Eventually Alan started his building business up here, and we were together. But it took almost a year before we got that figured out. I don't remember all the numbers—Alan is my number guy—but we bought the farm in 1985. Prices were good on cherries. No one can convince me that climate change isn't a real phenomenon, or that we don't have a great deal of responsibility for that. Being in agriculture, our climate, our growing practices, everything has been altered from 1985 when we started this. I started with prices, but part of what would determine that, too, would be the frost we would get, the cycles of the seasons, a normal season that you couldn't count on, but that with some variation had some normalcy to it. We don't have that anymore. We don't have that at all.

So going back to 1985, prices were good. '86 was decent. By 1987 we had been in this business for two years, and the prices plummeted. There was an oversupply and not enough demand. I didn't take economics much in college, but I understood supply and demand, and prices were very low, lower than what you could produce them for. We struggled with that. There were enough decent years, but the farm still wasn't paying its own way. I think at that point I was pregnant—Emily was born in 1987—and then our son was born just fifteen months later. That wasn't intended, but it ended up a good thing. Having two kids fifteen months apart takes a toll.

But we were very fortunate. I joined Alan in the building business, part time, basically. Anywhere from twenty to thirty hours a week. And we were able to have in-home help. One woman was a widow, a farmer, and she had sold her land. She became like a surrogate grandma for the kids. They learned to do drop-the-clothespin-in-the-bottle sort of things. All kind of games and stories, and tales. And we had some other women that just came into our lives—that we bumped into—and they became lifelong family for us up here. I'm digressing again, but it almost brings tears to my eyes.

Not growing up in agriculture, it's an honor to be accepted into the agrarian community. I know there are good people everywhere, but there are no better people. I have never met people with such integrity in my life. We've just really been blessed. So a lot of that became part of our life and helped us raise our kids.

Somewhere along the line—I think maybe in 1990—I went back to school. A good decision that I didn't know I was making at the time. I went back for my master's in social work, an accelerated program at that point. In two and a half years, not quite, I had a master's in social work from Grand Valley State University. They had just opened up. I was cohort two at the university center in Traverse City. I only had to—only!—drive to Traverse City for my classes. But I was in the second cohort, and it was one of the best decisions that I made in my life, not to have just my master's in counseling—which is a long story, but not reimbursable through insurance, Medicare, Medicaid.

I got my master's in social work, and at the same time I was running the farm and raising my kids and working with Alan in the building business. Also about that time I got my builder's license.

It was a joke that Alan finally succumbed to getting his license—he always wanted to buck the system. "I don't need to prove to somebody that I know how to do what I am doing"—but he finally did. And so as a fluke I said, "I'm going to go get mine, too." So I went and took the test, and I passed. Alan said, "There's two ways we can look at this. One, your test was easier than mine. Or two, you know more than you let on." Even now, that was easily twenty years ago, when we are doing something, I will say, "What do you want me to do now?"

"You've got your builder's license. You figure it out." That didn't work so well. He was kidding, but it was cute.

We were in the conventional nonorganic world. I was very active in the Farm Bureau and a lot of the cherry industry groups and committees in the state. I traveled to Washington, DC, a lot. Mostly worked in promotion and education, agriculture in the schools and things like that. Got a bit disillusioned. Prices were terrible. We were very frustrated with the industry. And then, eighteen years ago, I went to a conference up at the horticultural station in Traverse City and heard someone speaking about organic. I and another female farmer went, and we both came home, and our husbands were together. We walked into the kitchen, and we both just went off. We were so excited. What one remembered or the other, the whole story. We were talking about compost. We were talking about soil. How could we do this and things like that. My husband said, "Let's do this." And the other husband said, "No way."

So we went home and Alan, a week later, found a soil person, Joe Scrimger, and went and talked to him about it downstate. He was convinced, and that was the last spray—prohibited spray—that we put on the farm. It takes three years to transition, and we did. We started that whole process. So eighteen years ago one of my comments was, "Alan doesn't have a ponytail and I don't walk around barefoot."

This was a business decision. The farm was taking money away from us. So what money we were making in the building business—I wasn't in social work at that time . . . yeah, I was. I was in private practice and doing some domestic violence work on the side—but all our money was going into the farm. The farm was taking money out of our personal accounts. And we had these kids. And it was like, the farm has to pay for itself. The farm can't take away. It just can't. And so organic was the business position. If we can capture, if we can have the same or a little bit less of a crop, but we can get a better price, maybe we can make a small farm, an anomaly, a forty-acre fruit farm, support, or at least pay its own way for our family. So we did.

We were at the very beginning. The organic movement has been there for a long time, but nobody was producing organic cherries. Folks said it couldn't be done. We talked to an extension agent, a Michigan State extension agent, which is where our guru was that was helping us through different challenges. I was on the phone with him asking some questions, and he couldn't stop laughing. And I said, "No, I'm serious." And he couldn't stop laughing. He never did. I hung up on him. So we stumbled forward. The first couple of years in a conventional—or as Alan says, nonorganic—not organic farm, there's something called Ethryl, Ethephon, that you spray on the trees about ten days before harvest, and it makes the cherries abscise so that they let go. You come through with shakers, and you don't want to have to shake too hard. And you want the cherries to let go easily. So we'd been using that.

Picture us standing in a field at a friend's house, a group of about four farmers there, and they said, "How are you going to get the cherries off of the trees? You can't use Ethephon, can you? How are you going to get them off the tree then?" I felt such a . . . I won't even say, defensiveness, like a panic, and it's like, "How are we going to get them off the tree?" I can picture myself physically taking a step back from the group. It was almost like "step back, think," and it came out so innocently. Part of that goes back to my heritage. You don't pick fruit until it's ripe. My parents, trees in the backyard, Concord grapes up north and downstate, and everywhere else. I said, "Well, I guess we're just going to have to let it get ripe." It came out of my mouth, and I was literally looking down. And all of a sudden I looked up and I went, "Yes. We're going to let them get ripe. Then we'll shake them."

Crickets! I was so proud of myself, I was like, "Oh, my gosh. We're just going to have to wait until they are ripe. Okay. Got that. Check." It was not as easy as it sounds, though.

We faced umpteen challenges. And sure, in life, not just agriculture, but you have these events and people and information that you have in the back of your brain, and you just have to go back and forage in there. What are we going to do? I love flowers, perennials. And a book I found a long time ago, it's called lasagna gardening. You lay newspaper down and then peat and then leaves and grass, just all kinds of organic materials, and soil, and build it up, and when it decomposes on its own it makes an amazing bed. That was in the back of my mind from doing flower beds. We can't use Roundup. We can't use 2,4-D. We can't use our herbicides. And the big deal is, you can't have grass under a tree. Not sure why, yet, but you can't have grass under your tree. So we started lasagna-ing underneath our trees.

I drove to Toronto in a snowstorm with my two kids—I don't know where Alan was—to buy a shredder that would hold a square bale of hay. And brought it back here. We used to go up to the *Record Eagle*, the daily newspaper in Traverse City, and—I don't know how to say it—we would dumpster dive for the newspapers that were the leftover that the newspaper delivery guy brought back. They were bundled. We got to be really good friends with the production company and the *Record Eagle*, in Traverse City, so they would save the misprints for us. They would save extra advertisements. We couldn't do anything with glossy at that time. They knew that. We would go up every two/three days in the spring with two apple boxes, three- by three- by three-foot boxes and fill them with whatever was around. It got to the point where they would say, "Leave us a box. We'll fill it for you." They were so thrilled that this was getting used. It was such a great synergy. And so we would put that newspaper through the shredder and shred it and put it underneath the trees. And then we'd go back over it with a bale of hay and cover it.

It looked as though we had used Roundup. It was all brown underneath the trees with the hay. It was amazing. The shredded paper would hold the moisture. It kept the root system cool. There was amazing microbiology underneath it. You could just put your hand in it. No rain for four days, and you could stick your hand under there and it was still moist. There were earthworms and all kinds of creepy, crawly things that I can't identify, but there was a lot of microbiology going on down there. So much life underneath there. It was a lot of work. It was very time-consuming. It was a lot of trips to Traverse City to get the newspaper. But it worked.

Then they started doing more colored ink, and the organic certification NOP [National Organic Program] as well as our other certifiers said, "There are too many metals in the colored ink. You can't use colored ink." Well, for a while we could still get some of the inserts and pull the comics out. It was pathetic. Eventually we had to give up on it, and we couldn't do it anymore. I sold the shredder.

So we threatened, or whatever the word is, to buy the newsprint, and these huge, five or six feet in diameter rolls that they use to make the newspapers, buy that and—Alan always makes fun of me—but I pictured that you could just take a chainsaw right through it and cut it into newspaper size. So we could still feed it through the shredder. Sometimes you just have to—you can't get reimbursed for it—I mean the labor. So that was a good idea.

We tried black tarps underneath the trees, landscape cloth. We thought, "Fine, we'll use landscape cloth. We can plant a new tree." We discovered that the black tarp absorbs too much heat, and it was drying everything out underneath.

Now we plant clover when we do an orchard. We've invested in putting vetch in. Rather than fighting it, how do you make nature work with you? Or, ass-backwards, how do we work with nature? Because anything that you do has consequences. And so it's a different mindset that we have to adopt. It's not like replacement farming. It's not, "We can't use Roundup so how do we kill the grass under the trees?" Not everything is a replacement. You've got to think outside the box. It's been eighteen years and we still don't know what we are doing.

People come at U Pick time and, "This is amazing." Our cherries are amazing. I want to say. . . . It's like if somebody compliments you and says, "Your kids are amazing," and you say, "Thank you." That's just weird. I mean, to me. It's just like, yeah, I had something to do with it, I hope, but they are amazing on their own. It's kind of the same thing with the cherries. People say, "Oh, these are amazing." "Yeah, they are, aren't they? We're proud of them." And it's true. Our cherries are different, organic, than not-organic. And we know this.

The Brix count is higher. Brix is a measure of sweetness. Our non-organic cherries, they run thirteen to sixteen in Brix; a green pepper probably has a Brix of three. Our cherries run nineteen to twenty-one. They are still tart cherries. They are definitely a tart cherry. But it's a more complex flavor. I won't even say it's sweeter necessarily. They are more complex. That's how I can describe it. They are also meatier. It usually takes four pounds of frozen cherries to make a pound of dried. With ours it's more 3.2 or 3.4 pounds to make a pound of dried. I don't know. Nobody cares. You talk to different professors at different conferences that we go to, and they say, "We wonder why the Brix are higher?" We say, "We don't know." "What's for lunch?" "I don't know."

We transformed the farm from what it was in the beginning, some good decisions, some very bad decisions. Before we went organic we planted 180 sweet trees that are intended to grow to sixty feet tall, to be two feet in diameter. They are huge, standard sweet trees. Nobody grows organic sweet trees, cherries. We ignored them, and we were all about tarts. Tarts was our main business. And then one year they started producing. We literally ignored them. And they were the beautiful big, dark Schmidts—some people call them Bing, but they are Schmidts. We have the yellow variety, too.

Well, the German in me again, back to my heritage was, "You cannot waste them." So we stuck a cardboard sign out front and said, "U Pick." I think I measured them in quarts. I don't know what we did. I don't even remember what buckets we used or how we got started. Now, in our eleventh year of U Pick we have about 2,500 people that come in ten days. We're open from 9:00 a.m. to 7:00 p.m. for ten days. We start on a Friday. That was originally to get the locals a chance first, some of the people that are established customers. On that day the cars are lined up all the way down the road. We have people that have come for almost the entire time. It's "old home week." We have new customers, of course, all the time, too. It's a cherished event. It's crazy what it's become.

They are the ones that teach us to look up. They'll stand there and, "This is a slice of paradise." I can still hear somebody saying that this summer. That was a new one. And, "This is so beautiful." And a piece of me inside is going, "What are they talking about?" It's literally almost like they are putting their hand under my chin and raising my head, and, "Well, it is kind of pretty out here, isn't it? Ha! Who knew?" And the people say, "Thank you." That was so disconcerting for both Alan and me. We would stand there, and we were speechless. They would say thank you for growing food, for growing cherries. We just stood there and went, "Hunh!" because all we are, we were just ragged on all the time. "Bring more cherries and we're not going to pay you," and it's like we got questioned about things like agriculture and how the industry is operated, and it was just suppressing all the time, and now people are hugging us and saying, "Thank you!" I say, "Whoa, whoa. This is a little weird."

U Pick is rich. We have many of the same families and friends that have come every year. My kids—I know they will probably always be here for Christmas—but my children would never miss harvest. My son flies in from Denver right now. My daughter is just downstate, so she comes up, but they have flown in from Arizona, from New Orleans, from Washington, DC, wherever they have been in their lifetime so far. No one would ever miss harvest.

We make harvest fun. It's dangerous work. It's hard work. It doesn't matter if it's 94 degrees or if it's pouring rain. We still harvest. But we have an amazing crew. We have one young man, the nephew of one of my friends, and this is his eleventh year. He started when he was eleven years old, and he has come every year. He just graduated from the University of Oregon, and one of his goals was to get here for harvest, and he did. It's nuts.

But now the farm can't pay its own. Cycling back to climate change. We can't seem to grow them. There's nothing you can really do about frost. And the seasons—the weather is so erratic—I don't know. And it's not just us and cherries, not just the state of Michigan. It's all over the country, too.

The pollinators is another issue, certainly. For those that don't appreciate, they are not just honeybees. Pollinators incorporate a lot of insects. We have a pollinator habitat that's not quite an acre that's amazing. We planted that three, four years ago. It's full of pollinators year-round, and it's just amazing to watch. The vetch that we planted last year, which finally came in well this year, it's full of bumblebees. Bumblebees are the best pollinators there is. They truly are. Honeybees are very prima donna. In a wind they would not be out. If it looks like it's going to rain, they are not going to be out. If it's Tuesday they are not going to go out. But the bumblebees are just like frat boys: "Hey, man, there's pollen!" Anything that's going on out there, they are flying against a horrible wind, and they are still going for that pollen and getting to those blossoms. They are amazing. I am always pleased to see my guys out there, my bumblebees.

There's lots of good stories. We can make farming sound romantic. We make stories out of everything. Life is about stories. We can thicken the stories so wide they don't believe it. But I really do have my concerns about the future of agriculture. I appreciate the farmers markets. The folks that are doing truck farming, growing vegetables and herbs and a little of this and a little of that and everything else. I tip those guys heavy. There's no way I could have grown those green peppers. Eight green peppers that you are selling to me for three dollars? That's not right. They have more value to me than that. But we need them. We need the small farmers. We need people who support the small farming. We need people who support organic.

People ask us, "Why should we pay more for organic?" Particularly when we do farmers markets, and the wife is saying, "Oh, see, look." We always offer a tasting. "These are amazing. Oh, we should get like three of these bags and take them for guests," and so on and so on. The guy behind her, the husband, is saying, "These are pretty expensive." And looks down the row and, "Why should I pay more because it's organic?"

"You shouldn't. If they don't have value to you being organic, you shouldn't pay it."

My husband is very happy with the Wesco coffee. I'm very happy with the Starbucks, thank you. Even just black, decaf. But I'll pay my three dollars or whatever. He'll pay his ninety-nine cents for a Wesco.

"So if it doesn't have value to you, you shouldn't. And that's no criticism. And the farmer that's four booths down, they need to make a living, too, and sell their product. So please do buy theirs. And if ours have value to you, feel free. If not, don't." So usually, I quiet things down quite quickly. I'm not going to get into a debate with you.

One year back before we were organic we had an oversupply of cherries. The cherries were being priced at a nickel that we were going to get for the processor. So I don't know what currently it is, but it used to be about twenty-one cents to grow cherries, fourteen to twenty-one depending on the kind of operation you had and the equipment and different things. And it cost you 4.8 cents to harvest, just to harvest. Just to take your shakers through.

I had a fit. There was no way—I can feel it in my soul, even to say it—there was no way that I was going to be paid less than what it cost me to produce these. And—sorry for the naming—but Mrs. Smith's pies and Smucker jellies were not going to make a profit on my cherries when I couldn't make cost. There was no way that I was going to put my cherries on this huge forty-acre farm that was going to have devastating results across the whole nation. Mrs. Smith and Smucker's were going to say, "Oh, my God, Kobernik Orchards aren't going to give us their cherries." Hardly. But it was a stand. It was like, "No, I am not harvesting my cherries. I will leave them on the tree."

Well, there came those German immigrant parents going, "You can't waste that fruit! No!" So it's like one side on one shoulder and one on the other, and it's just like . . . Ugh! Long story, we called the Food Bank in Lansing, and I told them my story. I was just as feisty about it. And they said, "We'd love to have them. And we'll pay you 4.8 cents. We have donations that come into the Food Bank for gleaning and gathering and things like that." It was perfect. And then, benevolently, our processing company, which is nine miles down the road, agreed to pit them for free. And so we had a lot of cherries that went to the Food Bank in Lansing, and then they were distributed. As I understand, quite a bit of them went to the prisons, and the prisoners then make cherry crisps in these large commercial size—or they did then—and then they go to Senior Citizen Centers and things like that.

People found out and we started to get in the news. Some of the TV stations came out. But we were really adamant. We would not talk to anybody. This is not a feel-good story. This is a tragedy. Yes, there's a good ending, but if you only focus on, "Isn't this cute?" we're not talking to you. Alan was adamant. "I'm not talking to you." "Tell me what you hear I'm saying" (his experience from a social worker). "Tell me what you hear I'm saying." Making sure that they were going to take the right bent on it, so to speak. Because there was no way that we were going to be the cute little puppy in the pet store window. "Aren't they cute, those little farmers?" No. This is awful.

We still don't know what we are doing. We love it. I don't know what the future holds for the farm. We discuss it some. People ask us, "Well, your kids are going to take over the farm someday, aren't they?" "Don't know." We said if we couldn't make money growing cherries we were going to grow houses. My kids are twenty-eight and twenty-nine. I'm sixty and Alan's sixty-three. I don't know. Alan's uncle is now a widower. He's eighty-six. He still comes up every spring and he farms. He has one son that's forty-eight and lives out in Utah. He comes in May. He just left this week. So the two of them now keep their farm. Their farm is bigger than ours. I don't know.

Small farms can't survive without a second business. One or the other has to work and also for health care. I don't want to get into all of that, but we need to have affordable health care. We need to have universal health care. That shouldn't be something that you have to work for. Even twenty years ago there wasn't a farmer that we knew that didn't have—and I mean this respectfully—the wife working on the farm. Usually one partner or the other, part-time or full-time, was working.

But it doesn't mean you can't do it. You just have to find the right balance. You can have a five-acre patch. You can have an amazing spring and summer and you can teach school. You can work at the Crystal Mountain Ski Resort. You've got to be creative. Or you can do metal work. Or you can start a housecleaning business. None of this is demeaning. You can make damn good money, as you should. Just like you should make money, you should be paid adequately for some of those jobs. You can. There are some things I wish I hadn't done, or if we had made some different decisions along the line, along the way, but I wouldn't have traded it for the world.

My kids have grown up on an organic farm. I still think of that. I mean, because I didn't grow up here. But they grew up on a farm. And that's unusual for them. It helped them get into school. They got some scholarships because of it. For employment, it's a unique thing to have in their lives. I don't know. My kids did not get their work ethics—and they both have amazing work ethics, more so than Alan and I do—because of being on the farm. "When you grow up on a farm that's why you have a good work ethic." No. They got paid from when they were toddlers with their little pail out there picking, gleaning cherries. We always have paid them for any work they did on the farm. My husband would never dream of asking these kids to come to the job site and clean up his sawdust or his job site. I would never ask my kids to help me do my progress notes for therapy, or I don't know what. No.

We chose the farm. This is our business. If you choose to work on it, you will be paid. And if you choose to work on it, like you are going to do something, you are going to follow through and do it. Because you wouldn't get paid if you were somewhere else and you didn't follow through. But I feel bad for some farm kids who have grown up on the farm, and they were milking at 5:00 a.m. They couldn't do sports in the evenings, or there were some events they lost out on.

I don't know where the future lies. I have no idea. Climate change may dictate. We had 10 percent of our crop this year. We were frozen in 2012. We were frozen in 2015. In 2012 the whole state was frozen. In 2015 a lot of us were frozen. This year was a fluke. We ended up with 10 percent of a crop. Uncle Carl in Honor, they had none. And yet probably ten miles from here they had a full crop. It was just where the frost landed. Alan always says it was one degree that made the difference. The frost came too late. I don't know. So we are still trying to figure out what they want from us. We want a good cherry.

My Favorite Cherry Pie Recipe with Yummy Crust

RECIPE BY CHERYL KOBERNIK, NORTH STAR ORGANICS

Serves 6

Double-crust pie dough

2½ cups organic all-purpose flour

2 tablespoons sugar

1 teaspoon salt

8 tablespoons vegetable shortening cut into ½ inch pieces—chilled

12 teaspoons unsalted butter cut into ½ inch pieces—chilled

Combine flour, sugar, and salt. Add the chilled shortening and butter and cut the mixture together until the mixture resembles coarse crumbs. Sprinkle 6 tablespoons of ice water over the mixture and integrate, preferably with a pastry cutter, until dough sticks together—adding more water as needed. Divide dough into two even pieces and wrap in plastic wrap and refrigerate for at least one hour. Let the chilled dough soften slightly at room temperature before rolling it out and fitting it into a pie plate.

Cherry Filling

1 cup sugar

¼ cup cornstarch

pinch salt

6 cups fresh, jarred, or canned tart cherries

¼ teaspoon almond extract

¼ teaspoon vanilla extract

1 tablespoon butter

Heat oven to 500 degrees. Mix 1 cup of the sugar, the cornstarch, and salt. Stir in cherries and extracts. Spread the filling in the unbaked pie crust bottom and dollop pieces of 1 tablespoon butter on filling. Add top crust—brush with 1 tablespoon water and sprinkle with sugar.

Place pie on heated baking sheet and lower the oven temperature to 425 degrees. Bake until the top crust is golden, about 25 minutes. Rotate the baking sheet, reduce the oven temperature again to 375 degrees, and continue to bake until the juices are bubbling and the crust a deep golden brown, 30–35 minutes longer. Enjoy!

Photo by Madeleine Hill Vedel

3

Jenny Tutlis

Jenny grew up in Traverse City and did not farm or garden as a child. She studied art history and African studies in college. She first discovered her passion for gardening when she was a volunteer in a community of people with mixed abilities in Virginia. Years later, after a stint in the Peace Corps with her husband, she heard about CSA, Community Supported Agriculture. Intrigued, the couple explored different CSAs in Wisconsin before returning to Michigan to start their own in Leelanau County, initially on rented land, later on their own farm. Meadowlark now counts over 180 shareholders with almost 600 people owning those shares and being nourished by their food.

Jenny Tutlis, b. September 24, 1967
Interview: April 20, 2018
Meadowlark Farm, 6350 East Lingaur Road, Lake Leelanau

The whole idea of being organic is trying to
really pay attention and work with cycles.

I'm Jenny Tutlis, and I live and work at Meadowlark Farm, which is in Lake Leelanau, Michigan. We've been living there and farming for the last seventeen years. We have lived in Leelanau County for twenty-four years, farming. I grew up in Traverse City. I can't really say that my husband, Jon, grew up in Traverse City, but we went to high school together, met in high school, and went out into the world and did our different things and ended up back here after college and multiple experiences in the world. I went to Kalamazoo College, and Jon went to Earlham College. Neither of us studied agriculture. Neither of us came from an agricultural background at all. We didn't really have it in either of our family histories. I studied art history and African studies in college, good liberal arts degrees. Jon studied biology, so he actually had some relevant experiences in college.

When I got to the end of college I realized that although I had been interested in art education and I had done some amazing internships in art museums, I didn't really see myself doing that with my life. I was at a loss as to what I was going to do. Jon was still in college, so I decided when I graduated to just look for a volunteer opportunity somewhere. I would take a year to figure something out.

I wound up as a volunteer in a community in Virginia called Innisfree Village, living with people of varying abilities. I lived and worked with people there, and I ended up working in the garden. That's where it all began for me. I loved that work so much, and I felt within that first year of being there that this is what I loved doing. I loved every part of it. I loved learning so much, and it was an interesting time in the community there. There really wasn't anybody who was an experienced gardener. They had had someone previously, and that person had moved on. There was another young woman and me. We were both the same age. Neither of us knew anything, but we were both really passionate about it and learned a lot together. We studied and read a lot of books and also just learned from doing. She actually is still there. It's over thirty years now, and she still grows there and lives there.

I was there for a total of three years. After the first year Jon joined me there after he finished school. We were eager to get into the Peace Corps. We spent a full year applying and actually got married to go into the Peace Corps together. Marriage really wasn't on our radar at that time, but to go in together and be placed together we had to be married.

So we were like, "Really? Okay. That's a good enough reason to get married, I guess."

We did the Peace Corps kind of in between being at Innisfree. We were sent to Papua New Guinea, where we were going to be doing community development. We didn't really even care what our title was. We just wanted to go and learn and be immersed in a really different wild place.

But Jon got really sick when we were there. He got cerebral malaria and almost died. We ended up leaving the Peace Corps because of that and went back to Virginia to Innisfree and then stayed there for another couple of years.

Around that time—I think it was the late '80s—we started to hear about CSA or Community Supported Agriculture. I remember feeling like . . . it just made so much sense to me. It pulled together all these ideas that made sense to me. I was like, "Wow! That's so cool. I want to learn more about that." At that time there were CSA farms on the East Coast and on the West Coast and really not much in the middle. There weren't many CSAs in the Midwest or even just between the coasts. It was something that really took off on the East Coast.

Living at Innisfree we were growing food for the community there. But it was kind of an insular place. It wasn't like a closed-off community, but we weren't interacting much with people outside of the community. I remember thinking it would be really cool to have a CSA that could be working with the people there who had lots of differing abilities. That was an interesting challenge. But I wanted to also connect with the other community, which was outside of Charlottesville. When we proposed that idea to the community, people were like, "Well. I don't know. That sounds kind of too much." We decided at that time that we really wanted to learn more about this. "We want to explore this, and if we don't have your blessing to do that, then we are going to move on." Which we did.

We wanted to be somewhere in the Midwest if we could. There were some CSA farms in Minnesota, like the Minneapolis–Saint Paul area. We wanted to be in the Midwest because that was where we could imagine ourselves living eventually. And we wanted to learn how to grow in that sort of environment. We found a farm in Wisconsin that was a large CSA and also a community, and we went there for a year to learn about the CSA.

We'd had about three years of farming experience, but not about how a CSA works. It was an interesting experience. We learned a lot. The best part about being there was that there were other CSAs, and they had a really strong network together. We had the opportunity to talk to and learn from a lot of different people that had CSA farms and were doing it in really different ways. Just by talking to people and visiting their farms, feeling things out a little bit, we were able to learn what would work for us, what we were attracted to, and what we did not like.

After being there we felt like we were ready to start our own farm. We actually started to look at farmland in that area of Wisconsin, but it felt like if we were really thinking about settling we should probably move home. We had always loved Leelanau County and had hoped that we would someday land back there, so we decided to move back home, but not to Traverse City, to Leelanau County.

We were renting a farm, which I would never recommend to anyone to do. It was ridiculous, but it was all we could afford. We also weren't really ready, and we had no idea if Traverse City was ready for a CSA. Actually, when we moved back, we realized that there were a couple of small CSAs in the area: the Wells Family Farm in Williamsburg, although they didn't interact much with Traverse City. They were in the Williamsburg, Elk Rapids area. And there was a CSA in Bear Lake. Both were really small, so there really wasn't a CSA in Traverse City or Leelanau.

We landed on this rented place. The first thing we did was build a greenhouse. People always say, "How did you do that when you started to have children?" It was a lot because of our family. Our families being close, they helped us right from the beginning. They were superexcited about us moving home. Even though it was way out of the realm of their experience or interests, they were excited and very supportive of us and helped us in any way they could.

We rented that farm for seven years. The first year we just kind of did farmers markets. We were trying to get our name out there. The second year we started the CSA with some of our customers that were buying food from us at the farmers markets. We did it mostly through word of mouth. That's always been our favorite method of sharing information about the farm.

I also started writing articles for different publications about what CSA was. I felt like I needed to educate people at that time. Today a lot of people know what CSA is, but then I felt like I had to talk about the concept. So any small publication that I could get a spiel in about CSA, I would try and do that. But our die-hard loyal customer base—who are still people that we feed—came from buying food from us in markets. That was the best way for people to learn about us.

We had our daughter, Ella, the second year of the CSA, which was crazy but wonderful. She was born in April, which was also crazy and wonderful. We were still doing farmers markets as well. I remember going to the farmers market with her in a baby carrier. Traverse City market was all there was at that time.

We did a little market stand in Glen Arbor the next year instead of doing Traverse City, still trying to do the CSA and get people interested in the idea. It's a big step for people to commit to paying money before they receive something, investing in a concept, investing in people, investing in an idea.

We were living on the rented land, and we just kept investing. Every year we would pour everything that we made back into the farm. We were both working other jobs while we were farming, and almost every dollar would get put back into infrastructure and building. There are just so many investments to make to start a farm. We realized at a certain point that we had really sunken in there. We had bought a new well for the farm we lived on. We had built a greenhouse there. We had planted perennials.

I had always hoped that the people would consider selling even a chunk of it to us, because it was an eighty-acre farm, but at a certain point we realized that there was no way that was going to happen and that we really needed to try and figure out something more permanent. We were paying rent, you know, a ridiculous . . . not *waste* of money because we were building a business at the same time, but a lot . . . so we started looking.

It was the height of the real estate madness in Leelanau County where it was $10,000 an acre, ridiculously expensive. We tried to work with both conservancies, the Grand Traverse and Leelanau, about the idea of some community land trust. It's not enough to say farmland. You also need to invest in young people becoming farmers, you know, with all the statistics about aging farmers and people not taking over. At that point they weren't ready to talk about that. I mean, they talked about it with us, but they weren't ready to make any sort of financial commitment. Which they have now, both of them, which is great. I'm glad.

We started looking for something more permanent. Jon's family helped us financially. There is no way we would have been able to afford the farm on our own. We moved to our current location seventeen years ago. For seventeen years we've been on Lingaur Road. We don't do farmers markets any more. The CSA is the main thing that we do. We do sell locally to small wholesale accounts and restaurants, but the CSA is the heart of what we do. I still love it a lot.

My favorite thing is feeding pregnant women and nursing moms. When I learn that I am feeding pregnant women it just totally makes my day. I also love feeding families and having kids learn about eating food. I love the stories about people working hard to get their kids to eat vegetables, and finally they get it, and they learn that they actually love broccoli. That's very meaningful and important to me. A lot of what I do is educational, sharing ideas about how to eat well and what to do with vegetables, how to cook them, how to take care of them through my newsletter mostly.

We used to have school kids coming more. When our kids were younger we had connections with schools and we would have school groups all the time, and now that our kids are grown I don't even get phone calls any more. I feel like they maybe have connections with other farms that are closer. That's fine with me, too. It's always been hectic to have school groups come visit.

I didn't mention Eli. He was born a couple of years after Ella, in May, which was also crazy. Some crazy farming years. Another thing that is important to me is working with young people on the farm. I care deeply about teaching young people about where their food comes from and how to work, and how to work together in a group, and also how to be together with people of different ages. That's important to me. It's something really special about the farm that people comment on, and I feel it's the strength of what the farm means to people, that people of different ages are coming together with a common love and goal. That's powerful.

Our society is very segmented right now. People this age do this together, and people that age do that together. There's not a lot of mixing. I believe there's a lot of value in mixing and in being able to speak with people who aren't like you, who aren't your age. Our kids now are in their twenties, and there is a whole crew of kids who have grown up being a part of the farm and then becoming workers on the farm and working on the farm, and now a lot of that group have moved on to the next part of their lives as young adults, but I feel like the things that they have taken with them from the farm are super valuable and will help them learn how to be meaningful members of society no matter what they end up doing.

I feel especially passionate about young women and girls see-ing me as a woman farmer. That idea that farmers are all men is still really prevalent. Women are supposed to stay in the kitchen or they do this. . . . We're not that kind of farm. Jon and I have different roles on the farm, but they are not traditional gender roles. I feel like model-ing that to young people. That's the way we raised our kids. I've real-ized how important that is when I've had young people come back. They were able to see a less traditional role for women, and even if they don't want to be a woman farmer, they have seen a woman farmer. That whole stereotype won't change until there are more women farmers and more young girls start seeing that women can also be farmers. It's not just the man on the tractor.

For a while it was mostly through our kids that we recruited our crew. Friends of our kids and their friends. There was a connection that way. But that has shifted now. The last two years there has been a major shift. We've realized, "Okay, we have to look at things a little differently now." We don't have a lot of those young people anymore. They have moved on. We have to think about this a little differently and figure out what we want to look like, what we want to have, how we are going to attract people.

Because we don't do farmers markets now we don't have a public face in the community the way we used to, with people seeing us every week at a farmers market. I have done some advertising for workers. Last year we knew Eli was going to be moving out. . . . We are interested in attracting people who are interested in farming, so if we put that out into the world maybe it will attract some people who are serious about wanting to learn about small farming, about organic farming.

We have some on-farm housing. We had some people come. I have a listing. There's really only one that I know of that's a national list-ing. There's ATTRA: Appropriate Technology Transfer for Rural Areas. It's national. They build and maintain connections between farms and people looking for apprenticeships on farms. We had some immigrants work on the farm short term who were living and working in cher-ries on another farm. There was a gap between cherries and apples or something. A local farmer asked, "Do you need help?" and we said,

"Yeah, sure." But it was a really short-term thing. The whole visa situation seems really like a huge headache. We've had some people come to us who've been friends of friends. We haven't recruited them through any organization from other countries. I've always thought that it would be awesome to do that, but it also feels problematic. I don't really know of an organization to organize with them.

We are certified organic now. We were in the beginning, and then in 2000 when the rules shifted, it became a national law and things changed. Being certified organic had been organized and maintained through a state organization, and it was run by farmers. We regulated ourselves. It was still stringent and real, but it was grassroots. Then it became this national thing, and it just seemed super problematic, lots of red tape, rules that were not realistic. Ugh! The paperwork seemed like it was going to be this huge insurmountable task. We thought, "It's just not us anymore. Let's take a break from that." It felt overwhelming.

So we did not get certified organic. We talked about it and put it out there to our community of shareholders in our CSA and said, "We're thinking to not do this anymore, and this is why." And people were like: "We trust you. We believe in you." We realized then that this is a relationship that we have built here, and that's what's important to us rather than this large government organization stepping in and giving us some sort of rubber stamp. So we didn't pursue organic certification for a while.

And then there started to be more organic certified farms in the area, people doing what we were doing and also being certified organic. We started to look into it a little more. Things had settled down with the paperwork and the expectations, and we were like, "You know, I think we can probably do it." We looked at what it would take to have that happen for us. We also thought it was going to be really expensive, that that was going to be a huge stumbling block for us. And then these cost-sharing programs started, where states will basically pay for your certification costs if you fill out this paperwork and go through these steps. With the cost-sharing there was an incentive which convinced us it would be crazy not to do this.

We've always been organic farmers. We didn't change the way we were farming at all. We continued to farm organically because that's what we believe in. We just weren't going to jump through the hoops and do all the paperwork. But then the hoops weren't really that big to jump through. I don't know if it was just us getting older, or things settled down and the systems got more streamlined and easier to navigate. We realized: "This isn't really that bad." And the cost-sharing helped. And so we've been certified organic again, for the second time, for seven or eight years. I guess because we don't always know everybody who is purchasing a share—especially in our little wholesale accounts in the county; they don't really know our story or know us—that having the certified organic label is a selling point.

When we bought our own farm I knew—from being in the industry and then this farm that we were on in Wisconsin had animals—I had thought that I would be really interested in integrating vegetables and animals. But then I realized how much work that took. Still, though, even when we were on rented land, I always thought that when we got our own farm that we would have sheep, we would have horses. Those were the two animals that I was interested in having be a part of our farm, and of course chickens. But Jon would always say, "Let's just wait and see. Let's just try and get a little more established." It makes sense from an ideological standpoint to have animals be a part of the farm, but it's a lot of work. By the time we ended up being settled on our own place I would still talk about it, but Jon would still say, "It's really a lot of work."

"Yeah, I know. You are right."

We always kept chickens from the beginning. I was a vegetarian for a long time, and I knew that I didn't want to have a big meat production thing to be a part of what we did. And milk, I knew, was a huge commitment, and I just didn't see having a cow. I love plants. John and I both love plants. We knew that that was what we really wanted to focus on. And so we ended up never getting anything other than chickens.

Other people were doing animal work, and we built relationships with them. There were people doing goats' milk and goat cheese and people doing meat. It felt good to be able to support those farmers and not have that be on our farm. We had enough on our plate. We wanted to do vegetables and cut flowers. The two of those have always been from the beginning what we have done.

When we started we were in maybe one acre, or two acres, and now we have seven in cultivation plus three hoop houses and a greenhouse.

We are not getting any bigger. We are as big as we want to be. A couple of years ago people would ask, "How many shares? How many shareholders? How many people is it actually?" So when people were signing up that year I had them write down how many people were sharing a share. And it was like 585 or 586. It was almost 600 individuals. I was kind of blown away by that because it's like 175 or 180 shares and I realized a lot of people were sharing shares, which is great. That felt like a big deal. That's a lot of people. And that was just the CSA. That didn't include people who were buying our food in grocery stores.

So what to grow? It was always going to be vegetables and flowers, but as far as specifically—the whole kind of idea of CSA, I feel like is diversity—we've been fine-tuning and tailoring not as we go but with people's feedback. People give me feedback at the end of the season, what they really liked or what they didn't like, too much or too little of this. So we've tailored. . . . I'll try anything. I will try and grow anything. The one thing that I don't care much about growing is sweet corn. It's kind of a ridiculous crop to me. It uses a lot of land that we don't have. The soils in Leelanau County are just not strong enough to support healthy sweet corn. And people are used to it being a cheap crop. "Twenty-five cents for an ear of corn." Other people do sweet corn, and for us to do it organically is tricky. We always grow a little patch, but it's pretty tricky. And we just don't have the land to grow that much. But I'll try lots of other things. I really like growing artichokes. And we have been cultivating garlic for twenty-four years. We love growing garlic and sharing garlic with people. It's a main part of our boxes in the season.

I wait to listen to what people say with feedback, but I also like to challenge them a little. That's also a strength of CSA: that it challenges people to try something that they wouldn't maybe buy on their own. If they were to go to the farmers market or to the grocery store they wouldn't choose that. But all of a sudden they have it, and it's like: "Okay, what do I do with it?" And it doesn't work for everybody. I know that. I know that CSA is really hard for some people and it doesn't work for them. The people it does work for are excited about getting a box, and they look at it, and they say, "Okay, I have never done anything with fennel. What am I going to do with this?" And they read a recipe, and they cook with it. I try to help people expand their culinary horizons. But I know that people like standard staple food regularly, too.

Figuring out how much is too much and how much is too little is something I am always trying to balance. We learned early on that having too much was worse, really, than having too little. People don't like to waste food. They felt like it was valuable. It made them feel guilty to not use it. I'm still playing with that. What's the right amount for a family of four? And it really depends. How much people actually like to cook versus how much they think they like to cook. Or how many nights a week they eat in, how many nights a week they are actually cooking dinner, and whether the people in their house actually will try new things.

The summer Nancy Allen was creating recipes and cooking for the crew on the farm she would just show up to make a lunch for a large group of people. She would be like: "What's happening today? What do you have available?"

I know that doesn't work for everybody. I'm not a proselytizer about CSA. I don't even really talk about it unless there's an open door to talk about it. People are busy. People are busier and busier. With families, I don't know sometimes how people manage. I'm not trying to say that CSA is going to feed the world or is for everybody. If there's an open door, I'll go in, but I'm not going to be pushing down the door. I feel like the most powerful way for people to learn is from each other. Word of mouth. Friends sharing with friends is super powerful.

A lot of what is happening with the young people working on the farm—they might not even realize how it is affecting them until they are a little bit older and they go out and they are like: "Oh, yes, I remember seeing this grow or having this for lunch." And working on the farm, too, that connection with the earth is super powerful for the kids. It affects them on levels that they don't even realize. I think they are grounded in ways that they wouldn't necessarily attribute to the farm but that are definitely a part of it. Growing up in northern Michigan and then having that experience of being in a place, working with that soil, that water, and all that's happening around them while they are there . . . that stays with them forever.

One of the greatest skills that kids learn actually is how to see something in detail, not just kids but people who are on the farm for more than one season. We grow such a diversity of things, so many different vegetables and flowers. First of all it takes people a while to learn what everything is, discerning what is good and what isn't good. Seeing differences from week to week or from the beginning of the week to the end of the week in a crop is a really valuable skill in whatever they decide to do. Being able to really pay attention to detail, see detail and differences, is a big skill.

With the changing climate challenges come to us as a situation where we don't really know anymore. You can't expect from one season to another that anything will be the same. Not only the differences between seasons but also the beginnings and ends of a season. There are going to be really drastic fluctuations and that's going to increase. There's going to be really big differences. What that means to us is being as flexible and observant and trying to adapt as much as possible to those changes. The whole idea of being organic is trying to really pay attention and work with cycles, and so we are trying to observe changes, but also trying not to contribute to the changes.

We try and do things as efficiently and with as small a carbon footprint as we can. We are putting in solar panels, and we are going to have enough that we are not only covering all of the power that the farm uses; we are going to be generating above and beyond what we use. We are really excited about that. That's something we have thought about and tried to work toward for a number of years, and it's magically happening. A lot through the support of our community. The CSA community through the years that we have built the business and the farm has supported us financially in making some bigger investments in that growth, and the solar panels are one area that people are really excited about and helping us with financially.

About fourteen years ago when we built our first hoop house and then added another a few years later marked the major transition from having to work other jobs and pouring every dollar back into the farm and being able to farm full time. The season extension was the turning point. It's been fourteen years since we've had other jobs. We are able to pay our bills, and we are able to make investments in the farm. We are still low-income people, but we're fine. We are happy and content. That feels still like a huge thing, and it's still surprising. When we interact with financial institutions or people who are used to working with farmers, it's surprising to them that we can make a living and not have to work off-farm, because so many farmers do.

So that season extension works, allowing us to grow food in a season where there is not a lot of food happening. Our season extension is about our CSA. When we are doing season extension we are not selling much outside of the CSA, but it's for this committed group of people who want to eat local food. We do a winter share now and a spring share. That was the turning point.

A lot of that work Jon and I can do on our own with the help of volunteers. We don't need a huge crew to do it, whereas in the summer we need a huge crew to do all that we do. In the summer we have between fifteen and eighteen employees, and a lot of those are part-time employees. For full-time employees we probably have six. Our cycle is mid-April to the end of October with having help. It's pretty satisfying to be able to harvest food, especially greens, when there's snow on the ground. To be in a structure that's verdant and vibrant and alive, and then you walk out and like: "Oh, yeah. There's a foot and a half of snow still out here. This is pretty cool!"

Some of my best memories or thoughts about the farm are from when we are working on one big project all together; it's this coming together. A lot of what we are doing has this one common goal of growing and harvesting food for this community of people, this little community within this bigger community. But we have different tasks. It's a little group here and a little group here, but there are times that we do big projects together like garlic harvest. There can be some really sweet times with people all being together working for this one goal. It's really hot and sweaty, but everyone's happy even though it's hard, hard work. That's what it feels like.

Those are some of my favorite feelings of "best ever." When I have the feeling like, "This isn't us anymore. There's something bigger than us happening here. We are participating in it. We are like this tiny little piece, but it's bigger than us." That's a powerful thing, even though it's a small thing. It's this little community. It's this little farm in this little place of Michigan, but it can feel big, bigger than us.

II

COFFEE, TEA, AND CHOCOLATE

Grow with Care, Harvest with Love

Photo courtesy of Angela Macke

4

Angela Macke

Although Angela grew up on a farm where her parents grew their own food and her mom canned and froze for the winters, she did not return to farming until 1996 when she moved to this region as a Registered Nurse. Before that she was a travel nurse serving in different parts of the country. Her mother is also a nurse. Even after she started her tea farm on Route 72 where it still is, she didn't think of it as a business until Amanda Danielson placed orders for her restaurant. Guided by the rules and traditions of biodynamic farming since 2005, Angela's Light of Day is legendary as the only certified organic and Demeter Biodynamic tea farm in North America.

Angela Macke, b. December 13, 1969
Interview: August 24, 2015
Light of Day Organics, 3502 East Traverse Highway, Traverse City

God was really showing off when he made herbs.... At my last
count we were growing 252 different species of plants.

I was born in Adrian, Michigan. My mom was living in Oahu in Hawai'i while my dad was commissioned. He was a scuba diver in the navy. When they were first married they spent their first year in Maryland where my brother was born, and then they moved down to the Florida Keys, and then they moved over to Hawai'i, and that's where I was conceived and lived until I was four years old. And then dad got out of the [Vietnam] war and went back to school. He went to Michigan State for grad school, and that's where my brother Rick came along. Every two years there was another kid. There are eight of us. My baby sister is in grad school now at Notre Dame. There's about a nineteen-year age gap between us. I came from a big Catholic family, and I grew up in White Hall, Michigan.

Looking back now I'm convinced I had as close to perfect a childhood as you could. We had a twenty-acre farm, blueberries. My dad was a schoolteacher during the year. My mom was a nurse, but she didn't work outside the home because she was so busy taking care of us. And then they had the most giant vegetable garden every year, like Mr. McGregor's garden. Before we could do much we always had to go out and weed a row of carrots, pick a bucket of blueberries, and then we'd ride our bikes to Lake Michigan and go swimming. We had horses and pigs and chickens. We were all in 4-H. It was just an ideal place to grow up.

We learned how to share. We learned really about a self-sustaining community. We raised all of our own food. Mom canned and froze everything so we learned a lot of skills from watching. Grandma would come up from Florida in the summer, and I'd watch them can and preserve. And it was funny, even after watching them so many times the first time when I tried to do it—like five years ago I was so afraid I was going to blow up the house with the pressure cooker—they've gotten better since my mom's version. I've enjoyed growing my own food for our family. We have two boys. They are fourteen and sixteen.

I went to White Hall High School and then went on to Western Michigan University. I got a bachelor of science degree there and then at the same time went to Bronson School of Nursing, which is now part of Western's program. It was one of the old diploma programs. For every credit hour you had to spend nine and a half hours a week in the hospital, so by the time you graduated you were ready. The day I graduated I was offered a job in the emergency room. I worked there and then took my boards and moved to Hawai'i, and that's when I started doing travel nursing.

I spent twenty-two months in Hawai'i learning about alternative medicine, primarily because in my last year at nursing school I had been diagnosed first with Crohn's disease, and then lupus, and then rheumatoid arthritis, and then fibromyalgia, and then Hashimoto thyroiditis. I thought this had to be a bunch of hogwash. It wasn't truly denial; I just really thought there must be some mistake. I mean, you are given those diagnoses based on your lab results, and your symptomology, and I definitely presented with acute abdominal pain. It was true I had a Petechial rash; I had fevers. I met all the criteria for lupus and all those other things, but I knew in my gut and my heart that I had been misdiagnosed because it came on so quickly and I had been so healthy. It didn't make any sense to me. I thought it was something dietary or environmental because I had been healthy all my life.

I also had had mono in my senior year of high school, which I now understand is a red flag that your immune system is really compromised. And I think I didn't ever quite recover from that. So then starting nursing school and being exposed to all those cootie bugs probably wasn't the greatest.

But what I learned in Hawai'i was for the first time to understand about holism, not just that our diet of what we put in our mouth is a piece of the puzzle, or a success story for wellness. I learned about forgiveness and about my diet of thought: that the company I was keeping, the screens I was watching, the books I was reading, and the movies and the music, all contributed to disease or wellness. I learned about meditation when I lived there, and getting still because up until that point it was like Mach Five with my hair on fire, trying to get it all done at school, all of that.

I learned about meditation, and I learned about yoga and creating room, and the connective tissue in my mind; I learned to get really quiet with my body and my mind so I could listen to what was going on. And in a very short amount of time in combination with taking a food journal I realized that I was allergic to gluten, and so I got off of gluten and all dairy, and started on Matcha green tea. Within a four-month period all my lab work had zero converted, even the antinuclear antibody for the lupus. So that was huge.

Two years later when I left there I was completely healthy, whole. I had a real immersion in holistic health. Hawai'i is an amazing place, because when you look at the globe, it's like the center of the universe in so many ways. You get the influence of the east, of the west. I remember sitting in a hot tub at my condo there in Maui and Kihei—it's kind of a little local town—and it's neat because it's 74 degrees and sunny every day. It's perfect. But I remember in the hot tub there was somebody from Alaska, somebody from Japan, somebody from San

Francisco, somebody from Australia. It was just the melting pot. I was sitting in a melting pot in a hot tub simmering away. I felt more at home there than I had anywhere in my life. It was like anything goes, a really relaxed lifestyle, but also the hospital setting. Maui Memorial was very professional, but so loving. With so many Filipino women and Japanese giving nursing care, I felt like I learned to be a better nurse working and living there. Travel is always good. I enjoyed that immensely. I came back to Michigan for a little while and then I started traveling.

And I thought, "That's cool. I'm out of here." And then I was out of there and traveling up and down the coasts of California and Florida. And then I decided to start grad school. I had applied and been accepted at Emory University and Vanderbilt University and the University of Tampa to be a nurse practitioner, but I wasn't sure. They all had different programs. One was for nurse anesthesia; one was an ER practice; one was for a family practice position. And back then it was kind of a new program. There weren't a lot of nurse practitioners. And so I decided to give myself that summer and come up to Traverse City and work in the open heart unit, and try to figure out what I wanted to do. I came to Traverse City in 1996 after spending five years as a travel nurse. Every thirteen weeks for five years I had moved around the country to different hospitals and practiced intensive-care nursing.

I met my husband in my first day of work, my first hour of work. We dated for that summer, and then I went back to Sarasota Memorial. I had a commitment that I needed to finish up there. He came down and visited a couple of times, and I decided to come back the next summer and work at Munson. We were engaged that next December and married a year later. In 1999 our son Peter was born. He is now sixteen. And then twenty-one months later our son Leland.

They were just little, and mostly because I could have them both restrained—I'd have one in a front pack and one in a backpack—one of our hobbies every day was to trot out to the woods and do some wild foraging, berry picking. We had a big garden that we started on our twelve acres at home. It was my absolute escape. I loved being a mom, but I thought it was a lot harder than working at the hospital, just the constancy of it. It was exhausting when they were that age.

They weren't sleeping that much. They were very busy, healthy boys, active boys. They had to run a lot, like Labs, every day, but I enjoyed growing food with them. I had a good time. It was very satisfying to grow their food, mash it up to make baby food when they first started eating, knowing that I was providing food that I could grow for them. It was nutritious, and they were really healthy.

I started putting a lot of herbs away. Probably two years later I went to a family wisdom conference at the college, and that's where I met Amanda Danielson, who was about to open Trattoria Stella with her husband, Paul. That was in the fall of 2004. I had just donated some teas that I had made for these other moms at the conference. And Amanda came over and said, "Oh, this tea is great. It's exactly what we are looking for, for our restaurant."

I said, "Oh, thank you so much, but you can't have it because we are not really in business."

I had two kids on me just like she had her little daughter, Sophia, on her pack. But she was insistent that it would be a great fit. I told my husband about it and he said, "Why don't you do it just for their restaurant?"

I said, "I don't know anything about whole-sale-ing food. I don't know a lick about it. I'm a nurse. I know nothing."

But he was very supportive, and he said, "Be real, Ang. If you don't do this, you know you are going to do something else. Just do it."

So I did. I started with just a few blends for them, and then the word just sort of started spreading. Cedar City Market was carrying the tea, and then Oryana, and I knew I was in over my head because tea is so labor intensive, and I had these two little babies. I didn't know how I was going to do it. So we just started off slow, and everybody was patient and good as I learned. I definitely skinned my knees along the way. It was so humbling. I didn't know the rules of the game. I didn't know how to play it. And in the food industry they definitely knew.

The next year I had our land certified organic. I was desperately trying to find a partner. It was so hard to keep up with the herb production, and then what was happening was that the restaurants were selling teas, and then, of course, the customers wanted to get some, too. Web pages were just starting to pop up. In 2005 we were certified organic. And in 2006 we had our website, which was mostly educational. You could purchase teas on it. I remember we got like maybe an order a week, and it was really exciting. "We got an order! Yeah!" And it was in the basement of our house. We built a commercial kitchen there which is the only way I could do it. Our bedroom is literally right above the commercial kitchen in the basement. I remember watching the reruns of *The X-Files* until way in the middle of the night. It was kind of my secret time. The kids were asleep, my husband was asleep. I could just package teas and escape. I would be tired the next day, but it was fun. It was my little time for myself. I loved it.

I've always loved tea. My mom would always insist on pots of tea to do your homework. And then when I was in Hawai'i I really started getting into loose teas, particularly the Matcha. An herbalist I met there made recommendations for me that I quickly started putting together for myself. But for me it's been mostly an intuitive thing, what is available locally, what is going on, what I have a lot of to work with. You could just combine.

The biggest issue was about safety. Most of the medications I used to give at the hospital were plant-based, and I thought by going to a master-gardener class I would learn a lot. But they didn't really cover much of that. Backyard tea blending can kill someone dead easily. There are many things that are toxic. Nature is amazing. Burdock root is very nourishing, but the leaf is hepatotoxic. The root is actually the antidote for the leaf. But you wouldn't know that. God was really showing off when he made herbs. There are so many little nuances that you really need to know. People are constantly asking, "Why can't I do this?" You really need to do your research. It's not as easy as you would think, given the information that's now available today. For every herb you will probably see two books that say two different things. For example, raspberry leaf. Almost everyone agrees that raspberry leaf is one of the best things you can take when you are pregnant to help build a stronger uterine lining and all the vasculature you need. There are two arteries and a vein in your umbilical cord, for example. So there are certain herbs that are good for building a healthy placenta. But one book out of three might say that you should never have it during pregnancy, so it was really tough to get to the bottom of it and find out what's the truth about this.

There's so much folklore. There's so much oral tradition about herbs. And, as you know, during some of the events that happened on the East Coast—witch burning—they tried to eradicate anyone practicing herbalism. Farming, working with the soil and the land, is directly working with God. That's what paganism believed. Working with these naturally occurring cycles and rhythms was their communion. There are many very dark times in history when these incredibly wise herbalists who were teaching totally available natural healing to others were eradicated because they were a threat to the church, to the medical system at that time. It's really a bummer.

There are some great historians that know a lot about Hildegarde [von Bingen]. She was one of the best. A lot of her research is still considered really good today. And Susan Weed, another good herbalist, is out there. But my background being a licensed nurse really kind of set that level of accountability. It's been both a blessing and a liability risk for me. Probably the biggest reason we've been successful is because I'm a registered nurse. But because I'm a registered nurse, when people come in and say, "What can I take for this?" or "What do you recommend for that?" if I even address that, if I make recommendations, that's considered prescribing, and I could potentially lose my nursing license.

So you have to do the dance and say, "Well, historically this herb has been used for this." Or, "Many midwives have used this herb for this." Or, "In my own life, if I have a sore throat, this is something that I find relief with." Anyway, I learned, not exactly by trial and error, but it was just doing my research first, and then making up a small batch—like maybe a four-ounce batch or something, and tasting it, and paying attention to the effect on my own body. Each one of those individual herbal constituents has an effect, but then, what happens when you combine them? That was something that I really needed to take time with to make sure that all the blends were safe.

I worked with Cornell University and the University of Nebraska, their food labs, to analyze different things, just to make sure that I didn't end up with some crazy concoction. For me each one was inspired. I had to decide, what is my goal with this one? What feeling am I hoping to create in that person? So the first question I usually ask people if they are trying to decide which tea to choose is the same question I would use when I was trying to create all those blends. What time of day would I drink this? Am I drinking this to wake up or to wind down? I would start there. And what flavor fits your profile. Do you want something minty, or fruity, or flowery? There are a lot of things to think about. Every blend is an inspired blend.

There's a story about "Sun in the Winter." It's one of the four-year-old blends now. Winter in northern Michigan is brutal. It's not just the cold; you've got clothes for that. The part that you don't expect is the grayness. We have weeks with no sun. It's just gray and depressing. You wake up in the dark, and you go to bed in the dark; it seems like it's dark all the time. It's gray during the day. Anyway, I remember the kids were both in the back of my car in their little booster seats. It was a rare sunny day in the winter. We were driving into town. I could feel the sun on my arms in the car, so I pulled over and just parked and let that sun bask on me. I was just reveling in how good that felt. And I thought, and I said out loud, "I need to come up with a blend that makes me feel like this sun does on my face right now." The next morning, in the shower—I think almost all the good ideas have come to me in the shower, probably because it's the only time I was ever alone at that time of my life—I knew exactly what to put in it. I knew exactly: lemon myrtle, and cherries, and hibiscus. I had little pound jars, like my ingredients in my little apothecary in the basement. I put this blend together, and it was delicious. It smelled like fruity pebbles, this fruity, lemony delicious taste. When you look up all the historical, botanical herb medicines and why you would drink those ingredients, it was a mood elevator, and it was to help fight the flu, which are all pertinent to that time of the year. And I actually had a friend do a test. She's getting her PhD, and she had a friend doing a microbiology experiment for a student project. They cultured it, and in every strain of the flu it was negative. No growth after four days. So this blend was a mood elevator and it was good for combatting the flu, which was just perfect. We called that one "Sun in the Winter."

Each one has been done that way. I was planning on being the only tea company that didn't have Earl Grey offering, because I just abhorred it so much, but people would not stop asking for Earl Grey, so I needed to come up with something that was a little more mellow.

I ended up creating what we now know as "Creamy Earl Grey" with homemade vanilla, which is made with Maker's Mark bourbon and vanilla beans. It would sit for months and then I would take the caviar out and put that in and then use the pieces, cut up with little scissors and dried, and then you had this nice vanilla-based tea. I made homemade oil of bergamot—not by using traditional bergamot fruit—but using bergamot flowers that we grow, which are a cousin of the bee balm. We soaked those flowers in sunflower oil to create this beautiful oil, and then added calendula, lavender, and cornflowers. So each blend has a story behind it. "Blueberry Blessings" because I grew up on a blueberry farm. It was a Father's Day present for my dad. "In the Mood," an aphrodisiac tea. I've got more up my sleeve. We're going to have a "Good to Go" for the boys with the prostate issues. "Even Keel" for PMS. I'm always thinking of new ones and trying to phase out ones that weren't maybe the best sellers.

Michigan is amazing. We are second only to California in our biodiversity, what we can grow here, believe it or not, in this Great Lakes region. At my last count we were growing 252 different species of plants that all go into the tea production, somehow, including like bee forage, things that we want the bees to pollinate, for the flowers and the honey. The native species—like all the flowers—are really easy; they go gangbusters out here. Things like tea plants are more challenging because the tea is indigenous to Southeast Asia and grows best close to the equator. Anywhere where palm trees grow, pineapples grow, that's where tea plants really like to be, and we are a long ways from there. We are probably two thousand miles from the closest palm tree. So the hoop houses are great. They extend the growing season for us. And in the winter if we have the plants under a couple of layers of plastic and then it insulates with snow, they go dormant, of course, just like they do anyway, but they stay alive, the root system stays alive, so it's really great for us.

We get one big tea harvest right before spring break time; they start warming up in January, and then by March they are ready to be harvested. So we harvest, and then go on spring break. That's about our only slow time, and then all summer long it's berries: blueberries, aronia berries, raspberries, and raspberry leaf. Everything is used here; even the magnolia flowers are harvested to scent the tea. The jasmine tea is scented by fresh magnolia and lilacs and then Asiatic lilies and then hostas. People walk around and to them it may look like pretty landscaping, but it's all used in the tea production. It's crazy. It's challenging.

At the other farm a mile north of here by the river we are probably about a zone six, whereas here in this field with a fifty-mile-an-hour wind and 27 degrees below most recently in the last winter, it's pushing zone three to four. It's cold. And full sun in the summer, with the wind all the time. It makes a great solar farm. We are making all of our own electricity, and all the floors, all the trim, all the framing in all our buildings has been from wood we have harvested from the land. That's something we are pretty proud of. We aren't using any fossil fuels here and that feels pretty good.

Rudolph Steiner was the granddaddy of biodynamic farming. He gave a series of lectures back in 1924, a series of nine lectures for an agricultural course, and that's pretty much what biodynamics is based on. Most people know about the *Farmer's Almanac* because they've seen that. Kind of like *People* magazine, not a lot of serious content, but the biodynamic growing calendar is a very important tool that I use. There is so much to be done. I look at the calendar and go, "Okay, what does the farm want me to do today?" Because there's a time for everything. A time and a season. If it's a flower day I may work on picking calendula petals, or lavender flowers. If it's a leaf day I might work on the teas or lemon balm or peppermint, both cultivating and planting of seeds but also harvesting. For preservation purposes, like what we are doing, you have to do it or the product won't preserve as well. I always give the example of the potatoes. If you harvest potatoes on a flower day rather than a root day, when the gravitational force of the moon on the water is stronger, guess what they are going to do in your pantry. They are going to go to seed. And when they start turning green and going to seed like that they are hepatotoxic, toxic for the liver.

So there are really practical reasons for practicing biodynamics. I got interested in it when I went to a farm conference. I'd heard a little about biodynamics before then, but growing up Catholic, I thought, "I don't know. Cow horns. This sounds like it's probably against my religion or something." So funny to me now. Probably the same thing

I first thought about chakras when I first heard about them. They are just as much a part of our anatomy as my elbow here.

But when I learned that by practicing biodynamics I could potentially have a 30 percent yield increase, and nutritionally biodynamically grown food was far superior, I thought, well, that has my interest now. I started practicing biodynamics in 2005, so it's been ten years. Not only have we increased our yield by 30 percent, we have increased the soil vitality monumentally. I used to have the boys fill up these five-gallon buckets with soil and then dump their bucket on a tarp and we would count the earthworms. When we first started, we'd have six to eight worms in a bucket. And now we have like a hundred worms in a bucket producing all that great worm manure, worm casing so that the soil is much more fertile and aerated as a result. But when I am teaching about biodynamics people don't really understand what it is. So I say, "Let's break it down. *Bio* means life. *Dyne* means force, so we are talking about life forces, and these normally occurring cycles and rhythms. And just like human beings ovulate every twenty-eight days, so does the tea plant."

A conventional farm, a standard farmer that grows carrots—you go to the grocery store and you see conventionally grown carrots and right next to them organic carrots—you can see the difference between the two, without knowing the story of either one. A conventional farm always takes more from the earth than it gives, and an organic farm aims to replace what it took. You grow tomatoes. They are a nitrogen-sucker, so you make sure you replace what you took. But on a biodynamic farm, when you are farming with so much intention, from planting to sowing to preservation to supporting the plant in whatever cycle it is in—because there are flower days, fruit days, root days, leaf days—when you are practicing that way you are going to have a higher yield and the food is going to taste better. It's like natural family planning. You are more likely to conceive a child if you try during your fertile period. No wonder our yield has been improving, because we've been paying attention. We're in communion with the earth and the farm.

Biodynamic farms are taking into consideration every part of the farm. The farm is a living organism. It's not like "this is dirt." This is living soil. And my thoughts are part of the fertilizer. Just like back what I learned in Hawai'i, it wasn't just what I took into my mouth, not just those inputs. With the farmers, the manure they are putting back into the soil is also my thoughts. My intention and my prayers for the end recipient of this tea to restore their balance are all very crucial pieces that make a good cup of tea at the end. Not just that, but it's important to feel really good about your work. I'll go home just exhausted, but I feel like this was good work. I wake up in the morning and I'm charged up to do it again. So I know it's exactly what I'm supposed to be doing, which brings a lot of peace. It's half the battle. It's good to know that you are not mal-positioned.

We are the only certified biodynamic farm in Michigan, and we are the only certified organic and biodynamic—or organic even, or straight biodynamic—in North America. And that's not because others couldn't do it. The reason we are the only one is because tea is the most labor-intensive crop known to man. Seventy thousand tea buds picked by hand for one pound. Probably 300,000 of those cornflower petals picked for a pound. I never intended to get into all this growing. And every time my husband—when I would say I needed more of the cornflowers; I couldn't keep up; I needed more bachelor's buttons; I couldn't grow enough of them at first—he'd say, "Well, just buy some."

And I'd say, "You can't just buy some. The only country that even grows and sells them commercially is Hungary and they say, 'Yeah, we do have some and we would sell them for $300 a pound, but we don't export them.'" I'd think, "Jeez. It sounds like we need to be blue cornflower growers." As the business has grown, I probably receive one hundred inquiries a month from other tea companies trying to buy our ingredients because they ran into the same issues we did. It's hard to find good ingredients, and if you import them—even if you went to Hungary and met the farmer, and can see that he is practicing in the way that you would like to have him practice—when you bring those into the country the containers are bombed for bugs. So you might have a certified organic product, but they have to bomb the container, and then the warehouses where all these ingredients are stored are bombed monthly. So the only way I could insure good products was to grow them myself. It wasn't that I was trying to be a control freak. But I kind of had to be a control freak because there wasn't any other way to secure that the product was going to be what I was promising it was.

I have to work about ninety hours a week from the time we get back from spring break, so from April to November 1 it's seriously like eighty to ninety hours a week. Dawn to dusk. And then until two in the morning. There's so much to be done in the summer, like the nettles, for example. The stinging nettle is an ingredient that I have in a lot of our teas. You have to harvest wheelbarrow loads of it and get it drying and then throw it into the biggest bags you can. And then in the winter you take each leaf off the stalk. You have to harvest and dry, and then the work in the winter is processing. That's what makes it year-round work and why you really don't catch a break in the wintertime. Even though the farm's asleep, you need to process everything that you can.

Some things you have to process immediately: berries, for example. And herbs. People traditionally would just hang their herbs upside down in a barn, but we can't do that for commercial use. They would get dusty, and there would be bird droppings on them. So it's all dried in the food drier. So as far as help, our boys both help me now. I couldn't even afford to pay someone five dollars an hour to help me with this work, because then we'd end up having to charge $400 a pound for the tea. This is such a labor of love. It's not something where, "Oh, we buy in bulk and we get a better price." More product for us just means more labor. There's not a break. More product means more price. If someone wants to come personally and volunteer their time, I still can't give them a break on the price. So our desire is never to be big, just to be the best.

And then we found that advertising and marketing don't work, like print ads, but the most beneficial thing is word of mouth. Passing on what you saw, what you felt, what you tasted, passing on that sensory experience, how can you possibly explain this in an ad? You just can't. There is just nothing quite like it. As a result, we have some of the most meaningful exchanges with our customers. We really love them. They love us. They want to support us. And they send more cool tea people our way. It's just a very satisfying exchange.

It's the biodiversity that feels so good. Some people come and say, "Oh, it's not what I expected. I was expecting like rows and rows of the same thing," but that would be monoculture. It's a little bit challenging during harvest time, like the aronia berries that I was just finishing in the kitchen. With a thousand of those plants about eight hundred are around creating a defined area in the meditation garden, an edible landscape, but then we also have them as windbreak in other places, so you have to remember, "Did you pick all the aronia berries?" "Oh, all right. I forgot to do the ones over there by the back hoop house." But it creates such a good feeling at the farm. And the companion planting element is so good for the biodiversity, the support of the farm, and the wildlife loves it. I always plant about 20 percent extra for the birds and the bees and the butterflies. We leave our milkweed for the monarchs.

If I hire anyone to help, I hire other educators to help in the tea shop. I hire year-round help to help me after I finish putting the tea all together. I have to have help to package it, put the labels on, because the labels are all put on by hand. And then someone to help me with order fulfillment, to actually get those orders sent out by internet. That's an area of the business we'd really love to see grow. We know about our website that it's not just people randomly looking for cheap. It's people that are definitely looking for Light of Day tea because they have been here, or they have heard about it from someone else. Because the price scares people. They don't understand that one tin of tea is like two hundred servings. They don't understand about the labor part, that if they aren't buying Light of Day organic tea, that they are supporting a slave industry. Before slavery was abolished, there were many tea plantations in our country. But when slavery was abolished, it all went back to India, Sri Lanka, China. They are not paid a fair living wage even with fair trade certification. That's hogwash. Not with any of it, chocolate, coffee, tea. It definitely would not be considered a living wage. It's a crazy industry.

I took the name, "Light of Day Organics," from the song, "Joyful, joyful, we adore thee; fill us with the light of day. Creator of immortal gladness, fill us with the light of day." It's based on a poem. There's so much scripture that talks about the light. All good things come from the light rather than from the shadow side. And when I think about being filled with the light of day, and we talk about "in the light of day," that's where the truth is. The truth is always where the light is, and my goal from this, in trying to express it with the name, was that I really feel, especially with my medical history, my own colorful past, and watching others suffering, I feel that if people can be relieved of those pesky physical symptoms that keep them from doing what they are supposed to do . . . We are here for the experience. We are born into this exact time and space in history. We're here for a reason, for the experience, and we're going to have fewer experiences if we feel crummy and we're just sitting at home. If we can help people by easing their discomforts to get out and have more experiences, they'll wake up to do what they are supposed to do. They'll wake up and remember what they came here for, and others around them will wake up and also remember what they are supposed to do. And they will shine their light and not put it under a basket, but shine their light. We always have "radiate love; drink your tea, shine your light."

RECIPE

Hummingbird Nectar Sangria

ANGELA MACKE, LIGHT OF DAY ORGANICS

Equal parts wine and hummingbird nectar tea that is steeped 2 teaspoons per liter of hot water overnight and then refrigerated to cool.

A liter should be prepared and poured into a mold and frozen with raspberries and blueberries and cherries and floated in a punch bowl used to serve sangria.

It can be used half-and-half with either late harvest Riesling, Gewürztraminer, Rosé, or any favorite red table wine suitable for sangria.

Photo by Kim Schneider

5

Mimi Wheeler

Born on an island in Denmark, with parents whose business was running a small grocery to serve their local community, Mimi grew up with strong community values that led her first to a career in social work. The commitment to community-building and a passion for chocolate—quality chocolate made by hand from the best ingredients—gave her the incentive in her middle years to launch a second career as a chocolatier in the little town of Empire in northern Michigan. Once Mimi had learned about fair trade chocolate and the growers in Ecuador, her products became part of the organic and sustainable movement that is local in Michigan and also international as she and others support growers in other countries committed to these values. Grocer's Daughter Chocolate, her store in Empire, paid tribute to her heritage and to her present values. Retired now from her store, Mimi joys in her grandchildren and travels to Europe and to Central America where she helps support children in a school in Guatemala.

Mimi Wheeler, b. July 7, 1952
Interview: August 17, 2015
Grocer's Daughter Chocolate, Echo Valley Road, Empire

I wanted to create a community coming to my little store so people would meet each other and have face-to-face contact.

I grew up in Denmark, was born on the small island of Morsø, and moved with my parents when I was just nine months old to a small village called Hvam in a fairly poor countryside of Denmark. My parents had a grocery store, and it had a big impact on me to grow up in a community with a grocery store, hardware, a lumber yard, and a number of employees—many of them staying with us. We always had someone living with us who was cooking for the crew.

I loved the community of people. I think the community was very inspirational to me. I know that when I started my business I wanted to create a community coming to my little store so people would meet each other and have face-to-face contact and be waited on, exchange news, and get to know each other and be inspired by others—celebrating community, really.

My mom provided that a lot in the store we had. Both my parents worked in the store. My dad didn't like customers particularly well, but my mom had a lot of social work values and recognized good things in people and enjoyed their stories. She was also very involved in child welfare in the area and was a leader in the community. She enjoyed customers coming in and conversing with them and providing a good service. She set high standards for employees and was very popular in the community. I admired and loved her well.

I don't know how much I paid attention to food growing up, although I know that I loved the home-cooked, and I hated the camping trip that we took as a family with all the cans being opened. We arrived at the campgrounds and were cooking food that wasn't nutritious and wasn't interesting. I think I've always been a little bit of a foodie. We also had chocolate at special occasions. Especially at Christmastime we brought into the store some fancier chocolate that we had to weigh out in little bags. My dad would joke and say everyone had to be whistling because you can't whistle and eat at the same time.

A love for community and social justice led me to the career of social work. I worked in Denmark in this field for a few years and then met my husband from the United States. We moved here in 1980 when he became quite homesick. I worked in community mental health here a few years later after my children were close to school age. After that I worked in a private boarding school as a counselor/social worker, and during this period I obtained a master's degree in the field.

Throughout these years I had this dream of starting my own business. Since I had made chocolate desserts, made soufflés, cakes, truffles for a number of occasions over many years and had gotten a lot of praise for this, it dawned on me that chocolate was what I had to start doing as a new career. I named it Grocer's Daughter Chocolate.

I had a difficult experience in my work life about this time so I had to leave the job I had, and it was a great push for me to put all my energy into something different. I had a very supportive family—the mortgage was almost paid and the kids were out of college—so I was able to really put a lot of my full-time-plus energy into the chocolate business I was preparing to start. I knew that I had to do it with very small savings, so I really started up just spending a couple thousand dollars on a tempering machine and a few other pieces of equipment. I started in a commercial kitchen, and in lieu of rent I helped pay for some equipment and we did some remodeling. I had about six to eight months where it cost me very little to be in the space.

In that last year of work and transition to starting up the business I did a lot of research and read about chocolate. I had a chance to go to Provence, France, and I had earlier been to New York visiting a niece and had tasted truffles made by a French chocolatier named Joel Durand. This was the first time ever I had thyme-infused truffles and basil and rosemary in chocolate ganache. This struck me as a wonderful new way of making chocolate. I connected also with a few Danish chocolatiers, but generally they were not open to share.

I put together a new flavor profile most people didn't know. Because of my unique truffles, my enthusiasm, and being a middle-aged Danish woman starting in business, I got a considerable amount of attention right away. I had hoped to find a home in the popular touristy small town of Glen Arbor, but did not succeed in finding a home for my business there. Instead, I ventured to Empire. It was affordable to rent this building because I rented from a very generous landlord who was excited about a new business in Empire where he himself lived. Operating my business right on M-22 on the outskirts of Empire, a tiny town and the gateway to Sleeping Bear National Lakeshore and the famous sand dunes, was a great move. There was a growing recognition of M-22 and much tourist traffic. A lot of people stopped by, a lot of vacationers, and people were generous shoppers, happy and willing to stop and spend money. Various businesses contacted me, and I did holiday gift shipping of chocolates sometimes even outside the United States.

I had a small profit right away. I worked many hours, and the business was open seven days a week year-round. After eight or nine years the business was very sustainable. I had initially thought that I would not hire staff, just be maybe me making chocolate in the morning and then selling in the afternoon. I became way too busy right away and had to add people and had a few full-timers. It was mostly very joyful.

I was lucky enough to make a connection to Zingerman's Food Emporium in Ann Arbor right away through a young man who was a good friend of my son's. He had been to visit several times and was a chocolate buyer for Zingerman's. I didn't know much about Zingerman's or Ann Arbor until I started working with them. The first wholesale order I sent out was Zingerman's. I recognized when I started reading up on them, went down there many times and did some classes down there, that the values that they have resonated with me. It's really a social enterprise, interesting people, and community and networking. And that's who they are.

And Waleed [Alshamma] heard about me starting a chocolate business, and he said, "Can I come up for a weekend and play with chocolates with you and see what you are doing, because I'm looking for someone who has some of these ideas you have about herb-infused truffles." So he came up. I was using a very conventional average chocolate that many restaurants use, but they have no sense of fair trade values. It's not a very interesting chocolate really. Waleed helped me connect with a French chocolatier in Manhattan who was working with newly imported chocolate from Ecuador with a high cocoa content and that was fairly traded. I was seeking interesting flavors in chocolate and other foods for my production, and I wanted to buy products that were sustainably grown as much as possible. The cost was higher, but that was acceptable to me. It was worth it.

I worked exclusively with this chocolate maker for maybe four or five years and had a chance to visit the cooperative of cacao farmers in Ecuador with my Spanish-speaking son. I had a wonderful experience doing that and got to know people who produced this chocolate that I was working with. These had fair trade values in a cooperative, but the chocolate wasn't certified organic. I looked for but at this time was unable to find a high-quality chocolate that was organic.

There was too much attention paid to the process where the fermentation and the origin of the beans in the organic field was not that great, and was not at all affordable. But from the beginning I paid a premium price for chocolate. Later I added chocolate from Colombia and Venezuela.

My approach to learning how to work with chocolate was a practical one. I was not interested in sitting on a school bench and going to the Culinary Institute in Chicago or elsewhere. I wasn't into that. I wanted to learn on my own. Because I know so many people and I love to network I connected with a woman who had been a chocolatier but was no longer in this business. She early on said to me, "Let me help you with a few things." And she gave me ideas for which machines to buy and some of the technical skills that I acquired. But most of my learning was from books, and I learned from what I saw and from trial and error.

Clearly there were hurdles to overcome, and the technicality of processing the chocolate, "tempering it," was challenging early on. I remember a good friend who is an author, Anne-Marie Oomen, at some point saw my despair, because I had too much chocolate that didn't set up right. She said, "I love best the chocolate that didn't temper right. It's even more flavorful." It was good of her to say this, but of course it was untrue. I had an army of people behind me who were really helpful. Many friends were happy to volunteer as taste testers, and I made complex schematic charts for them to rate what they tasted.

There were only a few obstacles. I was very fortunate, and one of the gifts I probably have is that I am good at networking with people. I am good at asking for help. I had friends who had businesses that they had been operating for a number of years, and they said, "let us help you." Jack with a printing business printed inexpensive labels for me. Another friend helped me with the graphic design for a very minimal fee. I also did a lot of bartering back and forth with products and with needed services in the first years in business.

Timothy Young with Food for Thought helped me a lot with his advice for running a food business. A good friend who is an architect said, "This is the color you should paint your building." What had been this mustard yellow metal-sided building that was not attractive at all suddenly became this bright chartreuse eye-catching color that you couldn't miss. And that was a phenomenal idea. I had photographers who offered their service and said, "Pay me in chocolate." So enormous generosity surrounded me getting started.

My husband and a friend had produced a kitchen in the storage building that we rented for the business. Shortly after I had started the business a friend joined me in the venture. She purchased a part of the chocolate business, but after fourteen months she realized that this was not what she wanted to do, and she pulled out. We had not assessed our business compatibility. She was focused on wholesale in the local area, where I believed that the business would only be profitable if the majority was retail and web sales. It was a painful realization. She left in mid-December during a very busy holiday season, and I was unprepared for it. The word got out among friends that I needed help, and several close friends showed up the next morning and said, "Put us to work."

We started early shipping at holidays. That first Christmas was hard. In the beginning we sent some terrible stuff out. In the first year there were problems we didn't anticipate. People were very generous about accepting that something came broken or not packaged well. And I would always replace it. Anyone who was not happy with something we would send out an extra to make up for the mistake. I shared easily with customers early on that I was learning a lot in what I was doing. And there was a spirit of accepting.

We worked in wholesale a lot, but even in winter there were always a lot of people. Oryana's food co-op was a big customer. I love Oryana. I'm a big customer there and I know they keep some of these small businesses alive in the winter months. And, again, the community here is a wonderful community. So many of them will pay a dollar more for the chocolate bar that's made locally rather than the ones that have been shipped in from Kansas or somewhere else. So there's a high awareness and a pride in buying locally produced. And they know that of the dollar they spend on locally produced, so much of that dollar will stay in the community, whereas with the imported or the product purchased from outside, the money doesn't stay local.

There is a real generous spirit and a spirit of cooperation and also cross-marketing up here. I haven't lived very long anywhere else, but there are organizations in this region who facilitate this. One is

Groundwork Center, earlier called Michigan Land Use Institute. They connect food producers and farmers with businesses and schools and other services. They had an event where they hooked us newer food producers up with each other and came out with a catalog naming us all, who we were. Their catalog helped me find an organic cherry farmer in the region. I made the connection with this farm and became friends with the farm family. When the cherries failed, maybe five years ago, Cheryl Kobernik said to me, "Do you want us to save you a hundred pounds of cherries and then we won't sell them elsewhere because we know you need them?" Where the local area was bringing cherries in from Poland, I was able to get local cherries because I had the connection with another small farm family. There was a real camaraderie in that.

Cooks' House and other fine restaurants bought chocolate from me and served them to their customers. There were sometimes bartering agreements. We bought each other's goods. It was very rich for me to have my salt chocolate chips presented at Cooks' House. I also was not afraid at all of collaborating with other chocolatiers in Michigan and outside the state. Some I keep in touch with. We were learning together. I celebrate when I hear of someone's success.

I am very excited about the fact that a woman who came up several times to do an internship with me—she had a pastry degree—then decided to go into chocolates. She now has two very successful little chocolate shops in the Detroit area. I can't wait to go visit her. I was never afraid of sharing my recipes and my knowledge. I taught many classes in the store, at Northwest Michigan College, and at a local winery. I was happy to tell people how I make the rosemary-infused truffles. I was never afraid of sharing because I think that creativity comes from within, and it has to keep flowing for you to produce things that are delicious and interesting.

I also had the fun experience that Jacques Torres from New York came into my store one time. He is a big name in chocolate. He threw his card at me and said, "Come on to New York and spend some time with us." So I did. I spent two days with him and had fun doing so. Our approach is very different, what I did, what he did. I admire his technical skills and his team's empire of chocolate. He said to me, "I have no secrets. Anything you see that you want to know about, you let me know." This sentiment has been mine as well, but I recognize that it is unusual. I have never been worried about competition.

People would find us by coming by on M-22 in Empire on their way to Frankfort or to the Sleeping Bear Dunes or to Glen Arbor. I once had a Los Angeles magazine donate to me a whole back page of glossy print of free advertisement due to an inspirational meeting at Green Festival in Chicago. For a while we were wholesaling chocolate to a place in Los Angeles. That didn't make sense. The weather was just too different. It was too much for shipping. I was too small for them.

There was also a big Chicago magazine that wrote a story about us. A lot of journalists were hungry for good stories, and I was probably a pretty good story. I was also always proud that I tried to incorporate as much as I could from local sources. I found the organic cherries from Cheryl Kobernik at North Star Organics. I found preserves locally. I found spices locally. I found teas from two different sources locally. I found local cream that I used. I think at one time I was counting fifteen to eighteen things that I used in the product that were all produced locally. I took great pride in that. There are so many creative and quality-conscious customers and friends—often women—who have inspired me to create new chocolate bars using these lovely teas and more. I think again these lovely teas were inspiring me to use them. I think we came up with some interesting innovative products: Sunburst ginger tea dark chocolate bars. We would grind those teas very, very fine in a coffee grinder. And I found people who were very creative and resourceful. Mostly it was women who worked for me, and they came up with their own recipes that were better than what I was doing. I was so happy when together we made new inventions and people liked them.

I operated Grocer's Daughter Chocolate for about ten years and then I sold it to a young entrepreneurial couple. Jody Hayden had been in the coffee business and had started a successful coffee company, having traveled the world where coffee grows. She had moved away from the area after having sold the business to her former partner and was now returning home to family and the area. Jody came back looking for work and a new engagement. I knew how talented and resourceful she was, and I hired her to help me create a new website and help me make the business ready for sale. We traveled together to

Ecuador to the cacao plantations and the jungle several times. By the time we finalized the sale we had taken a group of customers down to visit a cacao plantation, visit the jungle, and see different ways where cocoa grew.

Now I don't miss owning a food business. It was a good era, but my life now is full with other priorities. I love where I live out in the country. It's tranquil, beautiful. I am an extrovert mostly and I love community. We've started hosting people here. We have occasional rentals. We own a home next door that we rent out. We have Airbnb guests. Now we have a couple of WWOOFers who are here for a few weeks helping out. I love to create big meals communally, joining together to tell stories. And my husband, Norm, provides music. He was very sweet and excited about what I was doing, very helpful, and never complained when I wasn't bringing any money home. My marriage is such that we do a lot of things separately. Norm is a musician and plays a lot with a lot of bands, and I don't come along very often. That's not my thing. I've been known to go and listen but not very often.

In the beginning I'm sure I did six days of ten hours and there was a little grumping from my children. My daughter would say, "Hey, Mom, I'm pregnant; I'm having a baby. How about helping me?" One hurdle was that it was like having a toddler 24/7. It was in my mind, in my head and my heart. I'm sure that early on, even on Sundays when I was not working—there was a woman working with me who was so happy to be by herself on Sundays and did a beautiful job—I still would call and say, "Mary, how are things going?" So I really did not have a break from the business. It was intense for me because of my brain structure.

I've been so excited about becoming a grandmother. There were two children who were married and were having babies in the same year or planning to, and I knew I couldn't run this business and be a grandmother and be very involved with my family. Today I have three little ones and spend a lot of time with them. And my energies now go toward hosting.

I am part of a women's circle that meets monthly. We get together and we have a greater cause. We put the money into helping, and a few of us help women in Kewadin, Michigan. They are Guatemalan. They are quite isolated from the community up there. Most of them are "pay for sustain." They are all deeply affected by the civil war in Guatemala. And Norm and I of course go to Guatemala every year. We go for a month.

Having a travel bug is another reason why running a business is not something I want to prioritize in my life right now. I'm very happy and thankful that I could have done what I did. But I did it with a lot of help. I was extremely grateful to hand over the business to Jody and D. C. Hayden, who come from a coffee background and have traveled the world and have very high ethics and value places and people. They are very dear friends.

It's a gift for me to go back to visit the store. I'm always welcome. When they come up with something new they often want me to come over and taste it, or if there's a new chocolate they are working with. I know Jody is going to take it quite a ways beyond where I was, and I am excited about that. I love it when she now and then calls me and says, "Can you help me with this or that?" And it's still recognized as the Grocer's Daughter Chocolate.

Chocolate Truffles

MIMI WHEELER, GROCER'S DAUGHTER CHOCOLATE

Approximately 20

150 grams heavy cream / 4/5 cup

300 grams high-quality dark chocolate, chopped to ¼-inch chunks
 (65 to 85% chocolate)

2 tablespoons unsweetened cocoa powder

Heat the cream and bring to a simmer in a pot or, alternatively, heat the cream in a small bowl using a microwave oven (watch carefully that the cream does not spill over).

Remove the container from the heat source. Transfer the cream to a small bowl if you used a pot for heating. Add the chocolate to the hot cream.

Cover the bowl and leave for maybe 2 minutes for the chocolate to melt. Be sure that the chocolate is fully melted. If any lumps of chocolate remain you will have to either warm gently again in the microwave oven or over a pan of simmering water.

Mix the ganache by stirring using a small spatula with small rotating movements until fully incorporated.

Cool the mix for a few hours on the kitchen table until consistency of firm mayonnaise.

Place a piece of parchment or wax paper on a small cookie sheet. Scoop the ganache with a rounded teaspoon or a small melon baller into small rounds and place them at an inch distance on the paper. Let them harden here for a few minutes before you hand roll them into perfect little balls.

Sift the cocoa into a little bowl. Roll each of the ganache balls in cocoa and place them in a cool place like the refrigerator until you serve them.

Truffles Infused with Herbs, Spices, Coffee, Fruit

It's easy to experiment with infusing truffles with other complementary flavors.

ROSEMARY TRUFFLES

Simmer a 2-inch fresh rosemary stem with leaves in the cream for a minute. Let the cream rest covered for a couple of minutes for the infusion to take place.

Pour the infused cream over a sieve to strain the cream and discard the herb. Reheat the cream before you proceed. This procedure would take maybe 2 additional tablespoons of cream.

COFFEE-INFUSED TRUFFLES

Follow procedure above and add 1 tablespoon of coarsely ground Java instead of the herb.

FRUIT- /LIQUOR-INFUSED TRUFFLES

Add fruit preserve or spirits to the cream and reduce the quantity of cream with the same amount that you've added. If you add one tablespoon of brandy to the liquid part of the recipe you will have to remove one tablespoon of cream. Proceed like previously described.

Photo by Madeleine Hill Vedel

6

Jody Dotson Hayden

Jody's story shares key elements with Mimi's in that both cared about food that was fresh, locally grown, and home-cooked (Jody calls it "scratch") from an early age, and both also cared about community and about social justice. Where Mimi's sense of community led her into social work, Jody's led her to Chiapas, Mexico, and the plight of the farmers and coffee growers whose indigenous crops were—and still are—threatened by Monsanto's genetically modified seeds. Wanting to combat the exploitation of coffee growers by middlemen, Jody and her husband founded Higher Ground, one of the first ten fair trade companies buying coffee beans from farmers' co-ops directly and paying them fair prices.

Born in Arkansas, she discovered northern Michigan through her first husband's family and their home on Lake Leelanau. She met her second husband, a native of Traverse City, while she was in Ecuador working with the coffee growers. The transition from Higher Grounds and coffee to Grocer's Daughter Chocolate was a natural and almost inevitable one. Like Mimi, Jody knew and had spent time with farmers in Ecuador and had their trust. Like Mimi, once she took over Grocer's Daughter Chocolate, Jody used local produce . . . cherries, blueberries, honey . . . in the chocolate and refused to use cheaper, commercially produced ingredients even when this meant higher prices. Grocer's Daughter Chocolate moved in July 2018 to a more spacious central location in Empire. Local residents and tourists on their way to climb the Sleeping Bear Dunes, their eye caught by the bright green exterior, stop to sample and savor the truffles and other chocolates.

Jody Dotson Hayden, b. October 23, 1975
Interview: August 31, 2015
Grocer's Daughter Chocolate,
Michigan 22, 11590 South Lacore Street, Empire

People want to get to know you, and they care
about the story behind their food.

I was born in a small town in southern Arkansas, El Dorado, Arkansas. I didn't live there too long. My family moved to Iowa, but I think just coming from that Deep South had a lot of impact on me. With southern culture you always have food cooking in your kitchen, and it's common for your grandmothers especially to be force-feeding you all the time. Which I obliged, because the food was really good, mostly scratch-made. It was rare that we would do processed food. So growing up we had big Sunday dinners with homemade buttermilk biscuits, fried chicken, collard greens from the garden, and sliced tomatoes, and fresh peach pies and things like that.

My mom carried that tradition to Iowa where we moved when I was a couple of years old. We were very much in a working-class situation. My dad was working for a big plastics company, and my mom did a lot of odd jobs. She ended up at a local Kmart pharmacy, but she always made a full meal at night. So my parents would work these full-time jobs and come home and make a dinner that always had a meat and a starch and a vegetable, and a lot of that was scratch-made. As an adult now, I really appreciate that because it's very tiring to work all the time and then come home and make all the food from scratch.

My mom always had a garden in the backyard. I only knew a few other people who were really committed to gardening like my mom was. We always had fresh vegetables. And that was part of my being raised. I remember for show and tell when I was a young girl, my mom sent me to school with a kiwi. All the other kids would take toys, and I arrived with a kiwi, and most of the kids in my class had never seen one, or tasted one. To me this was part of our diet, something that we really loved, and so I feel really fortunate to have had a family that cared about food and that exposed me to all kinds of foods when I was very, very little.

Fast-forward until I get older. Here we are in Empire, Michigan. I think what led me into the vocation I'm in currently was a commitment to social justice as well as food. My graduate program was based in Brattleboro, Vermont, at the School for International Training. It was an organizational/management degree focused on social change.

And part of that program meant that we had to spend a year in the field to graduate, and I ended up in Chiapas, Mexico, living there for a year with mostly Mayan indigenous farmers.

Anybody who has traveled to those regions would know that food is very important to those cultures. A lot of them are subsistence farmers, and at this point the struggle to keep *maíz* pure and indigenous was part of what they were fighting for. There was a big struggle against NAFTA happening. It was really a struggle to keep their indigenous seeds, the ownership of them, and not have big Monsantos, these companies come in and basically plant genetically modified crops that could eventually destroy all these indigenous varieties of corn.

I learned a lot about that. And I got to see it firsthand, what was happening in places like Chiapas. Those farmers were also growing really great coffee. At that time they didn't have a fair market to sell it to, and so a lot of it was going to intermediaries—they call them coyotes—at prices that are way below what they should be. And so my then-husband and I decided to start Higher Grounds Trading Company, which at the time was one of ten 100 percent fair trade coffee companies in the country. At that time fair trade was just getting its legs. Fair trade was a system of certification in which your company gets certified to pay a fair price to buy from farmer co-ops that are democratically organized, to buy from farmers that were very much encouraging women's leadership, who were not employing children unlawfully. It was just a really fair way of buying any commodity, and in this case it was coffee.

We started our company in Chiapas, and then we moved back to Traverse City, Michigan, in 2002. My ex-husband, Chris Streeter, still runs Higher Grounds Trading Company. He and his family had been coming up here since the 1940s. They had a house on Lake Leelanau, which they still have, and so when we were in Chiapas the rest of our families were—my parents were in Houston, Texas, and his were in Toledo, Ohio—and we knew that we didn't want to relocate to either of those places. And so we ended up here in Traverse City. We loved it, and we've been here ever since.

Chris and I built Higher Grounds, and it grew really rapidly for probably a lot of reasons. Traverse City likes to support food entrepreneurs, and people here care about where their food comes from. It was a small enough city that we could build relationships quickly and get to know people. This whole area is really great that way. People want to get to know you, and they care about the story behind their food. And so this little company just grew and grew and grew. I always tell people I think we did 90 percent education and 10 percent coffee. We educated people about what was happening in coffee. It was really important that we did that. We led trips to coffee-growing regions to meet farmers. That's something I still do in chocolate. And it's just creating those connections. When people know what it takes to grow coffee or sugar or chocolate or what have you, they are willing to pay more, to care about how it's made and where it comes from.

Chris and I decided to part ways in 2009–10. That was a friendly departure, but one of us needed to move on, and I chose to move on. I ended up in Minneapolis for a couple of years working for a larger fair trade coffee company. I was hired by a company called Peace Coffee. They are a 100 percent fair trade coffee company as well. When I went there I knew I was going to do a short-term project for them. I opened their first retail store, but then I was hired to do some internal projects, and I really loved it. There's a lot of great things about the Twin Cities, but I was happy to come home when it was time.

My current husband and I met when we took a trip to Ecuador together and fell in love there. He moved to Minneapolis with me for a year and then we ended up coming home. He's from Traverse City. His name is D. C. Hayden, and he was born and raised here in Traverse City. His family owns a cherry orchard. They are part of the conventional farming world.

But we knew that Mimi [Wheeler] was going to sell the business. It was really getting to her, and she had found a buyer that she thought would work out. That didn't come to fruition, and then she was ready to sell to whoever wanted to buy because she loved making chocolate, but she didn't like running a business. She told us that. It was perfect for us because we didn't want Grocer's Daughter Chocolate to go to just anybody. It's a very special chocolate shop to the community. It's very different from most chocolate shops. Had someone bought it who didn't know the history it might have changed the spirit of the shop, so we bought it for that reason. This was back in 2012. Time goes by so fast!

I had known Mimi, because as I was building Higher Grounds Mimi was starting Grocer's Daughter Chocolate. So I've known her since the very beginning. In fact we had a little business group that gathered semiregularly, just to talk about business issues. She was part of the group. I was part of that group. I was very familiar with her business all through the course of its life before we purchased it. And we also used the chocolate at Higher Grounds to make drinks and all in our coffee shop. So it felt like a really natural passing of Grocer's Daughter Chocolate to come from Mimi to us, and it feels like it has stayed in the family in a lot of ways.

We still make the trips. We took last year off. Last time I went to Ecuador I was seven months pregnant and huge, and we actually explored the cacao fields. I look at the photos of it and I think, "How did I go to some of these places?" Weird, traveling through a waterfall, to get to remote cacao fields. We hope to go back with our second child. I have a fourteen-month-old, and I'm due with another in October. We plan to take them both back next spring. And then we'll start the trips back up probably after that. The trips take a lot of time and attention. We want to do that. There is this wonderful dynamic that happens when you see someone, when you meet the cacao farmers for the first time, and you see how labor-intensive it is, what work goes into it.

I've had people tell me it really changed their life to go and see how happy and wonderful and welcoming the people are, and yet how hard their lives. It's a struggle. Even in the world of fair trade I still don't think farmers get paid enough for their work, not in South America, and not here down the road. Our farmers work so hard for what they do. So besides sourcing really great chocolate, what we think of as good prices for the farmers, we also source all the dairy we can locally from Shetler's Dairy, which is a family farm over in Kalkaska. Our honey is from Sleeping Bear Farms. Our maple syrup is local. We have cherries that are local. Blueberries. If we can get it local, we do. Of course, we pay more for that. We could make more money if we sourced everything more cheaply. And that's what a lot of chocolate companies do. But our first ingredient isn't sugar—which of course is another way to make more money—we do chocolate first and foremost and then we add really great ingredients to that. And for us it is really about supporting our local economy whenever we can.

I haven't been back to Chiapas for a couple of years because that was part of my coffee work, but the last time I was there—I went with Peace Coffee on a sourcing trip—the indigenous farmers are still really struggling. I don't know that there's been a lot of change. Fortunately there are seed banks now so there are groups formed to save seeds, but that doesn't necessarily help the day-to-day life of a farmer. If anything, what they are seeing is the spread of the genetically modified seeds, the unbridled spread of them. There's kind of a lawless situation where there's not a lot of recourse for the farmers, especially in Latin America. They are pretty much at the mercy of the larger companies. They don't have the cash to hire lawyers to fight. So there are a lot of educational campaigns around what could happen if one GMO comes in and takes over all these old varieties and then one plague comes in and takes out all of that particular kind of corn. It's a real issue. And certainly in cacao there have been famines that are widespread. The famines are widespread, and the plagues are widespread. Something can come in and wipe out a really large swath of harvest for a year. And that can cause famine because all of a sudden your cash crop is wiped out. It's a real issue.

Fortunately, I speak Spanish. A lot of times when we go to Ecuador most of the folks we visit speak Spanish and Quechua, their indigenous language, so we can communicate that way. We go and visit a lot of the same families from year to year. There's a family we are dear friends with that live in Otavalo, which is in the north part of the country. They have started their own little chocolate house for tourists to come visit. It's a really great honor to go and visit farmers, and to support our farmers here, too, it's really important to us.

It's tricky here for businesses in the winter. It really gets quiet in winter in this cute little shop. We do more online sales. People go home and they buy online. We sell to people all over the country. We ship directly. We also sell to grocery stores, and so we do a lot of those kinds of orders in the winter. I think most of the businesses in Leelanau County face this. You make all your money in the summer, and you spend it all trying to keep going in the winter. There are a lot of places that close in the winter, but for us, we have employees that rely on us all year-round, and we just try to keep it going. Our summers are really great because we've got lots of people, both locals and visitors, coming. We kind of feel like ambassadors for the region because we're on the very southern edge of Leelanau County, so people coming up M-22—which is a famous road—to visit in our area, sometimes we're their first stop entering Leelanau County. We get to tell them all of our favorite places to go for cheese and wine and cider. It's really fun.

Our staff includes four full-time year-round and then there are a couple more that are part-time year-round. We have summer staff that come and go. But one of our summer staffers has been here since she was eleven. She comes back every year. Now she's going to be a sophomore at Macalester in Saint Paul, so she's kind of our senior staff member right now. She started working for Mimi. She begged for this job and Mimi found stuff for her to do until she was of legal age to work, and then she got more formalized in the business. She always says how she wants to own this chocolate shop someday. So we have really great staff who come back, just because they love everything about it, our family culture, how we source things.

There's not a chocolate school per se. You can go take workshops. In this case most of it is handed down from person to person. Mimi had learned to make truffles on her own, and then she taught some gals who work for us and who had worked for her. And that kind of continues on and on. What we've learned is that there's still a ton to learn, always, and there's lots of techniques and things that we've adapted from other chocolatiers, by calling them or watching them or asking them. If you just stay here and don't talk to anyone you work in a vacuum, so we're constantly looking to see what other people do, calling people when we are trying to figure something out. We adapt new techniques as we go. But we are very traditional in that we hand-make everything. We don't have big fancy equipment. And we don't use any artificial ingredients or flavors. And we hand-roll most of our ganaches. It ends up being about thirty or forty thousand truffles a summer that we hand-roll. So it's really labor-intensive. Hand-rolled and hand-dipped.

When/if we introduce new flavors it's because we are inspired by the season, so we may play with a peach or a plum or some hops because there's a hops festival coming up. It's rarely something that's outside of our little gardening zone. It's usually something that we've tasted that inspired us to try something new. Or a holiday flavor. We do a really popular peppermint thing at the holidays, an organic pep-permint candy that's fantastic. We have to order candy in July because they run out. It's really wonderful.

We use Food for Thought preserves from right up the road with blueberries, and pear ginger, and apricot. We incorporate lots of fun local flavors. I've always loved to cook. I wouldn't say that I'm like a candy maker, but of course I love chocolate, and to me chocolate and candy are a little different. Candy to me has got mostly sugar—don't get me wrong; there are some things I really love in the world of candy—but chocolate is certainly more like wine or coffee in that if you get it from different places in the world it tastes different, and if you add different kinds of sweetener it tastes different. Beans are roasted to a different degree, lighter or darker, and you are going to get a different flavor.

Chocolate has become this—it really is a sweet, it is certainly a treat; it's not a necessary food in our diet—but it's kind of fun in that it has its own genre of flavors. To me candy always has sugar forward. To us, with chocolate you want to taste the chocolate first. There is a medical doctor from New York City who says that chocolate should be the fifth food group. And he spoke at the Writers' Conference in Traverse City this past spring. I didn't get to go, but I had a friend who was there and sent me a message saying, "You've got to listen to this guy, because he's really espousing the benefits of dark chocolate." And that's more and more common, good for your brain, your memory, your heart, for your happy endorphins.

The seasonality of any business up here is not easy, but I don't think that's unique to us. I think it's common to business. I think for us the chocolate has an attitude, and so trying to figure that out—when I say that—it's temperamental based on weather conditions in a room, humidity and heat, and so oftentimes we are behind on getting our wholesale orders out especially in the summer. And it's really hard for us to tell our customers and remind them that all of this is handmade.

We may make fifty pounds of chocolate in a day, and part of that will go out of temper. We can't sell that because we are not proud of it. Even though it tastes fine, it doesn't look like we want it to look. And we don't always know why. Our chocolatiers have done everything. They are on chat rooms asking other chocolatiers what they do. We are changing our room environment. We are controlling it to the best of our ability. Sometimes the chocolate just doesn't want to behave. The humidity is critical. If it gets too humid in the room it will go out of temper in a heartbeat.

I don't know the source of the expression "out of temper" for chocolate, but we like to joke that it's ill-tempered. It has a bad attitude. It's just a batch of chocolate that's having a bad day. So the fat or the sugar will bloom, which means it comes to the surface, and there's something about the environment of that room that causes that. Oftentimes the humidity. And there are white streaks or sometimes red streaks on the top of the chocolate. It doesn't have the sheen that we like. The tempering process is a heating and cooling, a controlled heating and cooling of the chocolate crystals, and, done well, it makes this beautiful snap and shine. If it's not done perfectly or even if it's done perfectly and then it sits for a little while in a room that's too humid, it can go out of temper. Become ill-tempered. Bad attitude chocolate, which is a funny thing to think about. A little piece of chocolate with a temper tantrum.

Being in coffee in the time we were was fun because at that time fair trade was brand-new. There was only a handful of companies in the whole country that were doing fair trade. So it was fun and it was hard to get our arms around because the growth happened so quickly. This business I feel like you learn as you go, and so you get really good at saying no to certain things. Even though this business could grow probably just as quickly, it's not necessarily the goal any more. Your values change as you get older. And for me, I have a child and another one on the way. It's really important to me to have a quality of life that's balanced, and not overwork our staff, and give people a really authentic experience when they come to Grocer's Daughter Chocolate. I love what we are doing now because it's a great family business and it's wonderful chocolate. I am so proud of what we make, and it hasn't grown so fast that we can't keep all of our principles in place. In fact, we just say, "No, we don't want that account. We don't want to grow that way." That's a really fulfilling place to be. It's not without its struggles. We still try to figure out winter every year. But it's getting easier. We're getting better at it every year.

Pulled Chocolate Chicken Chili

JODY HAYDEN, GROCER'S DAUGHTER CHOCOLATE

six to eight large servings

2 pounds boneless chicken (I like to buy chicken from a local farm)

*you can use bone-in chicken but you have to take more care when shredding

4 tablespoons olive oil (or healthy fat of choice), separated

1 medium onion, diced

3 heads of garlic, minced

3 tablespoons Grocer's Daughter Chocolate Chocolate Chili Rub; 1 tablespoon reserved

2½ cups stewed tomatoes (I like to use canned tomatoes from our garden)

2 chipotle peppers, chopped, in 2 tablespoons adobo sauce

½ cup raisins (I prefer golden raisins)

¼ cup nut or almond butter (I recommend Naturally Nutty from Traverse City peanut or almond butter)

½ cup Grocer's Daughter Chocolate 70% Esmeraldas dark chocolate chunks

1 teaspoon cumin seed

1 cinnamon stick

1 teaspoon sea salt (or to taste)

In a heavy-bottom pot, cook onions in 2 tablespoons olive oil (about 3 minutes), add garlic and cook a few more minutes.

In the same pan, brown chicken in remaining olive oil. Dust with 2 tablespoons Grocer's Daughter Chocolate Chocolate Chili Rub while cooking.

Add stewed tomatoes, chipotle peppers, adobo sauce, raisins, nut butter, Grocer's Daughter Chocolate dark chocolate chunks, cumin seed, cinnamon stick, and remaining Grocer's Daughter Chocolate Chocolate Chili Rub.

Rub. Cook for 3 hours at 350 degrees, checking progress every hour.

Remove cinnamon stick and shred chicken with fork. Serve over blue corn chips, tortillas, or polenta. Top with sour cream, salsa, and fresh cilantro.

III

PASTRY AND CHEESE

Flour and Fermentation

Photo by Madeleine Hill Vedel

7

Susi McConnell

Baking is the constant in Susi's story, from baking in her home kitchen as a teenager to becoming a pastry chef for the Leland Lodge, Hattie's, Carol Worsley's Thyme Out, and Martha Ryan's restaurant in Suttons Bay. In Europe she worked in restaurants as diverse as one in a Swiss ski lodge and one on a navy base, but pastry is the thread throughout until she developed celiac disease. A time working at Angela Macke's Light of Day Organics introduced her to biodynamic gardening, her passion today as she grows her own fruits and vegetables.

Susi McConnell, b. September 18, 1949
Interview: July 18, 2016
South Highland Drive, Lake Leelanau

*When you grow the seed that's planted in your greenhouse and
then plant it in your garden, the cycle is a really spiritual thing.*

I was born in the United States. My father was Lithuanian and he came over during the Bolshevik revolution, so I have all that background, and my mother was German. I'm from a family of nine children so we've always had gardens, lots of vegetable gardens and food, and my dad also owned a bar in Saginaw, Michigan, which was in the Lithuanian part of town. There was a little enclave of Lithuanians: a grocery store, my dad's bar, and a couple of plants, like Lufkin Rule and Baker Perkins. It was kind of like a Cheers bar. People would come after work, and they served food.

So when I think about food, it was always around. My mother made a lot of food. Maybe she wasn't really happy with that, but when you have that many kids . . . and we always had plenty of food because we had a huge garden. She canned everything. We had a cellar that was filled with canned food. My father always made sauerkraut. She made pickled pigs feet. So we had a lot of ethnic foods, too.

My parents' garden wasn't organic. I'm sure my father used chemicals. When I was a kid I had to work in the garden, which I wasn't happy about. When I graduated from high school in 1967 there was the '60s movement to get more natural. That's when I began becoming aware of organic stuff. When I went away to college I was very into making my own bread when I went home and bringing it back and eating it. I became really aware of food, and the health benefits. I started yoga at eighteen, not very well, but I did, and was very aware of the body/mind thing. But that was that whole era, too, the late '60s. There was an awareness there. And I hung around with people who had that awareness. That's pretty much where it all started.

And I always loved plants. I went to a high school that was not very good. They never asked you what you were interested in. They just sent you off to college. I probably should have gone into botany or some form of agriculture, because when I was a teenager I had a room full of plants. I always had plants around me. I wish I had done that. Instead, I became a master gardener. Right now I have plants that are forty-two years old. I have a cactus that is even older than forty-two. I have plants that are as old as my children. Many generations, and they have babies, and I give their babies away. They are family to me. I have a long lineage with plants.

As a teenager I was a little bit interested in cooking, but more in baking. I would bake and do things at home, but it wasn't until I left college and went to Europe that the food bug really hit me. I had worked in restaurants since I was fourteen, as bus girl, and again in college I had worked in restaurants. I majored in theater and English, nothing to do with food. But when I was in college I became a vegetarian and got into health food. Adelle Davis was my idol. So I really got into health food. And then I went off to Europe for just a couple of months. I thought I would take a break from Western Michigan University between my sophomore and junior year. I was entering my junior year. I went to Europe with two girlfriends who were sisters. We sailed to Europe on an Italian liner, the smallest on the ocean. The food was wonderful, and it was everybody going to kibbutzes, like a student ship.

I ended up in Leysin, Switzerland, where I got a job as a cook in a ski lodge that was owned by Australians and Americans, up in the Alps. That was my first experience with commercial cooking. We had to make three meals a day for the staff and the guests. It was like a young person's place. People would use it as a stopover from India. Everybody was in transit. We were all travelers. I worked under an English chef there. She was traveling. She worked for a noble family, and she was taking a break. I learned a lot from her. Her name was Penny. She was exquisite. She had classical training. So that was fun, working under her.

Then I got a Swiss boyfriend, and after realizing I wasn't going home, I wrote to the college and had to cancel my scholarships because I was not coming back. I don't know if that was a good move or not, but I didn't go back. I ended up staying a year and a half in Europe, and then I came home, and again I got restaurant jobs. I teamed up with my then husband. We had known each other, and we started dating, and in 1974 we moved to the Traverse City area. Again, I got a job in restaurant work.

We got married and started a family, and in the early '80s I got a job at Leland Lodge, for the first time as a pastry chef. I had met Martha [Ryan] and we started a business together, a very short business, we were going to bake for area restaurants—but it fell through. We were kindred spirits. We were a lot alike. We raised our kids together. When we were working at SugarLoaf it got really slim about March when SugarLoaf closed down. We were on unemployment. And Martha would call me and she'd say, "What kind of food have you got left?" and I'd say, "This is what I have." And she'd say, "This is what I have." And then we would have communal dinners. So that's how we made it through the winters. We both had young children, and we were collecting unemployment. Our husbands didn't have great jobs.

Time went on and I got this job at the Lodge. Back then they decided that they were going to go gourmet. So they hired a chef who had just graduated from La Varenne in Paris. Her name was Melissa Yard. And she hired me as a pastry chef. I learned a lot from Melissa. It was a great experience, and she really gave me full rein. That job lasted five years. In the meantime they sent me away to Hyde Park, New York, to the Culinary Institute of America for an advanced pastry course for one week. And that really opened doors for me. I had been doing things the long way because I was self-taught. That brought it all together, and I learned a lot from the people I was with. To be in the course you had to have been in the business for five years, so it was everyone that had been in the business. And I was with a lot of country club chefs from very fancy Jewish clubs, and I learned so much from them. We swapped recipes. It was a great experience. Also I was with people who had their own bakeries.

That job lasted five years until they decided that gourmet wasn't their item. I left with another chef, and we went to Hattie's in Suttons Bay, where I was hired in as a pastry chef after Nancy Allen left. Nancy Allen was doing the line, and trying to do pastries. And she didn't like that, and so I took her place as a pastry chef, and the woman who left the lodge with me took on the line work. I ended up working for Jim Milliman for ten years. I loved it. That was a great job.

Then I was in a real bad car accident, and I had to retire from Jim's. I couldn't stand for long periods of time. So I left Jim's, retired for a while, and then I worked, actually, in a gift store in Leland for a bunch of years, five, six, seven years. And then Martha came back into my life. She had gotten a job out in Glen Arbor at a little place called Thyme Out. It was a little pastry shop, and Martha was going to run the kitchen and I would do the pastries. I was hired in to do that. So what I did was I worked in the wintertime at the gift store, and I would take the summers off and work in the pastry shop. It was the best job I ever had. It was for Carol Worsley. I worked in this beautiful country inn kitchen, and she gave me whatever I wanted. Any recipe I wanted to try—she was so supportive—she would buy whatever I wanted. My job was just to fill the pastry case. I could be as creative as I wanted. I had been collecting recipes since the early '70s, so I drew on all these old recipes and on new recipes.

Carol sent me to a French pastry school in Chicago. The chef was Sébastien Cannone. He came to the Detroit area for a class I took, and I also went to Chicago. Carol Worsley sent me to both of those. I didn't like some of the French customs. They used dye, red dye, and they used too much fondant on the cakes, rolled it on. Their pastries have a lot of steps to them. They are usually a two-day process. A lot you don't want in a small place. The classes were very good, but I found that a lot of it was for big hotels, and especially the Culinary Institute. Massive recipes, for ten cakes; croissants for a billion people. A lot of recipes I could not even use. We could break down some of them. It was better having smaller quantities.

Thyme Out was a wonderful job. I loved it. And then after the fifth year Carol kept closing sooner and sooner, and pretty soon she was only open from July 4 to Labor Day. I couldn't survive on that.

By then Martha had decided that she was going to open a restaurant. She got backers, and she said, "Will you come with me and be my pastry chef?" So that's why I left Carol Worsley, and that summer, after I was off all winter, my job also ended at the gift store. They wanted a full-time manager. I took that winter off, and all that winter I worked with Martha on the menu, what we were going to have. I worked for Martha for five years until I developed celiac, which meant I could not work with flour anymore. I was getting too sick. It was the worst thing that ever happened to me. That ended my pastry career.

For five or six years I had also done wedding cakes on the side in the summer. But that was it for pastry. Then I went to work for Angela Macke at Light of Day for three years after I retired from Martha's. I learned a lot from Angela. I got into biodynamic gardening. I don't do it as fully as Angela does, but I follow the calendar, and I harvest and plant according to the calendar. I've always been an avid gardener, and I'm always inspired to make whatever is in my garden into something. So when we built our house I planted massive fruit trees. I planted currant bushes, strawberries, black and red raspberries, apricot trees, apple trees, pear trees, plum trees. So what I had done to myself was to become a slave to my garden and my orchards. I had to process everything because I couldn't stand anything to go to waste. So I repeated what my mother did. I canned everything.

But I got even more creative. I used this in all my jobs as a pastry chef. All my jellies and jams, I used them in all my preparations. I made liqueurs out of them. It's very satisfying to use all your products in another way. I candied all my flowers so when I did desserts I'd have candied violets, or whatever flowers I had. I did candied leaves with mint. I grew roses so I could do roses on wedding cakes. I candied those or used them fresh. That's always been a passion and that hasn't left me. So if one year I don't have apricots, I make nothing apricot. I don't go buy anything. It's only what I have in my garden. That's been really fun and challenging. If I have too many tomatillos I'll make a tomatillo chutney. If I have too many tomatoes and I'm tired of canning I will dry them, I will freeze them. I will make condiments. I will make ketchup. Whatever you can do, I will do it. I'll make syrups, lavender syrup, pancake syrups out of fruit.

So then I had all these gardenings, and I had to get animals so I would have my own manure to make compost. That's not really the main reason I have horses. I have always loved horses. But that's what I do. I compost everything. We have a great compost area.

Now I'm into saving my seeds. I have my own organic seeds, because I do everything organically, so I save my seeds and replant. We're on seven years of our own garlic. Every year you save your biggest and your best garlic and you plant it in the fall. My garlic now is so big that I only have four cloves to a head. They are like elephant garlic. We use all our own potatoes, our own seed potatoes. And this year I started saving onion seeds. I grew my own onions from seeds. So that's my latest thing.

I am a Virgo, and I was very into astrology years ago. Virgo is an earth sign. I feel very close to the earth and so this is so important to me, to grow all my plants in my greenhouse from seeds, and then to take the plants, put them in my garden, and then harvest them. It's the whole cycle. And then when you grow the seed that's planted in your greenhouse and then plant it in your garden, the cycle is a really spiritual thing. Food has become more that way for me. It becomes more nourishing because it's something that I have grown. And it's especially wonderful with the garlic because it's now our own garlic. It knows my soil. This is our climate, our microclimate here. This is our environment. This is home. That's how I feel. It's all inner-connected.

When we first moved here in 1974 we immediately became members of the co-op, Oryana, that was in its beginning stages. We became members because I ran a co-op down in Saginaw, Michigan, before I moved up here. So we joined Oryana and have been with them ever since. And so we've known that group of people ever since that time. A lot of people moved up here in the early '70s, all of the same mind-set.

People bought farms. Some people did farming. Many foodie people and back to the land. Healthy eating. For a while there was a co-op in Suttons Bay that was started by Kathy Powell. It was called Sweet Water. For some reason, that didn't last very long, only a couple of years. It was in the Bailey building downtown. But there was that whole awareness at that time of people wanting to get back to the land and away from the craziness of the cities.

I'm happy that I have led the life I have, with a total awareness of my environment. We are all inner-connected, and I wish everyone could feel that way, about taking care of their property, their land, their bodies. I try not to preach to people. Either you are into it or you are not. You have that realization or you don't. A lot of people don't.

Blueberry Crumb Cake

SUSI MCCONNELL

Serves 8

1 pint blueberries (2½ cups)

½ teaspoon grated lemon zest

2¼ cups flour

1 cup sugar

6 oz. unsalted butter cut into small pieces

1 teaspoon baking soda

1 egg

½ cup plain buttermilk or sour cream

1 teaspoon fresh lemon juice or vanilla

Preheat oven to 400 degrees. Butter a round 10- by 1½-inch baking dish, or a 10-inch springform pan.

In medium bowl toss the berries with the zest. In a large bowl combine 2 cups of the flour with the sugar. Using your fingers or a pastry blender rub or cut in the butter until the mixture resembles coarse meal. Set 1½ cups of the mixture aside for the crumb topping.

In a small bowl lightly beat the egg. Stir in the sour cream and lemon juice. Add to the dry ingredients in the large bowl and stir briefly with a wooden spoon until blended. Fold in 1 cup of the blueberries.

Spread the batter in the prepared dish and scatter the remaining 1½ cups of blueberries on top. Sprinkle the preserved crumb mixture over the blueberries.

Set the dish on a cookie sheet and bake in the middle of the oven for about one hour or until the crumbs are golden and a tester inserted in the center of the cake comes out clean. Serve warm or at room temperature with crème fraiche on the side.

Photo by Madeleine Hill Vedel

8

Anne Hoyt

Anne's story starts in the Old World, in the north of France and in the Swiss Alps. It was her husband, John, who was from Michigan and also who was a cheese maker before Anne developed those skills. Leelanau Cheese was the first local cheese in this region, and for many years remained the only one. Slow at first to be recognized in the era of Velveeta when no one in the region and few in the country appreciated local artisanal cheese, their Raclette is now sold nationally and acclaimed as one of the sixty-six best cheeses in the world. In 2016 it won a super gold at the world cheese competition in Spain. After twenty-five years of intensive cheese-making, Anne and John plan to downsize but also reinvent the Leelanau cheese wheel and to add new cheeses in collaboration with a new *fromagère* in 2020.

Anne Hoyt, b. August 4, 1961
Interview: July 19, 2016
Leelanau Cheese, 3324 SW Bay Shore Drive, Suttons Bay

In a perfect world it would be local and organic and at a good price.

I was born in the city of Roubaix in northern France on the Belgian border in 1961. I moved to the center of France for a couple of years when I was eighteen, and I worked on a farm. It was basically a commune and we were trying to be 100 percent sustainable, which didn't work, but we tried. We were raising our own chickens, rabbits. We had hens for the eggs; we made our own bread. We had a vegetable garden as much as we could. I loved the work there. It was wonderful. The hardest part was working with the people, as always. There are always some who do more than others. I am in that category of those people.

It got old very fast, and actually the owner of the farm kicked us out after a few months. He kicked a few of us out, so we ended up in the street. I was just nineteen. We had to find jobs, so we found different jobs in the city. As soon as we had enough money to get out of the city we bought a little bus, lived in the bus, and started picking fruits all over the south of France and the Bordeaux area. That kept us going in the food industry. Picking fruits was a lot of fun, but very seasonal. I finally ended up with my partner at the time in a farm in the south of France near Roquefort, where they make the Roquefort cheese in the département de l'Aveyron. And we started a little farm.

We raised chickens. We bought chicks; we had two thousand chickens a year. We raised turkeys for Christmas, about a hundred. We had fifty hens and a huge organic garden. Everything was organic although we didn't say it, but that's the way it was. It was naturally organic. And we sold everything at the farmers market. It was just simple and easy, a lot of work, but unfortunately we were not making enough money. We were hardly paying the bills. We did that for five years. It was an interesting life. I loved it. I loved the farmers market. I was already a vegetarian, but I was raising good chickens, and I was actually killing them and getting them ready for the farmers market. I believed it was the right way to do it, even if I didn't eat it. That's something that I was comfortable doing.

It was a great life, but not making any money. It's always an issue. You need to make a living. A better living than just eating your own vegetables and poultry. Then you need to be able to fix the car and the equipment that breaks down, and all kinds of things like that. The cash flow was not there, so from there I moved to Switzerland, still with that partner, working in the Alpage. We were shepherds. We took care of very young cows, heifers. We didn't milk, we didn't make cheese or anything like that. We just took care of the young cows, feeding them, making sure they were all right in the mountains. We were spending a lot of time running up and down the Alps. It was a wonderful job. I loved it.

When I was on that job, in Switzerland, I met my husband, John. I broke up with my boyfriend, and I started my life with John. I worked with him. He was already a cheese maker. He had been going to school. Let me tell you about John, because he's a huge part of my life, of course. He's from Detroit. He left when he was eighteen years old to go to school in France to learn French. And from that he met a lot of people and ended up making wine and working in vineyards in Switzerland. He met some cheese makers and thought cheese-making was more interesting than making wine, so he went to school and learned cheese-making. We met on his first job.

It was the most beautiful place at 2,000 meters in the Alps, no electricity, no running water, milking cows by hand, and I just fell in love with the job and the place and with the guy. And we started working together, making cheese. It was again seasonal work, so we would do that for several months, then go back in la Vallée and pick grapes, and then we would have all of that time off, all of that money we made in Switzerland, wonderful Swiss francs, and we would go travel in India, in Nepal, in South America. It was a wonderful life, but we didn't have a home.

After a few years of doing that we wanted to have our own home, and a garden, and a cat, so we found a solution to that. John always wanted to come back to the United States, and anyway, the idea of starting a cheese factory in Switzerland or in France would have been pretty déjà vu. On the other hand, in the US, it was very appropriate to do, especially the type of cheese we make, Raclette, very unusual here in this country, so we came. It took us a while in the US in 1988 to get it going, because of course we had no money.

John being from Detroit would come up here on vacations, so we came, and of course I loved it here. It was so beautiful. We just came camping and going back to Detroit, but then it was, "This is it. This is the place I would really like to set up something, if I'm going to stay in the United States." So we came, and we found a little house, and we found jobs. I worked at an herb farm, Woodland Herb Farm in Northport, for a few years and I had different jobs, working at the Homestead, just keeping busy, until we were able to get Leelanau Cheese going. From the time we came to Michigan and we started Leelanau Cheese it took five years. We could not find money. A family member, John's sister, loaned us money, and I can tell you it was not much at all, but it was enough to get it going. Of course we had to find milk.

I absolutely didn't want to have cows. Being so far away from home [France], I had the feeling that if I had cows I'd never go home. Not that I go home often, anyway, but I know that the cows' part, milking cows, is a full-time job, and making cheese is a full-time job, so I knew there was not enough of us to be able to do it all.

So we had to look for milk, and milk in this area is not what it used to be. There used to be a lot of dairy farms, but they got replaced by cherries, and now replaced by vineyards and hops, so now there's just a handful of dairy farms. It's not Vermont. And then we needed to find a place, too, so we found Omena. We were both working at Leelanau Wine Cellars, and that's how we found that location. We started Leelanau Cheese in 1995, and it's been a challenge. Every day is a challenge.

In 1995 we rented something that used to be a garage, a little place that became a little creamery, but we couldn't age the cheese there, so we built a cheese cellar in the hill, a very small cheese cellar. Already in the first year it was too small. We couldn't keep up. For some reason we got popular fast. I guess being the first cheese makers in this area, even though the local food movement was not really moving at that time. I remember going to some restaurants with my products, and the answer would be, "Well, I get all of my supplies from Sysco. I don't think I want to change." I had that answer a few times. It was really hard to sell your produce in stores and restaurants. They didn't really believe in us.

The little shop in Omena was very popular. We sold a lot of cheese there. But I found that trying to sell it in restaurants and grocery stores wasn't easy at all. There was no farmers market. Farmers markets are very new here. They didn't exist at all. We went to events with our cheese. There was a little wine festival. There was a jazz festival in Suttons Bay in those days. We did both events, but no farmers market. And now I don't have enough supply to do farmers markets in the summer, but I would love to do the farmers market.

It was a completely different scene. There was hardly any local food when we started. And not only were we making cheese, but we were making an unusual cheese for this area, so people would come to a shop, and they would ask for cheese curds, they would ask for orange cheese, and I would say, "But, orange is a color. It is not the name of a cheese." And I would explain how the cheese is only orange by adding color to it. Natural or not, you add the color to the cheese to make it orange. The milk comes white. So it was a challenge at the beginning to sell our products. Some local publicity helped put us on the map, and then we took first place at the Michigan State Fair, which does not exist anymore. That was awesome for us, being so small. And then we started doing cheese competitions and getting successful in those competitions and winning some awards. Every time you win another award you get a little bit of publicity. It really helped. So as we grew, it got too small really fast, in Omena. We were looking for other places, and we could never find the right place.

Then Black Star Farms started. They knew we were looking for a place, and they asked us if we would like to move in with them. Those were the years when wineries were popping up. We were definitely going to make them different from the other wineries to have the creamery there, so we agreed. We moved to Black Star Farms in 2000. We had been in business for five years when we moved there. Then the local food industry became a lot bigger, still not a lot of people making cheese until Idyll Farms started about three or four years ago. But until then we were the only cheese makers in this part of Michigan, not only in Leelanau County, for many, many years. The next cheese makers were by Grand Rapids.

Although people still didn't understand. We are very genuine here. We actually go to the dairy farm. We pick up the milk. We come here and we start processing, and we make everything from scratch, and we make things exactly the same way we did in Switzerland. We are using stainless instead of copper kettles, and we age the cheese the same way we did in Switzerland. It's a washed rind. It's very labor intensive, and we don't rush it. If a cheese is not ready, we leave it in the cellar until it's ready.

We do pasteurize, and the reason we pasteurize is first that we make cheese year-round. If we don't make cheese in the winter I have nothing to sell in the summer, which is high season. And in the winter we give haylage, which is not the worst, but it is a fermented food. With fermented food you get problems when the cheese is aging, so you have to pasteurize to kill both bacterias. But we do add the good bacteria, to put the cultures back in the cheese, so we make up for the pasteurization. And we make up for the pasteurization also by aging the cheese properly. I think a huge problem for artisan cheese makers in this country is the aging part. They can never build the right cellar and aging rooms, so they have huge problems aging the cheeses. Fifty percent happens in the creamery, and 50 percent happens in the cheese cellars. It's very important, and it's worth spending the money on the cheese cellar you really need. But we do everything the same way we did in Switzerland, except for pasteurization.

I have had many people coming from France, or Switzerland, who believe our cheese is made out of raw milk. Actually, raw milk is not going to make a difference on the flavor. Flavor-wise, it's all about how you make the cheese, and then how you age it. Raw milk doesn't make a cheese more potent or stronger. Raw milk is all about the nutrition you get from the raw milk, and I totally agree with that. I wish I had that quality of milk here in Leelanau County, so we could do raw milk. But raw milk is not going to make any difference in your flavor or the quality of the cheese by itself. We don't really have a choice. The nearest organic milk I could find would be, I think, about two hours from here, so that would be a four-hour drive to get a batch of milk, and it's not really sustainable at all. Sometimes you just have to make choices. We use the milk from two very small dairy farms, nothing industrial, and they take good care of their cows. That's the best we can find here. That's the way it is.

We are still the only cheese maker except for another cheese factory in Northport that is extremely small, I think even smaller than when we started. The cheese industry is small, and I think it's going to stay that way because of the lack of milk. We get people coming here all the time who want to start a cheese factory. They want to start making cheese, but when I ask them where are they going to get the milk, they haven't thought of that yet. It's kind of important. No milk, no cheese.

The year we started, Stone House Bread started. So we were always put together. Leelanau Cheese and Stone House Bread, and of course cheese and bread was perfect, so we did a lot of things together at the very beginning. And then the local movement grew mostly with farms, vegetable farms, and CSAs [Community Supported Agriculture]. You started seeing more and more of that. And lots of bakeries. In the local foods we always had cherries, we always had places like American

Spoon Foods and other fruits, using the preserves. That was a part of the local movement, but I didn't even see the growth happening. It just happened. All of a sudden there was a farmers market. Farmers markets started really small and got bigger, and now I hear they are too big and they are looking for a new venue for the market. There's a farmers market in every village now in the summer, and it seems like it just happened.

The restaurants are looking for local food. What bothers me, I have to say, is first of all we need to define "local food." I think we should separate the food made here but with the ingredients coming from very far away—like coffee and chocolate, for example. The food is made here, so it is local food, but the ingredients are coming from very far away—that is important to me. Also, the quality of the local food. I don't think that people used to care about that too much, as long as it was local. It's safe; it's sustainable. It's local, and they don't really care how much they pay per pound and all of that. It just has to be local. It doesn't have to be good.

In a perfect world it would be local and organic and at a good price. What a dream! At a price we can all afford. Because we are feeding people. And we need to keep that in consideration. We are not only feeding the rich people. We want everybody to be able to afford our products. So, local, and organic, and at a good price, that would be a dream come true. Right now I try to keep the price of our cheese affordable. When you are at the grocery store, and you are looking at a wedge of cheese, you want to say, "I am very comfortable with that. I can definitely buy a wedge of cheese and eat it and not buy it as a souvenir." I want to keep it that way. Business-wise I have a lot of contact with a lot of friends. Everybody is telling us to raise our price, but my goal is to actually sell the cheese we make. I'm not going to keep it in my cellar forever and take care of it. I want to make it and sell it. I want people to enjoy it. That's very important to me.

We ship and do mail orders, not during the summer, but very busy for the holidays. We are food makers. We are feeding people. We want to provide a good-quality product at a decent price. I wish my cheese would almost be even cheaper. I cannot go any lower than that, because then I can't pay my bills. And I don't make any money even after twenty years. But I think it's important. People go to the farmers market, and because they are buying it at the farmers market, they agree to pay more. In France it's at the farmers market that you find everything cheaper because you buy directly from the producer, so everything is going to be cheaper. It's not packaged, and it doesn't have to go through a middle person, so everything is cheaper. But here it's the opposite. At the farmers market everything is more expensive. And the quality is not always there either. We went through a lot of stages: no farmers market, then a little farmers market, then big farmers market. I hope soon it's going to be farmers market with good local quality produce at a good price. At a normal price that everybody can afford. And not because, "Oh, I bought it at the farmers market, so I agreed to pay twice the price." I think we'll get there.

Oryana [food co-op] has been here for a very long time, already in the '70s. We sold cheese at Oryana's when they were on Randall Street. Now that place is getting bigger and busier and doesn't sell only organic products. They do research the source of their products and they do a very good job of it, but Oryana is not necessarily a cheap place either. You need to find what works for you. Our cheese is pretty much the same price in all of those places. There are just two stores where we were not able to keep the same price as everywhere else. We just did not agree.

But we do all of the work. When we deliver the cheese everything is packaged, labeled. We put it on the shelf. We price it. They don't have to do anything. We sell everything. There is no return so they don't lose any money. It's not like getting a truck and you need somebody to open the boxes, and if it's bulk they need to cut the package and the label and price, so their markup would be a lot higher. I want to keep the markup as low as possible by doing most of the work myself so I end up with priority in the stores that sell well enough because I really want to sell my cheese. I make it, and I still work a lot, and I am still working seven days a week, twenty years later. I haven't found a way yet to get some time off, but, at the end, I want to sell my cheese. I think if you have a right price out there for the quality you can sell it.

Right now we have two full-time employees, one person working on weekends with me—and that's saving my life—doing a lot of cellar work on weekends. And I have two part times. The training depends on what they do. The cellar work is not only about the training. It's about understanding what's happening in the cellar with that cheese. Not everybody gets it. It's something very particular and unique. You can work in the cellar for years and never really understand how it works. What matters is to find the right people who have the right feeling for the job.

We are being inspected a lot more than any other food places like restaurants because of the pathogen problems. So, as small and as clean as we are, they are very often checking on things, for the good, I suppose. Sometimes I think they could go check another place and leave us alone, but they are doing their job, and I am grateful for that, too, because it's easy to let it go. The cleaning and the sanitizing is so important, and how to train somebody on that. From silly things, from handwashing. You would think—everybody thinks they know how to wash their hands, but they actually don't. It's understanding what's dirty and what's clean. It's two different problems and situations. Teaching people who never worked in the food industry is really hard. We just hired somebody a few months ago who actually is a chef and he has been working in some very good restaurants, and he gets it. He never worked in a creamery before, but he just gets it. It's not for everybody, and you never know when that person comes along. I suppose if you are in Vermont or in Wisconsin it might be easy to find somebody who has been working in a cheese factory, but not here.

Thinking back, I was eighteen when I left my hometown. The best thing about my life now is—as much as I don't like being in the front, dealing with customers—the best thing about it is at the very end of the chain. From the time we go to the dairy farm and all of the time we take care of the cheese in the cellar and it ends up there, it's the people coming back to keep buying the products, and the customers who have been buying from us for twenty years, and they keep coming, that's the best thing about it. We think we are doing something right.

If the goal, as I was saying, is to sell your product, and if people keep coming back and coming back to buy your cheese, and they keep telling you how much they love it, and they always have a story about what they do with the cheese, or a restaurant has been using the cheese for years. If that happens, people are happy, they keep coming back, I'm happy. Cheese-making is an everyday challenge. We work with the milk we get, with the atmosphere in the cheese cellar, a lot of things happen in the creamery. It's an everyday challenge. We also learn all the time. At the end, if the product is good, I'm happy.

Swiss-Style Potato Gratin

ANNE HOYT, LEELANAU CHEESE

Serves 6

1 teaspoon butter

1 pound potatoes, peeled and thinly sliced in rounds

Pinch of salt and pepper

2 cloves garlic, minced

8 ounces Raclette cheese, grated or thinly sliced

⅔ cup dry white wine; 3–4 tablespoons milk

Preheat oven to 385°. Grease small casserole dish with butter. In a medium bowl, gently toss potato slices with salt, pepper, and garlic. Place a layer of potato slices in the prepared bowl. Sprinkle with a generous amount of cheese. Repeat with another layer of potatoes and another layer of cheese. Top with remaining potatoes.

Pour wine and milk over layered potatoes. Sprinkle the top with remaining cheese. Cover the dish with foil and bake for 30–40 minutes.

Uncover and bake for an additional 15–20 minutes or until top is golden brown. Serve immediately.

IV

CHEFS AND RESTAURATEURS

Farm to Table

Photo by Tracy Grant, Karuna Photo

9

Jennifer Blakeslee

Jennifer, chef/owner of Cooks' House, describes food as a second career that she came to in her thirties. The constant in her life was and is horses, from early childhood to the present when she spends summers as a private chef to a family in Colorado. But her first career until an accident sidelined her was dancing. Her daughter today is a dancer and also a rider, so the tradition continues. Travels in Europe and South America educated Jen to different ethnic cuisines, and after opening her own restaurant in Denver she became sous chef at a Michelin star restaurant in Las Vegas where she met Eric Patterson, her business partner. Happily for all of us, they decided to open Cooks' House in Traverse City instead of in California or Colorado or any of the other fifty states. In 2018 Cooks' House celebrated its tenth anniversary. In addition to her other travels Jen now spends a lot of time in India.

Jennifer Blakeslee, b. December 20, 1964
Interview: April 14, 2017
Cooks' House, 115 Wellington Street, Traverse City

*We just wanted to have the best produce basically
that was in season and then try to do it locally.*

I am chef and co-owner of the restaurant Cooks' House. Born in Detroit, I moved to Traverse City when I was two. My dad took a job as a prosecuting attorney in Traverse City, so that's what brought us up here. I grew up here and went to high school and graduated from high school here. And then moved away immediately for about twenty-five years, and came back.

My parents divorced when I was about seven years old. One of my parents lived on one side of Traverse City, and my other parent lived on the other side, but I grew up basically in Leelanau County. I've always had a horse, and I kept my horse on a farm, so I started doing a lot of farm work, baling hay, harvesting corn, shaking cherries in the summertime, and milking cows. It was great when they first started getting the electric milkers.

As far as food goes the biggest influence came from my grand-mother, who was an amazing woman. I spent almost all of my sum-mers with her in Canada. She was my mom's mom. She had property in Canada, and she also ran a wildlife sanctuary in the Indiana Dunes on Lake Michigan. She was an amazing cook and grew everything all the time. She had herb gardens and vegetable gardens. We would spend one whole day driving to the country to get eggs from the Amish farmer. She had a big influence on me early on.

I didn't really do anything serious with food until I was about thirty years old. It was a second career for me. When I graduated from high school I lived in Chicago, and I danced with Hubbard Street Dance Company for a couple of years. When I broke my toe I had to retire from dancing. At age twenty-eight I found myself in Colorado in the mountains and I started cooking in restaurants. I cooked with three amazing chefs that had all been out there. They were all just super inspirational and had a great approach to cooking. We were cooking for twenty to forty people a day, and had no food costing or anything like that. We had amazing ingredients to work with, and we could do whatever kind of food we wanted. That was my introduction to the food world.

From there I moved to Denver where I opened a restaurant with one of my friends. I was the chef of the restaurant, and, looking back on it, I had absolutely no business at that time taking on that position. But if you want something bad enough you just try every-thing. It worked in that restaurant. I think they are in their eighteenth year now, and they still use the original menu that I wrote when I was there. It was a very small place. Thirty seats. A lot of outdoor seating, which is easily done in Colorado because of the weather. It was all

Italian food, so we made all of our pasta from scratch. We bought a lot of our produce from local farmers, so that's where an awareness of the local, sustainable sourcing started for me, and also the idea of eating in season. After that job I had the opportunity to live in Italy for a little while, and that started me on a cooking path almost around the world.

I spent quite a bit of time in Italy, and then because I have a sister that was in Berlin, I found myself in Germany. The man that owned the restaurant in Denver had a second house in Mexico, so I would spend a couple of months at a time working in restaurants in Mexico. I know a little bit of kitchen Spanish, a little bit of kitchen Italian, but I can't really have a proper conversation in either language. From Denver I was able to travel the world and make good connections with many people. Also while I was in Denver I went to culinary school at Johnson and Wales University and got a bachelor's in culinary arts.

From there I had an opportunity to work as the sous chef at André's in Las Vegas, which is a Michelin star restaurant. Chef André had classic French cuisine, great pride in the food, and we had all the right tools that you could need. The entire staff was passionate about what they did and invested in everything. While I was in Vegas I cooked with Chef Eric Patterson. That's where we met each other. He had been at André's for about twenty years. We worked really well together so we decided to do our own place, and Cooks' House is it. In 2018 we will celebrate our tenth anniversary. Eric is from Kansas, but we decided to come here. Originally, we were looking back at Colorado because I was most familiar with Colorado at that point, and I loved Colorado. And then we started looking at the wine and all of the agriculture here in the different seasons, and we decided that Traverse City would actually be the best choice for what we wanted to do for a restaurant.

Right from the get-go we knew that we wanted to do local cuisine, almost maybe to the point where we were trying to redefine what local cuisine was, which is a task that we are still working on. We've talked to the tribe considerably: the Anishinaabeg or Three Fires Confederacy comprised of Ottawa, Chippewa, and Potawatomi. Hopefully, at some point we'll write another book that redefines what the original cuisine of this area was.

We knew that we wanted the food to be seasonal and from small farms. We were both really interested in foraging as well. Eric and I have very different cooking styles. He's been very classically trained French. I have some of that knowledge from being at André's and doing culinary school, but most of the cuisines that I have experienced are different ethnic cuisines: Mexican cuisine a lot, Indian food, and then the German and the Italian. It's more what is the ingredient and what does it want to be. And then we kind of both put our two cents in, and that's how each dish is created.

When we started we literally just opened the door. Two people came in. And then the next day six people came in. It's been word of mouth. We haven't done any advertising. We have a lot of repeat customers. Our client base is all over the board. We have culinary students. We have a lot of farmers that eat here. And then we have people that just want to experience—I don't know—fine dining. But it's not fancy here at all by any means. We wanted to be approachable to everyone. I mean, we don't have a dress code other than your clothes. You just have to have some clothes. It's pretty casual.

The local and sustainable movement didn't exist when we came here. I think maybe after two years someone called us from Condé Nast or another magazine, and they said, "Oh, since you are one of the forerunners in this local, sustainable thing . . ." But I would think more of Alice Waters being like the mother of invention, you know. We didn't really know what that was. We didn't do this like, "Oh, we're going to be a local and sustainable restaurant." We just wanted to have the best produce basically that was in season, and then try and do it locally.

In the beginning there was quite a lot of leeway as to how to define what exactly local, sustainable was. I think we include about a hundred-mile radius of Traverse City, but everything that we cook is seasonal. When we started out we would just go to the farmers market and try to make the connections with the different farmers. The farmers markets have been here about ten years. The farmers didn't really know what to do with us either. I mean there was no connection at that time with the farmers delivering to local restaurants. Those relationships have all grown over the last couple of years.

At first we would go to the farmers market and get peaches that were in season and tomatoes. We would buy as many as we could because they were just so beautiful. And then we would think, oh, what can we make with this? And we would have several different dishes with tomatoes in them or several different dishes with peaches. Now we understand what's going to be available roughly within the season, but of course it's all dependent on weather. And now the farmers will come to us in December, January, and we'll look at the seed list, and we'll see if there's some stuff that we're not sure what it is. "Can you grow that for us?" and we'll make a commitment to buy it. And then whatever that ingredient is, is what the dish becomes. It's centered around that. When we are out of that ingredient, it's gone, and the dishes change.

As a chef, it keeps you thinking all the time. What direction can I take this next without repeating it? But it gives you a lot of flexibility, too. The menu is changing all the time. If we get a quart-size bag of dried beans, when the dried beans are gone, then the menu item changes. It just depends. It could be a couple of days. It just depends on the amount. The tomatoes we have now for almost two full months. Asparagus, a couple of weeks. And then the morel season of course. It depends on how much it rains and how much the sun comes out, what the weather is.

We try to buy wines locally. I think Château Grand Traverse was the first winery. That was just starting when I was graduating from high school in 1983. There was a Late Harvest Riesling that was super sweet, like hummingbird nectar, and all the women loved it. But definitely people's palates here have grown and changed over the years. The breweries and the wineries, all of them are represented on the beer and wine list. We do dinners with all the wineries and breweries. We have fourteen of these dinners, twice a month through all of the off-season, so like November through May. We do five courses, and we write the menu around whatever the breweries and wineries want to showcase. They'll bring in their library wines now, things that are a little bit more special, that are from their own stash. We only need three bottles to get around the restaurant, because it's so small, for one course. So we're trying amazing wines that the winemakers and the brewers are very, very proud of. They are here through the whole dinner, and they talk about their craft and where they came from and what direction they are going. It's a pretty intimate setting. It's nice. We will come up with five new dishes that pair well with whatever wine they want to show. I had a short crash course on wines at the culinary institute, and I'm gradually learning a little bit more all the time, but I have to practice my beer and wine knowledge constantly. It doesn't come easily to me.

There's a good rapport among the chefs here now. I feel like when we came here maybe the community dictated more what that relationship was. In the beginning, when we started, the community's idea was: "Who is the best chef, this person is a better chef than that person." I don't like that. I think everybody brings their own individuality to the plate. It's such a passion, and it takes so much of your life, and you work so hard to get where you are, to be in this place, before you can ever open a restaurant. My experience is completely different than Myles Anton [at Stella's]. And Myles Anton is amazing. Or than Guillaume [Hazael-Massieux at le Bistro and la Bécasse]. However, probably in the last eight years, all of us chefs do a thing where we get together on a regular basis, and we do a chef's potluck. Each of us brings a dish. We did it at Little Fleet sometimes, but now we just go to each other's homes. Somebody hosts in a different place each time. And we just talk about our crafts and how we can do it better and the different ways we can support each other. It's been a really nice ride with everybody. There's lots of information sharing.

And we share employees with each other, like if someone needs a dishwasher, or if someone needs a line cook for the night. So we have a really fantastic rapport with everyone. With Jen Welty, when I first moved here, Jen and I worked at Black Star Farms together. We were in the wine-tasting room, and then we also made cheese together with John and Anne at Leelanau Cheese. So Jen and I were together all day long and just talking. And she would say, "Well, what do you want to do?"

"I want to open a restaurant. What do you want to do?"

She'd say, "I want to open a bakery."

It's just fun to see where we've gone in the last eight years. We're very supportive of each other all the time. We have a nice friendship out of it, too. I think that is more common now than it was ten years ago here, with the "Who has the best chili?" for the chili cook-off. There is networking now, and friendships between the chefs and the farmers, and the artisans: the bakers and cheese makers.

One of my favorite days here a couple of years ago was when Eric and I were here early in the morning. I had dropped my daughter off at school. We were just sitting here and organizing, doing the morning routine, and in walks Madeleine Vedel, first time, and going 100 miles a minute. "I make this cheese, and would you like to try some of this cheese?" I thought, "Who is this amazing, crazy woman?" We tried her cheese, and it was just this fantastic cheese. We weren't even halfway through this cheese tasting, and in walks Sue Kurta from Boss Mouse. And so the two of them met for the first time. And we sat down and we tried all of Sue's cheeses. And we weren't quite finished with that when Larry Mawby came in. He brought all of his bubbles. We pretaste a week ahead for our wine dinners. So he brought all these bubbles. So we got to sit there with Madeleine and Sue and Larry Mawby and eat cheese and drink bubbles. How much better does it get?

We are small. We can seat twenty-four in the dining room or fifty-two all day if the seatings work out right. So no more than fifty-two a day. It's perfect. We have five servers in the front of the house, and we have about five cooks now in the back for twenty-four people at a time.

Our original wine list was written by a master sommelier, Ron Edwards. He's in Petoskey now. We did have one somm, and she just left. We have a girl who started out as a busser, and she's now working on her second-level somm test. She's taking that on and growing into it. We're keeping the wine program growing. In addition to the local wines we also have wines from around the world. They are all from very small places. A couple bottles of this, a couple bottles of that.

I also private-chef for a family. They have several homes around the United States: Nantucket, New Jersey, Colorado, Texas, Jupiter Island, Florida, so I usually do a lot of the holidays: Fourth of July, Labor Day, Thanksgiving, Christmas, at one of their locations. They have a chef that is on staff most of the year, and then I come in just for the special event deals. Now I'm up to bringing about six people from Traverse City with me every time that I travel, as well. One other cook and then, usually, three or four servers. It's a great working vacation. They are a wonderful family.

I always bring my daughter with me when I travel, and that is great. She's been coming with me basically since she was two. I think this is going to be her first summer that she actually works down in the horse barns. She's fourteen now. It will be her first deployment summer. It's a great opportunity for her. I don't have a horse anymore. My last guy got too old. He was living in Colorado. He became like the head of the herd and stayed out there. But I do ride every year when I go back now. I use their horses. I usually get the boss's horse. That's pretty lucky. It's a very nice animal.

So my daughter's fourteen, and being a chef, you are working eighty to a hundred hours a week. Back when I was still at André's I realized one day—it just popped into my head—"Oh, when my daughter turns five, I will see her on Sunday. And that's it." And I had to make a choice there to figure out how to balance that, as I'm sure that most women do. The cooking thing comes pretty easily to me, and I love it, and I don't realize how many hours I am into the day. I could stay here for hours and hours and then I'm like, "Oh, I'm a mom, too. I have a kid, too." I'm trying always to find that constant balance.

I have an amazing child that's very happy, but if she doesn't have what she needs, she lets you know. So sometimes she's like, "You are working too much. I need a day with you." "Okay. We can do that." I'm always trying to find that balance, so I guess, in four or five years—she's starting high school next year—in four or five years, she's going to be graduating and then, that's that. Not that my job as a parent will be done by any means. I know that it's a lifelong bond, but it will free me up for a lot of time for being here at the restaurant. I've been lucky to flip my whole schedule around so that I can do this and be a mom. I feel very fortunate for that, but I look forward to the time again when I can just spend a lot of time here in the kitchen because I just really do love it so much.

Over the next couple of years the restaurant should be running pretty smoothly. We started a couple of series two years and four years ago. Young Chefs' Dinner which has younger chefs that are working on the line for other people come in, and they each are responsible for a course, so that's been a really fun way to get a lot of different cooks in through the doors here, and keep that little stage-ing food knowledge expanding and growing and networking with all the different cooks. And then we started a Guest Chefs Series with chefs from Las Vegas, California, Chicago, and Detroit that are coming here to do dinners. There's also an Indian woman that comes here and does an Indian dinner. Those are the things that I'm putting my efforts into right now. We have ninety farmers that we buy from. That's all running smoothly. We don't have much turnover in staff, and we're booked pretty solidly on a pretty regular basis, so we just have to let all of that be what it is right now and be thankful for it.

I might like to have a second place, somewhere that I could play around a little bit more with the ethnic foods, and that would be super casual. I'd like to try a place where the food items are still good, cooked properly and locally sourced, but in the $10 to $12 meal range, a plate more. Other than that, I'd like to continue traveling. Travel, travel, travel!

Appetizer with Panache: Savory Squash Crème Brûlée with Bhelpuri

JENNIFER BLAKESLEE, COOKS' HOUSE

Serves 4–6

1 quart cream

¾ cup sugar

8 egg yolks

1 12-ounce jar tamarind concentrate

2 small onions—diced

4 cloves garlic

2 tablespoons grated ginger

⅔ cup jaggery

⅔ cup sugar

Salt

2 tablespoons chunky chaat

2 cups lime juice—fresh squeezed

4 large bunches cilantro with stems

¼ cup shredded cabbage

¼ cup diced apple

¼ cup diced and cooked potato

¼ cup lentils

¼ cup cilantro

Make the Brûlée

Preheat the oven to 325 degrees F.

Put cream in a medium pan and heat gently over medium heat until it begins to simmer, and then turn off.

In a medium bowl, whisk together ¼ cup sugar and the egg yolks until well blended and it just starts to lighten in color. Add the cream a little at a time, stirring continually.

Pour the liquid into 6 (7- to 8-ounce) ramekins. Place the ramekins into a large cake pan or roasting pan. Pour enough hot water into the pan to come halfway up the sides of the ramekins.

Bake just until the crème brûlée is set, but still trembling in the center, approximately 40 to 45 minutes. Remove the ramekins from the roasting pan and refrigerate for at least 2 hours and up to 3 days.

Make the Bhelpuri

Make the tamarind chutney by putting one jar of tamarind concentrate, 1 onion, 2 cloves garlic, ⅓ cup jaggery, ⅓ cup sugar, 1 tablespoon salt, 1 tablespoon chunky chaat, and 1 cup lime juice into a blender and blend until smooth.

Make cilantro chutney by putting 4 bunches cilantro (stem and all), 1 onion, 2 cloves garlic, ⅓ cup jaggery, ⅓ sugar, 1 tablespoon salt, 1 tablespoon chunky chaat, and 1 cup lime juice into a blender and blend until smooth.

Mix remaining ingredients in a bowl with a pinch of salt and enough of both chutneys to dress.

To finish:

Burn the brûlée as normal. Once the sugar crust has cooled, place a spoonful of bhelpuri on top and serve.

Photo by Madeleine Hill Vedel

10

Jennifer Welty

From early childhood Jen loved baking, working with flour and sugar, salt and butter, seeing dough rise. But for a number of years she didn't think of cooking as a career, even when she supported herself by working in food establishments. She held a bakery job in Atlanta where she also briefly attended culinary school. Later, as a single mom, she held a bakery job in Ithaca, New York, but quit and moved back to live with her parents in Columbus, Ohio. There she was the first woman to be hired as a baker by a renowned Belgian-owned bakery. She worked there almost three years before deciding to go back to college at Ohio State. At OSU she met her future husband, a fellow student and also an instructor in one of her classes. An internship in viticulture at Black Star Farms led her to Leelanau County, and the rest is history. Together with Nic she started 9 Bean Rows as a farm, then added a bakery, taking their produce and baked goods to the farmers market. Over time they added a restaurant. Summer 2018 they sold the restaurant, now renamed Wren, to Adam McMarlin (see *Edible Grande Traverse* no. 54 for a full story and review). Since then they have been expanding the bakery, adding an outdoor pavilion with a wood-fired stove and other wood cooking equipment to make pizzas and more. Long lines form routinely at their stand in the farmers market as loyal fans of the breads and croissants and other baked goods wait patiently or impatiently, hoping the supply doesn't run out before they get to the head of the line.

Jennifer Welty, b. November 3, 1975
Interview: April 13, 2017
9 Bean Rows Bakery, 9000 East Duck Lake Road, Suttons Bay

It takes a village to raise a restaurant, a bakery, a farm.

For me to go back to what first got me into food, I have to—this is great—because it involves a book. When I was a child my favorite author was Richard Scarry. He has cartoon books, and I opened the page and I saw the pig which was the baker with the rolling pin. And this pig in the cartoon was rolling and beating and making and doing, and I loved that pig. I also loved another part of the book which was Halloween. For Halloween, the baker, the pig, got dressed up, but they all got candy. And the food, and the candy . . . I would sit and look at that. And then I grew up and I forgot about it.

The second time I recall thinking this is what I'm doing with my life—before I knew I was doing it—was being fifteen years old going on sixteen. Up until then I had led a pretty easy, American white life, but my dad had just recently lost his job. My sister was on her way to Emory University, and my dad was trying to figure out how he was going to pay for it. So we had no money. And it was Michigan. We were taking pop cans back and doing everything we could, and there wasn't a lot of food in the house. But there was flour and salt and butter. Going in and perusing the cabinets and pulling out anything I could find out of there and looking at it and knowing I loved sugar, well, the first things I would come up with were those very crisp, kind of like pie crust with cinnamon and sugar on top, and that's what I had. I thought well, this is pretty good. And I flocked it out. And that's what I did for that year to get by.

Of course I went on after I was out of high school straight into college when I didn't know what I wanted to do. Cooking wasn't what I was going to do. I liked earth, so I ended up going to a college in Athens, Ohio, Ohio University. I thought I was going to do archaeology. But, you know, I didn't even want to go to school. I just wanted to be free and play. In fact that was my first Grateful Dead concert that year, and I just wanted to go on a Grateful Dead tour. My mom did not want me to do that. She said, "You are going to college."

I said, "No, I'm not."

And she said, "Please, just give it a try."

And of course I pretty much always listened to my parents, and I did then. I ended up going to college right out of high school, but within six months I was out. I was not ready to be there. It was a waste of time and money for everyone.

I hit the road. I traveled, and went to music concerts for a few years, and did those things for a few years. I did all the things that people think of when they think of the '60s. I just did them later, in the mid-'90s. And along the way, needing money, I found myself working here and there, and not too long of stints, anywhere from a gas station takeout food, to working in a small sub shop. Those were my first jobs with food, and I don't recall that anything I did was that great.

But in 1997 I made the decision to go back to college. I went to culinary school. I was living in Atlanta, Georgia, at the time, actually in Athens, outside of Atlanta, and commuting into the Art Institute of Atlanta. For the first six months I attended very wholeheartedly. I enjoyed it, but my life was very tumultuous, in and out—six people all living together trying to split rent, roommate issues. You know, you are eighteen, nineteen, or twenty years old, and those are the things that happen to you. But the worst thing that happened to me that did change my life dramatically, was that . . . I had been in culinary school for a while. I had actually gotten a job working my first bakery job at the Flying Biscuit Café, which is a restaurant owned by a famous singer/songwriter couple, the Indigo Girls. It's down in Atlanta, and I was there for a few months living in a house that was not even built yet. I was living on the third floor of this house thanks to the gracious nature of one of my colleagues at school who was letting me live there because it was an easy commute to college.

I woke up one morning at four thirty to get to the job at the bakery where I was the biscuit maker, nine-hour days, all day long, all biscuits, all day. The day before the job my mom had come into town to visit. I hadn't seen her in a really long time, so we ended up spending the night in a hotel, and she was going to drop me off at the job in the morning. But before I went to that job I had to run back to that house that wasn't finished yet to grab my stuff. And I grabbed my stuff, and when I got to the top floor I found my roommate had hung himself on the third story by an electrical cord. I had seen him the previous day twelve hours before. He had waved good-bye and said he was getting a pizza.

When I went to the bakery that morning, I just said, "You know, I don't think I can do this anymore." I didn't want to walk to work in the middle of the night at 4:00 a.m. in downtown Atlanta, because I was very spooked by everything.

So I took off again. And I did lots of things, more music, more leading not a very great life, but a very transient, free life. I was having a bunch of fun, maybe too much fun. Along the course of the way I found myself in and out of trouble—some of it was my own undertaking, some of it was other people's—but I met my boyfriend along those years and we ended up having a child together. But then he left. He had a drug problem like so many people in that era. He and I parted ways. In 2000 we had gotten married, and by the middle of 2001 we were getting divorced.

Right before that I was working in Ithaca, New York, at another bakery. That seemed to be my calling. I kept finding myself in bakeries. But during that time I found that I loved the kitchen. I had worked at an incredible bakery called the Ithaca Bakery, downtown Ithaca, Cornell campus right there. Going to work was like walking into a family. It didn't matter how bad your day was, what you were going through, how bad your husband was, whatever, you came into this place and you made dough. And you made a biscuit. And you were loved by all the people around you, and every single one of those people had their own story.

Homi and her friend, Lo, were from Laos and had been there thirty years making pastries since they moved over in the horrible part of the wartime there. Homi was a wonderful pastry chef. I have never to this day been able to understand her talent. She was ambidextrous and could frost a cake with two hands, and I always considered it like Edward Scissorhands. It was just magnificent. I loved the job. I loved working in the bakery. I thought, with a six-month-old, I can make it.

But then life got the better of me, and I said, "Maybe I do need to return home to my family." I returned, a little bit head down, tail in, but knowing that I had had a great experience in New York, and was loved. I recall driving the U-Haul truck back to my parents, who, I'm sure, were happy to have me back, on Christmas Day. I just remember thinking how ironic. It was very funny. All Christmas songs on the radio the entire way back. It was a surreal moment for me. But as soon as I got back into Ohio—which is where my parents were at the time; that was home for them and for me again—I set out to look for another job. I set out to finally be an adult. I was twenty-four years old. I thought, "Okay, I'm not going to make $9 an hour or $8 an hour anymore working in a bakery. I'll do something else." So I walked into what changed my life.

I put on a suit and tie. I had dreadlocks. I was a hippie. I tied up my dreadlocks. I put them into a bandanna, and I walked into a place that I knew to be a good bakery at the time, and I just thought maybe they will take me. The moment I got there—Valerian was his name—it was a Belgian-owned bakery in the middle of Columbus, and when I mean Belgian, I mean Tadeus, Charlotte, Gigi, Stanisalis, Valerian, and Yannik. Those were the owners and the family. And Valerian said to me right when I walked in the door with my résumé, he said, "Stay here." Fifteen minutes later this other person, Tadeus, comes running in the door from down the street from wherever he was—it turned out he was running from the other facility they owned—and he said, "When can you start?"

Of course I said, "I can start tomorrow."

He said, "Can you work at 3:00 a.m.?"

I said, "Yes. I need this job and I'll do whatever it takes."

I was hired on the spot because their baker was leaving for France the next morning. He had a whiskey problem, whiskey by the oven, as classic bakers do, so they were shipping him back, and I was lucky to get my foot in the door of this place. The more I look back on it, how thankful I was. I was working on a Lopi oven. This one had like a sixteen-foot diameter, twelve-inch hearth where you have the wheel on the outside of your oven, and the breads are loaded into the oven. The wood fire is underneath, and it's a continuous flame that burns twenty-four hours a day. And I knew of this place. That's why I went there in the first place and I thought, how lucky! It turned out to be a fabulous job in so many ways. Tadeus became one of my very good friends. I wouldn't say he taught me a lot about baking, because he was a very busy man, and when I came along I was here to save the day for him. So it was one week of training, and, "Good luck to you. Get this job done."

There were two other people in there trying to get this job done with me, and about six months after I was there I looked at Tadeus and

I said, "You know, Tad, we can save a lot of money because I can do their job and you don't need them anymore."

And he looked at me and said, "You think you can do that?"

And I said, "Yes."

And by the way I was the only woman baker they ever had hired, that they would ever hire, because it was fifty pound sacks a day and I was actually turned down by the Ithaca Bakery in Ithaca, New York, because they didn't hire women bakers because of the physicality of it. If you couldn't consistently lift 100 pounds they didn't want you. They wanted to hire you as a pastry chef, or to make muffins or doughnuts. But not as a baker. So feeling fortunate to get in the door, but then six months later looking around and understanding the entire process and saying, "I can eliminate this and this." Those people didn't lose their jobs. They moved to different places in the kitchen because it was not only a bakery. It was a café. They served breakfast, lunch, and dinner. They served classic wines. They did spaghetti à la Gigi. It was French. It was Belgian. It was hip for Columbus at the time. Now fast-forward, not so hip anymore. I learned a lot about who I was and the strength I had.

Two and a half years went by. I started to see where I was in the company. You weren't going to get anywhere because it was a family-owned business. Even if you were their number one, great, but you weren't going to penetrate that French family. I made the transition from an $8, $9 position to an $11 an hour position with insurance for my child and me, which was very good at the time. I was thankful for that. But I also had a love of food and farming. I needed to move on.

So in 2004, after several years there, I made the decision to go back to college. I enrolled in Ohio State, which was a mile and a half away from the bakery, to pursue a degree in crop science. I wasn't really sure what I was going to do with it, but I knew that working long nights as a single mother I was not going to get very far. Fortunately, I did have family and I lived nearby the bakery. I was renting a house from the owners of La Chatelaine with my cousin who would spend the night there while I was in the middle of the night working. I would come get my daughter on my break, take her to day care, and that was good for what it was at the time.

I went back to school, and of course, if I'm going to do something, I'm going to do it great. I ended up doing my bachelor's, which was pretty piece-of-cake work—I mean, I wouldn't say that it was super strenuous on me—but I managed to get a degree in about two years because I had some other coursework done elsewhere. I wasn't sure what I was going to do after that, so I enrolled in graduate school. Well, why not? In crop science with a focus on viticulture. What do I like besides bread? I like wine. I like fermentation. I like this food culture, the simplicity behind it. So I started in the graduate program at Ohio State right after my degree. I was fortunate enough to be given a stipend to live on because of my scores, because of the research I was doing.

This is where it gets juicy. I was in school as an undergraduate. I had already made the decision to go to grad school. I was in a crop science 300 class, and in walks my TA, my teacher's assistant for that class—the professor never showed up, ever—but here is this guy. His name is Nic Welty. And he comes in and he runs the class. I see him in this class. And an hour and a half later I sit down in my next class, which was a 600-level graduate class that I was taking as an undergrad—because why not?—and so, there comes Nic Welty. Although in this instance we were in the same class. He was not my TA. We were taking the same coursework. So here he is, my TA, and there he is in my class with me. Things are going along. We didn't know each other, other than, "Hey, give me your assignment. Turn it in. I'll grade it." That kind of thing. But then one of our professors, Dr. Metzger, said in the middle of one of our final exams, "If anyone knows where Nic Welty can live over the course of the holiday break—he's looking for a place to live." And I say in my head, "Okay. I've got three bedrooms. There's only two of us. I have an extra bedroom." So I slip my number to the professor and I say, "Sure, he can stay." And I don't think twice about it, just go on my way, take my exams, and leave on break. And then three weeks later I hear a knock at the door, and he just shows up with his luggage.

"Oh, okay," I remember I said that. "Come on in." So for the remainder of the school year we became friends. He became a person I competed with in my class to get a better grade, and I always beat him. But the reality is the man is a million times smarter than I am. Who knows why he was there, to be honest. He had graduated from Carnegie Mellon with a degree in economics, biology, and chemistry. And then he decided to go to grad school for plant genetics. He was offered jobs on Wall Street with his degree from Carnegie Mellon out-the-door, but decided that he didn't really want that kind of life. His family was from Ohio, and he liked to grow pumpkins and had that little side business. So he found his way to grad school. We ended up with a connection. I would say that maybe six months after he moved in we went on our first date to the Bagadales Club.

He was such a strange guy. I fell in love with him right away. So there we were in Ohio, and I had said to him, "Have you ever been to Michigan before?"

He said, "No."

I said, "There's good fishing."

And he said, "Okay. I'm in."

I should say that prior to meeting Nic when I was finishing up my crop science degree, I needed an internship. And I chose Black Star Farms in Suttons Bay, Michigan, and they chose me. I had sent an email to them, and I had sent a résumé and I said, "This is who I am. I like food. I like wine. I'm in the viticulture research world, and would you take me on as an intern?" Surprisingly, they said yes. The reason I chose Michigan was because I wanted to be in the wine industry in this part of the world. I wasn't setting out to go to Napa. My research was on the cold-hardiness of *Vitus vinifera*. So if you are looking at cold-hardiness you aren't going to Napa. You are looking up here. So I came to Don Coe, and Lee Lutes, and I knew some of the guys at Black Star Farms. They took me in under their wing, and for a year I worked the bottling line. I worked in the tasting room. I tied vines. I did a little bit of everything. I was there for whatever they needed me to be, and I fell in love with the place and the people.

So then I went home after my internship and started my graduate program. I was hanging out with Nic and we are talking. He's getting his degree, and I'm not that enthused about mine. I enjoyed a little bit of the research that I was doing, but my heart kept calling me back to Michigan. I thought, "I'm not a scholar. I can do the work easy enough.

I'm smart enough, but that's not where I want to be." So I turned in my resignation at Ohio State, and I said, "Don, would you take me back?"

And he said, "Absolutely. When are you coming?"

I came up with no real job in mind knowing that they were going to let me work in the tasting room for $10 an hour plus tips, and I would be happy. Nic said, "Oh, I guess we are moving to Michigan then." He finished up his master's degree at Ohio State, all the while I was living up here. We bought a house together. He went up and saw it, looked at it. He drove back. I drove up and bought it. This was before the crash. It was a no-income, no-asset loan. They didn't care. You could just buy a house. And we did. We still own the house today. We did not go under. It's one of our rental properties now. It was a commute for him. He came up every single weekend, doing his master's, getting it done, just to see me and our kid. Then when he was finished he moved up full time and began working at Black Star Farms.

He also took some roofing jobs and odd jobs. We decided we would work together at this farm enterprise. Black Star Farms' tag line is that they are an agricultural destination. So with my love of cooking and then my degree in crop science . . . Nick and I had always talked about the idea of: "Why aren't we growing the food that we cook? Why is this the missing link that seems to be prevalent in the United States?" We were looking around before we even moved up here and asking ourselves, "Is there anybody out there doing this?"

This was back in 2004. Nothing was really happening, not much anyway. It was just starting to be an awareness. I knew of Dan Barber, and I knew a little bit of what he was doing, and when I first read it, I thought, "Oh, my God, there's other people who think this way? What the heck?" But when I came up here to northern Michigan I wasn't exactly sure what I was going to do. Was it going to be wine? Was it going to be grapes? Was it going to be food? Was it going to be farming?

My husband with his background which is economics, chemistry, biology, also was raised on a soybean, corn, and wheat farm. He made his first thousands of dollars with his pumpkin business when he was thirteen. He was a day trader and ended up working that, too, which is why he managed to be able to buy our house in 2006 with some

$40,000 he had saved from being very frivolous at college. Because he never paid for anything at college. He got into a fraternity, and he ate all the fraternity food. He took all the T-shirts they would give. So that's how we ended up being able to come up here and just figure it out. And figure it out we did. We were lucky enough to have Don Coe as our mentor. He was one of the managing partners and has since retired from Black Star Farms.

He embraced ideas. "Hey, Don, what do you think if we start farming and we do what's called a Community Supported Agriculture farm?"

"What's that?"

"Well, this is how it works."

And we went through the whole process of telling him what it was, and he said, "Yes, let's do that. Let's put a hoop house up on this property." Black Star Farms let us work for them with our idea.

But then fast-forward. This was 2006. In 2008 the economy tanked. Don looks at me and says, "We don't have the money to keep you on. This is just bad timing, and, Nic, I am so sorry. Would you like to use any of the equipment and resources we have on the property and continue it as your own business?"

We didn't even need to think twice. Yes. We had two years under our belt garnering a reputation for solid work and a good product. Something was happening. We didn't need anyone to pay us. I remember filling out the paperwork to go on unemployment. And then like three days later we thought: "What are we doing? We are able-bodied people. We don't need anyone's help, no way, and we're going to do this on our own." And we just never did. We might have gotten one unemployment check. And I remember thinking: "This is an awful lot of work to get this little money. We could have already had another business by now if the time and money and energy spent on something like that paperwork was put toward something positive." So we did.

In 2009 we hit the ground running selling at farmers market. Prior to that Don and I had invested in a wood-fired oven at Black Star. We spent $10,000 on it. The one that I was trained on, the one at La Chatelaine, was an $80,000 oven. They came over from Italy to build it. It was magnificent. But here I was with this $10,000 gem. So, well, what can I do with it? What are we going to do? We know we need to make money. Why don't I go back to baking? We'll see if anybody around here likes what I have. We added our bread into our CSA.

We went to our first farmers market selling vegetables with a few loaves of bread, and then we just got bigger. We never had money, though. We always got by. We took this business and said, "We'll pay ourselves nothing. We'll find more people. We'll keep it growing." And we've been doing that since 2009. Now we're in 2017 and have expanded from a farmers market to a small café in Traverse City to a restaurant in downtown Suttons Bay with full bar, liquor licenses, big money. We also have a bakery quite close to the restaurant downtown that has more acreage for our farm. It's been a lot of work. I never, ever have thought about giving it up even though it's been so much work, even though there's been days where we don't know how to make payroll because we just did this, or we just bought this, or some tragedy happened.

The very first year that we opened the bakery I had a child, our first together. I was breastfeeding him. I was back at work full time five days after he was born. I was upstairs nursing and all of a sudden I hear screaming. It was my daughter. "The bakery is on fire." I forgot. I had gone downstairs and fired up the pot. I was going to fry some brioches, and I completely forgot to turn it off. And it just caught the building on fire. Fortunately, nobody was hurt. Within fifteen minutes we got the fire out. And it took down a wall.

We've dealt with adversity ever since we began this business. Not having a lot of investment dollars—no investment dollars—right off the get-go, I've been lucky enough to have my mother and father. They were fabulous. They helped us with our first hoop house when they could afford to. So no investment dollars, build up some money, then here's some, then here's a little more. We've been managing to make it work. We're in a climate where people up here are starting to know a little bit more about food, and obviously across the country everybody is trying to eat more organically and locally. There's more competition now, which just makes everybody better.

The farm is expanding. The restaurant actually, as we sit here, is taking a little bit of a turn, just for a temporary hiatus. In 2012 when everything was going pretty good for us we decided that we wanted to move out of this café, and we wanted to open a real restaurant. The café was too tiny. We were stepping on ourselves and there was no room to do anything. So I thought, what about a place really close to our farm? What about something that's right in our backyard? And this building that we're sitting in right now was for sale. I had known of a guy named Paul Carlson. He and I had worked together at Black Star Farms. He was working for Don Coe at the time doing exactly what I had left Don to do. When I had worked for Don he was doing that job. When the economy swung back open there was room again. We met, and we established a relationship, and I pulled him in to be my chef at this restaurant because I am not a chef. I am a baker. I can cook great food, but I don't know anything about running the line at a restaurant.

Three and a half years later, this past fall, he quit. He wanted something different. It was one of those moments where I was crushed, really crushed. Because I put my heart and soul and love into something. But we have a new plan. You have to be able to be versatile. You have to change. Life is not static. It must continue. So rather than trying to look for a new chef within the six weeks we have before our season hits, and staffing a restaurant—most of the staff left when he left—we decided we are going to bring it back to our old school roots. We're going to be French café again for breakfast and lunch. We are going to hang in there until we find that next chef.

I am very proud of the job that Paul did while he was here for us. He did a good job cooking. The good news is that we have a community that has supported us from the beginning, and we're heading into another season where I believe the quality of our food will never change. It will always be good.

The story that I want to end with is where we are going in our future. I always say "we" because while this is my story, I'm not the only one involved. It takes a village to raise a restaurant, a bakery, a farm. It takes everybody, and we have been fortunate to have so many great people. What will we do for the rest of eternity? We are going to make food. We're in the food business. We're not going anywhere outside of that.

There will always be change. A good baguette will never change, but everything about food evolves: gluten free, tastes change, people change. We will still be here making food. And we'll be doing it with the community, focusing on local farmers, what we don't grow, what they can grow, people that make quality cheese like Anne and John Hoyt at Leelanau Cheese, people like Loma Farm that grow great vegetables when we are out, Reed from Second Spring Farm, looking at the agricultural landscape that we have, and being able to look around and say, "What can we add? How can we make it better?"

I had a revelation way back when I first read about Dan Barber, and also, to be honest, on my very first and only trip to Europe. I was in Athens, Greece, for a month, and was looking at food in a different way culturally, and saying to myself, "Why doesn't Leelanau County have a prosciutto? Why is there nothing that grounds us?" Yes, we have cherries. We have commercial cherries. But where is our prosciutto? Where is our Parma? Where is our Parmigiano? Where is that thing that you can say has the terroir? What is Leelanau County?

I'm waiting for that to happen here. It hasn't happened yet. We're starting with the wine industry. We have some morel mushrooms. Yes, there are some Porcinis that are grown out on the outskirts of Manistee. Idyll Farms started something making that goat cheese a few years ago. Is that something that's going to be the future? But Anne and John Hoyt were the ones that taught me that this is how you make a cheese. You make it this way. You make it every day. This is what it is. And they are the first people—well, obviously, Anne, being from France, she understood food. That it takes time. That it's not just something that's here today and going to be gone tomorrow. That this is a product that will be here and will be what Leelanau County is.

So when I think about our future, I think about Leelanau elevating itself to be that kind of place that people want to travel to as a destination, but also that has something that gets exported all the way across the country because it is sought after. And believe me, I believe in eating locally. But I also believe that if you have a great product, put it out there for the world. We're all better for it. I mean, the very first time I tasted some foods overseas I said, "This is ancient. This goes way back. This is not mom and pop and Swanson's food, and the crap I was raised on." Love you, Mom! In the '70s in America, nobody cared about cooking. I will say that my mom's recipe for hamburger pie in my mind goes down as one of the world's worst faux pas that could possibly be invented. Pie crust with some hamburger in the middle. I don't even know where she was going with it. And my love of food is because of the people that I work with every single day. We are surrounded by people that are kind and giving and thoughtful, also that have talent. To get to work with them every day, that's pretty fabulous.

Winter is hard. It's not a bad thing; it's just how it is. It is important to recognize that we are a tourist industry. We need more people who want to be here to support that industry, because without it, we don't have anything. I won't make the money. I won't be able to make the bread. We realized very early on that our summer sales—oh, my gosh—that bakery does $150,000 of business in the month of August. And then in the month of January we are lucky to do $16,000.

Keeping or losing staff has never been a problem for us. Fortuitously, because people wanted to leave—a student back off to college—and then people were willing to work a little bit here and there. I also made a point to try to grow one full-time job every year. When Don Coe laid us off in 2008, I knew I never wanted that to happen to anybody else. If this could be avoided, it would be. It was just me and Nic for a couple of years, and then we added a couple of people, and then a couple of people more. It's the service industry. People come. People go. My hard-core bakery staff, I slowly keep them, and they are here full time. All in all, we are very lucky that way.

RECIPE

Sea Salt Fennel Sourdough Boule

JENNIFER WELTY, 9 BEAN ROWS

2 small loaves or one large loaf

This recipe requires a scale. These are easy to find in the bakeware section of your nearby multipurpose store. By starting with weight measurements the home and professional baker can easily scale up a recipe from a loaf or two for family use to a dozen. It is helpful to have a lightweight mixing bowl on hand to place on the scale and weigh the ingredients, which you add in one by one, putting the scale back to zero before each addition.

11 ounces bread flour

5 ounces rye flour

3 ounces sourdough starter (if you don't have sourdough starter then you can replace this with 1 tablespoon baker's yeast)

.3 ounces fine sea salt (or 1.5 teaspoons)

11.5 ounces warm water (aim for 75 degrees F)—this is not quite 1.5 cups

.3 ounces or 2 teaspoons fennel (for inside the dough)

.15 ounces or 1 teaspoon fennel (for topping the dough before baking)

coarse sea salt for topping

In a large bowl combine the flours, starter, and water. Knead until the dough comes together and looks shaggy. Let rest for 20 minutes.

Add the fine sea salt and knead for 15 minutes or until medium gluten development is attained and it passes the windowpane test.

Add the fennel seed and knead until completely incorporated.

Let the dough bulk ferment for 2 hours at 75 degrees in covered, oiled bowl.

If making 2 loaves, divide the dough and let rest for 15 minutes. Shape into a round ball (boule).

In a small round basket lined with linen and dusted with flour, place the boule seam side up. Cover with a cloth and let rise in a draft-free place for 1½ hours at 80 degrees.

While the dough is rising heat the oven and a Dutch oven to 500 degrees (or as hot as your oven will get).

When the dough is ready to bake, remove the Dutch oven carefully. Flip the boule into the Dutch seam side down. With a sharp knife or razor blade score the bread ¼ inch deep in any decorative pattern you wish. Sprinkle with coarse sea sat. Place the lid on the Dutch oven and return to oven.

Let bake for 30 minutes. Remove the lid and return to oven for 10 minutes or until the bread sounds hollow when patted on the bottom of the loaf.

Photo by Madeleine Hill Vedel

11

Martha Ryan

Martha has done so many things in the food business—from working front and back in restaurants, working in Carol Worsley's Thyme Inn, serving as the food service director of Leland Public Schools for twenty years, baking and managing Stone House Bread in Leelanau, and most recently (2008) opening Martha's Leelanau Table, her own restaurant in Suttons Bay—that I find it almost impossible to fit her rich history into one of the rubrics in this book. As a baker who mastered the sourdough preparation of Stone House breads she belongs to the story of Bread and Chocolate. As the food service director she was both cook and manager. Now, with Martha's open all year and serving three meals a day, she clearly is an extraordinary restaurateur, owning, managing, and also cooking. What she shares with every woman in this book is the commitment to food that is locally and, whenever possible, organically grown, and which is then prepared by hand in her kitchen, not purchased packaged or frozen from commercial providers. The menu changes as the seasons change. Her restaurant celebrated its tenth year in July 2018.

Martha Ryan, b. August 26, 1950
Interview: August 23, 2015
Martha's Leelanau Table, 413 North Saint Joseph Street, Suttons Bay

I had a sense that I should not be buying apples shipped in from Washington, when there were apples sitting in Leelanau County that were fresh and grown in Leelanau County.

I was born in Kalamazoo. My mother was born in Kalamazoo. She and my dad both had been living there. They lived in a little house, and I was the second child born to them. My brother and I were what they called at the time "Irish twins." He was born June 26, 1949, and I was born the following August 26, 1950, fourteen months later. Growing up my brother and I were really close. And then there were three other children. My sister Kerry was born four years after me, and then my brother Dan six years later, and then my brother Tom was born ten years after me in 1960. He was like my baby because I was ten years old. I got to take care of him a lot.

My mother was a nurse. She went into nursing school during the war because that was her way of serving. She worked at Borgess Hospital in Kalamazoo. Some friends introduced her to my dad, and that's how she met him. He had already started to work for Kodak, for Eastman Kodak, and he sold X-rays to hospitals. Their paths crossed and that's how that started.

We lived in Kalamazoo for a short time, and then my dad got transferred to Cleveland. I think we moved to Cleveland in about 1954. I grew up in a suburb just outside Cleveland. I have good memories of that time in our life. Then in 1964 my dad got transferred again to Detroit, and we lived in Rochester, just outside Detroit. It was a great time to be in Detroit with Motown and the Supremes and the music and all. And my mom, all the time we were growing up, she never worked until my brother Tom was pretty much a teenager. She never went back to work until everybody was on their way. Only then she started working as a nurse outside the home.

As I was growing up she cooked. She took a lot of pride in feeding us really good food. My job was never to assist her with cooking. My job in the family was to set the table, clear the table, help with the dishes. I watched her cook a lot, but I never really had an interest. I didn't peel potatoes with her or do anything like that. She did it all. And I think that was the model for mothers in those days.

We didn't have a lot of relatives around us because we had moved so much with my dad's career. My mother's family wasn't around very much and my dad didn't have much family. So I was unaware of different ethnicities. We were Irish, Catholic, English . . . you know . . . nothing very ethnic, no special foods. But in Cleveland we lived in a very ethnic neighborhood, Parma Heights, with Polish, Hungarian, Yugoslavian, all of this rich ethnicity, different cultures and different foods. My best friend growing up, her father was Italian and her mother was Hungarian. Jayne would always invite me to go with her to family weddings. I had never seen anything like this, big Italian weddings with all the fun and dancing and singing, and the food. That was my introduction.

And then one of my mother's brothers, my Uncle Neil, he married a Lebanese woman from Flint. Her name was Bobby (Roberta) Ferris. She was probably five feet tall, dark black hair, beautiful hair. My Uncle Neil was Irish Catholic, and they produced twelve children. They had five girls in a row and then seven boys. They lived in Kalamazoo. We would visit them at least once a year. They had a cottage on Gull Lake. We'd always go, and I remember my Aunt Bobby always having a baby on her arm or on her shoulder with a diaper or a blanket, and I just thought it was growing, like always there. I didn't know what was going on there.

She was always baking and cooking, no matter how busy, how many children she had. She was always pulling something out of the oven for us, always the hospitality and the good flavors. When I think of her now I think of bread. I always think of bread or pie or something coming out of the oven.

We lived in Rochester outside of Detroit, and then I went away when I graduated high school. I went to Michigan State. I was there 1968 to about 1973. I loved college. I studied sociology, anthropology, and human resources, very useful to me later. It was great; Michigan State was wonderful. I needed a part-time job, and very close to campus was a small little submarine shop, Hobie's. I started to work there. This was my first experience of food service. The owner's name was Ernie Saint Pierre. He was from Massachusetts, I believe, and he had this idea of the grinder, and it was kind of unknown in the Midwest. So he started this idea and he had a couple of partners: Jack Leone, whose family was big importers of Italian products, and then another guy whose name was Rick Lorenz.

Rick had just recently graduated from Michigan State in the hotel and restaurant school. His family owned the Mayflower Hotel in Plymouth, Michigan. He was this amazing young, ambitious, food-and-beverage guy, and he was the person that taught me the initial beginning of my food service business. He was relentless about cleanliness, and efficiency—and I was just a young kid saying: "What's going on? Why is he bugging me so much?" I learned a lot from him. That was my first experience of working in food, and I liked it. I liked the excitement of it. Later I worked in some other places in East Lansing, but that was my first place.

I had had a dream since high school which was to go to France. I had a friend that I had met working at Hobie's. Bill was taking French, that was his minor, and we would talk a lot about going to France. We planned a trip for a summer break. We saved money and did a backpacking trip together in Europe in 1972. Eleven weeks, which was seventy-seven days. We covered England, Ireland, France, and Spain. Of course, France was our main focus. There were many, many food experiences that shaped me at that young age. But the one that Bill and I talk about and reminisce about was one afternoon when we had hitchhiked, because it was safe then. Sometimes we rented a car or took the train, but this one time in France we hitchhiked.

We were outside Paris. I think we were making our way away from Paris back toward the coast to go back to England. These two men picked us up. They were very young. They were both teachers, and I would guess they were probably five to ten years older than us. We were in our early twenties. They were professional; they were working. They invited us back to their house because it was late in the day. One guy was taking the train, he was going out later, and he said, "I can give you a ride later to get you where you are going."

So we said, "Okay." They invited us back to their house for dinner. We were always looking for good food, so we thought this was going to be great. It was our first experience of home dining the French way, course after course after course of beautifully prepared French food. That changed our lives. We didn't realize it at the moment, but it changed how we looked at food. It was amazing. Then we came back to college, graduated, and went our separate ways.

I got married in 1974 up here in Leelanau County. My soon-to-be-husband, Jim, had some friends who were living up here. We vacationed up here, came up for a week or a weekend and saw Leelanau County and immediately decided to move here. We moved up in May of 1974, and got married in November of that year.

There were only a few big places to work then. Sugarloaf was the main one that was year-round. Both of us got jobs at Sugarloaf. It was a very thriving, going concern then. They prided themselves on being year-round, four seasons. The dining room was called the Four Seasons Restaurant. While working there I met my friend Susan McConnell. She and her husband, Tom, had moved to the area around the same time that we did. Susan and I were working as waitresses in the dining room. We were paired as a team. They were doing team-service then where there was a front person and a back person. I was the front person and I would go to the table, get the drinks, talk to the people, put the order in, and then Susan would bring the food out to me. Susan did everything in the kitchen, and I did everything in the front. That type of service was supposed to be so that you never had to leave the floor and you could give all this great service to everybody.

Through that relationship Susan and I became fast friends. We ended up living very near to each other for many years while our children were growing up. Susan and I always fantasized about doing some kind of food business together. But we didn't really have a clue. We were young with our young families. Susan had gone to Europe also when she was in college, so we had a similar background there. And while she was in Switzerland she had worked in a ski area in a restaurant and learned how to bake. Fine baking became her passion. We had that in common. We both liked to cook. She was a good home cook, and I was a good home cook. We cooked all the time for our families. We all had families, and we worked. Everything was good.

Then, one evening, we went to a meeting. Our children were just getting ready to go to school, at the local school in Leland, and the school board had called a meeting about having a new food company take over the food service in the school. Susan and I were both interested. We went to the meeting, and we were appalled at what we heard. They had had a cook at the school for over twenty years, and what they wanted to do was to buy food that was prepared somewhere else by an outside company and bring it in, and all the person had to do was heat it up. They were sure that this was going to save the district money by eliminating labor and having a product that was palatable and flexible. They could pick whatever kind of foods or meals they wanted, and it was frozen, completely frozen. Susan and I were up in arms. We spoke up at the meeting.

We said, "No, this isn't right. We don't want our children to eat this kind of food, and we want local people to work in the kitchen." We just jumped in with both feet. It was kind of funny. And then, not too much longer after that, there was an ad in the paper for a part-time assistant in the school cafeteria. Susan called me up and said, "Come over, I want to show you this." So I went over to her house. She hit me on the arm and said, "Look at this, look at this. This is what you ought to do. You should do this. It's only four hours a day. You should apply."

I said, "Oh! Look at that. Okay." So I went in and I applied for the job. It was four hours a day, and I thought: "Well, here's your chance to put your money where your mouth is. You can actually do something in your community."

I applied for the job, and I got the job. The superintendent said: "Gladys will call you a couple of days before school starts to tell you what time to come in and what you need to do." And I said, "Okay."

The night before school started the superintendent called and said, "Gladys has retired. I need you to come in at eight o'clock tomorrow morning."

I said, "What do you mean Gladys has retired? You mean there's nobody? I'm coming in alone?"

He said, "Oh, don't worry. I've got some hot dogs."

And that's how I started my career at Leland Public Schools as food service director. The good thing was that there was no one there to set the bar for me. There was nobody there to say, "This is how we do it." There was no one there at all except the teachers. So I ended up working at the school. I did not want the job at first. I told the superintendent no. He should post the job and look for someone else. This was too much for me. I only wanted four hours a day. He said, "Oh, okay."

He posted it, but not very many people applied for it. And then after about six weeks I said, "You know? I think I will apply for that job. It might work out."

I worked there twenty years from 1982 to 2002. It was a great experience. But even at that point I had a sense that I should not be buying apples shipped in from Washington, packed in a warehouse and then shipped to me from Gordon's or Sysco or other companies when there were apples sitting in Leelanau County that were fresh and grown in Leelanau County. I tried a couple of times to contact local farmers, but there were purchasing agreements, there were legalities with the health department, there were all these things that were roadblocks to buying locally, but happily that's all changed now. It's all different now with "farm to school," local produce programs.

The school environment taught me many things about food service and also about life and how to get along with people. A school system is a very political environment, and food service was always at the bottom, right with transportation and janitorial. But the thing about food service was it cost the district. They didn't like that. I had to make the foods that I served, the meals that I served, break even while selling them for 50 cents or 75 cents apiece. It was a challenge.

It was hard not to use frozen food because a lot of the government food was frozen. If you were going to make it on your budget you had to use government food. But I got around a lot of it by creative cooking. I cooked most of the soups from scratch. I baked bread. I did as much as I could, given my parameters, to make very healthy food for the children and the staff. And the staff was always very supportive.

The funniest thing I did—we had commodity peanut butter at that time; now, of course, they never have peanut butter on account of the allergies—but then we had commodity peanut butter, and I found this recipe for an African peanut soup. I thought: "Oh, this will be good. And this will be a good way to use this up." I served it, and of course no one had ever heard of peanut soup, and so no one would eat it. The kids would not eat it.

I learned a lot about feeding children, because they are very traditional and they want very simple foods. The government would buy up surplus food from farmers and use it for the army and use it for schools. And that way they would subsidize the farmers. It was killing two birds with one stone. They were buying foods that would otherwise go to waste and supporting the farmers, and then using it to feed industries that they wanted to support. One thing was canned asparagus, and canned asparagus is really not palatable. I found a recipe and I made guacamole out of it. I would never have been able to afford avocadoes for guacamole. The first time I served it on our taco bar everyone was a little suspicious. But it tasted good and it looked good. And the superintendent would come by and he would say, "Martha, I don't even want to know what you are doing, but it tastes good."

And I said, "Well, if I have to use these products, I'm going to find a way."

You had to be really creative in that job. One of the people who mentored me was a woman who was like a counselor to small districts like myself. Leland was considered a very small district. Her name was Katie Peterson. She was hired by the school board to come in at the beginning and show me the ropes of the food service, school food. And because of her I joined an organization called Michigan School Food Service Association, MSFSA. I was a member of that for all the twenty years that I was at Leland. I got involved with Katie on the board. I represented Leelanau County up to the Mackinac Bridge, this little area—it was Area 8—in Michigan, and so I represented all the school food service people in that area. I went to meetings in Lansing and sat on the board, and I soon became involved in the legislative committee. I was very excited about that, and I went to my first legislative lobby in Washington where we lobbied for child nutrition. That taught me a lot about the way the government works, and how they feed children.

I believe the food service program of feeding children in schools started right after World War II, because a lot of the soldiers enlisting for service were malnourished. And so they decided to utilize the abundance of surplus that they had from agriculture and combine with the schools to make healthy children. And of course that all kind of backfired a little bit, but I think they are on the right track again now. Ronald Reagan wanted to count ketchup as a vegetable, but that did not go over very well.

Another big influence in my life was a teacher at Leland, Mary Lou Landry, who was a Spanish teacher. Mary Lou got me started again on my love of travel because she did trips. One year she took high school kids to Costa Rica. For a Spanish teacher, that was a great place to go. The next year she was going to go to Paris and Madrid, and she asked me if I'd be interested in going. Of course I was very excited because I'd never had a chance to travel again since I went on my trip in 1972. Now I'd be able to go back to Paris and Madrid, both places where I had been. Mary Lou had never been to France, and she was a little concerned about the language and everything. I said, "Yes, I'll go."

We ended up taking about twenty-five or thirty students, and I helped her chaperone. We had some other parents go. My daughter went. She was in high school at the time. After that we hosted another trip, and we went all over Italy. Again, we took a bunch of students. Then I did a couple of trips on my own because Mary Lou was busy. We did England, Wales, and Ireland. And then it was 9/11. 9/11 happened when I had a trip planned, and we had to cancel it, or put it on hold until everything had settled down. Nobody knew what was happening. Finally, we were able to reschedule. I wanted to do Middle America or South America, but all the students wanted European capitals, so we did London, Paris, and Switzerland. And that was a beautiful trip.

A couple of years after that I retired from school after twenty years. I didn't think I'd be traveling any more. But I discovered that the company that I had worked with, EF—they were the biggest company that did educational tours for high school students—they also had a part of the company that did adult tours. I would keep getting brochures in the mail, and I kept throwing them away. One day I was cleaning and I was taking a break, and I sat down and looked at this brochure, and I saw a trip that was a walking tour of Tuscany. And when I'd gone on the trip all over Italy, Tuscany was the one place I really wanted to go back to. So I called the company, figured out what I had to do, and jumped right in to do an adult tour. Immediately, before I knew it, I had thirty-four people signed up, because it was right around the time when *Under the Tuscan Sun* had come out, and everybody wanted to go to Italy. And from then to now, fast-forward about ten years—I think that was in the '90s—I've done fifteen trips with adults. I love it. It's become a passion, being able to travel.

While I was in the school, I worked during the school year, and then in the summer I worked in several restaurants as a waitress. I also catered. I started catering for a friend of mine, Sue Hammerslee, who lives in Northport. She had a bed-and-breakfast, and her daughter was getting married. Sue knew me and she knew that I loved to cook, and Sue loved to cook because she cooked for her bed-and-breakfast. She asked me to cater her daughter's wedding for three hundred people and I said, "Sure. I will try." I had no idea what I was getting into. Since then I've catered many weddings, but I've never catered a wedding as large as three hundred, and I hope never to do it again. But I did get into the wedding business a little bit on the side. Sometimes I married people twice. I catered their wedding twice because they liked the first job I did, and then their marriage only lasted a few years, and then they came again. So that was kind of funny.

There was a hiatus, six years, between the time I retired from the school and when I started Martha's. At first when I left school I worked for Carol Worsley in Glen Arbor. Carol was just opening a business called Thyme Out. Carol had actually worked with Julia Child as one of her food preparers when Julia was on the road, when Julia was doing her cooking classes. I was just taken with that. I thought: "Oh, my goodness. I need to work with Carol, because Carol worked with Julia Child." And Carol also worked with Simca, Simone Beck. I brought Susan McConnell with me to work with Carol. Susan continued to work for Carol in Glen Arbor for several years as Carol's pastry chef. Carol also owned a bed-and-breakfast in Glen Arbor called Thyme Inn. It was a beautifully restored inn that Carol and her husband, Don, refurbished. There was a beautiful kitchen that Susan got to work in. She worked for Carol for several years until I stole her back.

I worked for Carol at the opening of her shop and then I needed a year-round full-time job, because I wasn't working at the school any longer. I had once worked one summer for Bob and Ellen Pisor in their bakery in Leland called Stone House Bread because I wanted to learn about sourdough. And I can't exactly remember the year, but I was on vacation from school—I was still in school—it was in the summer, and I was going to school, and I was working two jobs. I was working, I believe, at Key to the County in Lake Leelanau and going to school and working at Stone House. And that was the furthest I had ever spread myself. I needed to learn the sourdough. I did the mix and the bench at Stone House. I didn't work the ovens. There were also two interns there that were learning to bake and later went on to form a bakery down in Detroit that is still open.

I worked for Bob just that one summer. And then Bob came to me and asked if I would be interested in working full time at Stone House Bread in the bakery to run his retail outlet there. And I said yes.

I worked there for six years from 2002 to 2008. While I was there it was a small café, initially just a bread store selling the product. The oven was there and they baked the bread. Everything was right there. After a couple of years Bob decided he had to either stop or expand, and so he found a place in Traverse, and that began a project of moving the oven to Traverse City and opening the new bake house in Traverse City. And I was there through that whole change.

I remember it was a two-ton oven that they moved out in one day. I saw them do it. I was working the cash register and everything while they did it. They didn't miss one day of baking. They already had another oven installed in the new place, and they moved this one. It was an amazing thing. They took half the staff, too; they all went to the bakery in Traverse. And I remember Bob saying when he walked out the door: "Well, Martha, now you can have your café." And I was like, "What? What's he talking about?" Then Bob's wife, Ellen, helped me and we remodeled Stone House. There was a big void, because half of the building had been the oven, and now there was just a big hole in the floor where the oven had been, and so we put a big curtain over that end until Ellen and I figured out what to do. Bob was so busy running the new bakery that it was pretty much Ellen's job and my job to come up with this plan.

I didn't realize at the time what experience this was for me. I was just trying to do my job. I was making a modest salary. Bob gave me health benefits. I was fine. I think I was still waitressing on the side. I actually came up with a menu for the café. We started making sandwiches and soups on a hot plate. There was no oven. I didn't have much to go with. And Bob was a real stickler for simplicity. I kept saying, "I need a kitchen." And he was like, "Martha, you can do it. Just do it." So I did. I kept it really simple, and I made the menu to fit what I could do. And that was fun. That was very successful. I kind of became an expert in bread.

One of the other things Bob had me do, before the café, was outside sales. That meant going to places that did not sell Stone House Bread and convincing them that Stone House was for them. This included restaurants, cafés, delis, wine stores, and so that was all over the place: Charlevoix, Petoskey, Traverse City. As the bakery was growing, Bob's geography of where the bread could go was growing. They had a fleet of vans that would go everywhere. New people took over when I was leaving, Tony Spearing and her husband, and now Tony owns the bakery, and she has expanded it and expanded it, and it's doing great. I still use Stone House Bread, organic sourdough bread, for all my sandwiches. That was an invaluable experience.

After I catered the wedding for Sue's daughter I did more weddings but not only weddings. This area is very rich in parties and a lot of people having fun in the summer, and so I started catering parties. Some people that I catered for a lot in Omena were Judy and Bruce Balas. Judy and Bruce became good friends, and I would always cater a couple of parties for them in the summer and for other people in Omena also. We would sit around after a party and talk about: "Wouldn't it be a fun thing to have a restaurant?" We talked about it for a few years and then we actually started to think seriously about it as a group, Judy and Bruce and myself.

I would take a plan to my accountant, and he would shoot all the holes in it and tell me to come back when I had a real plan. We did that for a couple of years. And I would keep on dreaming, collecting recipes, and thinking about it. The main thing he told me was that I had the cart in front of the horse, and so I had to figure out how to put the horse in front of the cart. And it took me a while to figure that out. And then we became serious and we started looking at properties. That lasted quite a while also.

There was a restaurant in Suttons Bay that was for sale. We thought: "Oh, we'll go look at this. Maybe it's good because it's already a restaurant, and a lot of what we'll need is right there," and so we went to look and we made an offer. We had done our due diligence, and we looked at everything, and the numbers. We made a low offer and the people were very upset with us. We were standing in front of the restaurant when Judy said, "Look at this, Martha. Look across the street. Look at that."

And I said, "What?"

And she said, "Look at that old house. What about that?"

And I said, "Oh, no. No, Judy."

And she said, "Well, I've already looked at it. Let's go look." That was the beginning of Martha's Leelanau Table. That was in July of '07.

Judy, among her many skills, is an architect, and so she was able to see the bones of this building where I could only see a 110-year-old decrepit building. We talked about it, and it happened that the building was foreclosed, and our realtor told us that somebody else was making a bid, and that if we wanted to get in we had to jump in right now. And so it all happened kind of fast. We made a bid, and we got it. And then all the fun stuff started happening.

We planned and designed. It took us a year. We opened the following July of 2008. Why did I want to do this? I had worked in many, many restaurants in all the summers in Leelanau County. Probably thirty years of working in restaurants. And I loved the business. I absolutely loved the business. There's nothing quite like it if it grabs you. When you see it perfectly executed, it is hospitality, excellence in food preparation, and wonderful human resources. The experience of hiring people, having a staff, working together, and I thought: "I have the skills to do this, and I can make a go of it."

Fortunately, it was at the beginning of the food surge in Leelanau County. I had been purveying food and seeking out food from local farmers for years before this happened, and I knew many local farmers and little people here and there who grew things in their gardens, who had fruit stands, or stands on the side of the road. That has quadrupled with everything that's happening now. It has exploded. And I knew many of the wineries, the people that were starting the wineries in the '70s in Leelanau County. That business has also quadrupled or a hundredfold. It's crazy. There used to be ten or twelve wineries in Leelanau County, and now there's over thirty. And there's no end in sight, really.

For me to be able to offer all these beautiful things from this beautiful place, Leelanau, to friends and visitors is a great experience. And I guess everything in my life moved me forward, but I really couldn't have done it without all the people that helped me. Right now in the restaurant my son and his girlfriend, Andi, do most of the cooking at night, and I cook on the line a couple of nights a week. Andi's a graduate of the culinary school in Traverse City, a recent graduate, just a few years ago, and so she's got a lot of knowledge and talent. And Matt started out when he was in high school working in Leland at the Blue

Bird, and he worked at Carlson's Fisheries, and he worked at the Merc, and then he's worked at some other restaurants along the way, but mostly he's learned his craft at Martha's by experimenting and working with me. We work on menus and new recipes together. He's turned into a real chef.

I'm a self-taught chef. I think there's two paths to having a restaurant. One is to do everything by the book, and the other to teach yourself. Basically, I worked in many, many restaurants, and saw things that I would not want to do. Now that I have my own restaurant, those are the things that I focus on. I want to have a friendly kitchen, not an abusive kitchen. I want to have an open kitchen. I want to have a clean kitchen.

I am actually torn between the front of the house and the back of the house because while I love to be in the kitchen, I really like to be in the front. One of the things that I was really good at when I was a server was telling the chef who was in the house, because when you are in the back cooking, you don't have time. You can look at the book of reservations and see, but you don't really see who's there until the people are there, and a lot of times the servers are too busy. They don't really know who is there. And so I would go see the chef and I would say: "Locals, your favorite people, are at table two, and they would really like it if you would come out and talk to them."

Or if we had somebody visiting, somebody special, whatever it was, anybody. I had a knack for names and faces. It's a talent that you either have or you don't, and you learn it. Like my friend, Sue Hammerslee, she told me, when she had her bed-and-breakfast, she kept a file on everybody, and she knew what they liked for breakfast, where they were from, if they had a dog, all these things. I do that myself with the restaurant, but I keep it in my head. It is kind of a knack, but I can look at people, and the minute they tell me how they met me or when they came into the restaurant, I know what they are talking about. And I remember who they are. It's kind of a strange thing, but I remember what people like to eat. I don't know how that goes, but it's funny.

I worked hard on my business plan to come up with some words to describe the feeling. What I wanted was for people to always feel welcome, that it was a place where they could meet their friends or their family, or bring their friends and family to have a meal, whether it was breakfast, lunch, or dinner.

The old building that we chose had a lot more history in it than I realized, as we found out. The family that lived in the house primarily, I met several of the daughters. They come back, and they sit in what was their living room. The floors are the same, they are the 110-, now 118-year-old floors, and the stairs going down to the basement are the same. And they've told me stories. Their grandpa used to make dandelion wine. He used to make other kinds of liquors, and things that he would keep in the basement, in the room that I use for my wine cellar now. These women say that they would sneak down there, and they would have to crawl back on their hands and knees up the steps, so they know the steps very well. When we redid the building they were some of the first people that came by to see what we did to it. It was pretty amazing to talk to them. And they still come. Most of them don't live in the area anymore, but they come and visit at Martha's when they are here. It's fun to see them because I think they feel like we gave new life to their old house.

We bought the Martha's building in July '07 and made the plan in July, August, September, got the builder, got the architect, the design, and then that winter we planned the inside. I was off, I wasn't working, and I bought equipment, made lists, checked everything off, made more lists, checked it off, and then the whirlwind when we actually could go into the building, and they had the walls done, and we could see what it looked like, and the equipment began arriving. And everyone was losing weight because they were working around the clock to get it done. And we just couldn't believe what was going to happen.

They were supposed to be done with it Memorial weekend. And they weren't because of all kinds of legalities, paperwork. I didn't have my liquor license yet, and the health department, all the codes and everything had to get signed off on, and all the finishing touches, and finally we were approaching Fourth of July weekend, and I said, "You know, we've got to do it. We have to open." And we opened on July 3. I enjoyed the design process of planning and getting ready, but I vastly underestimated what kind of business I was going to do.

I undershot it by quite a bit. It's been growing quite a bit since then, and there's no way, really, that you can tell other than multiplying out. Like, how many eggs are you going to need? You can't even imagine how many eggs we go through for breakfast.

I've gone through a couple of different scenarios in the winter months. A couple of years ago we closed during part of the winter months. I didn't want to. Everybody except my son said to close. He said, "Don't close, Mom." My accountant said, and Judy and Bruce said, "Close. You are not making any money in those months." But the problem I had, when you close, people go somewhere else. And then they get used to going somewhere else. So now, that's our challenge this year. Last year we stayed open. Just be open the minimum weekends, but don't close.

The best thing, what works, is just immediately after Labor Day we will cut down to five days a week, still doing breakfast, lunch, and dinner. And then sometime in October—I've been open now seven years so I can look and see exactly; it's probably the third week in October when it falls off—so then we'll close on Monday, Tuesday, Wednesday. But in the odd season I will have cooking classes which is a fun thing to do. I can't do it in the summer because I'm open, and I can't have people in my kitchen because I'm open all the time.

The problem is staff, trying to retain my core group while I have to hire a multitude of people in the summer, get them trained and ready in a matter of weeks. My human resources degree has come in handy because I aim for retention. I aim to get the same high school and college kids back, and I've had some good luck. I've had kids start in high school, go all the way through college and stay with me, and that's really gratifying.

I like to be able to train people in the food service industry so wherever they go they can say that they worked for me and they had a good experience and they learned something. A lot of my cooks started out as dishwashers, entry level, and have gone on to different jobs and still are with me, but it's a difficult thing to hire people, to sit and have just a fifteen-minute interview, look at them, and then decide. You have to ask the right questions and listen and make a judgment. It's very difficult. One of the hardest things I do is interview, but I've had some good luck.

When I travel I like to do a cooking class abroad to see how they do the cooking classes. We did one in France. We did one in Barcelona. And now on our trip in April, we're going to Ireland. I'm really hoping to go to Ballymaloe and get an afternoon cooking class. No, that's not really what I want. I want to take a long class and stay there a couple of weeks, but even just to go there is a dream that I've always had.

Hungarian Mushroom Soup

MARTHA RYAN,
MARTHA'S LEELANAU TABLE

Serves 6

¼ cup olive oil

¼ cup sweet butter

8 cups shitake, cremini, or button mushrooms or a mix, sliced

2 large onions chopped

4 garlic cloves chopped

4 tablespoons paprika

Cook down about 15 minutes.

Add ¼ cup dry white wine and stir to deglaze pan.

Add ¼ cup flour and cook until browned, about 15 minutes, stirring often.

Do not leave unattended.

Add 2–4 tablespoons chicken stock with 4 cups water, 2 cups heavy cream.

Photo by Michael Poehlman

12

Amanda Danielson

Amanda's aunts in her words were extraordinary cooks. Growing up in multicultural Detroit with Lebanese and Polish grandparents, Amanda encountered multiple culinary traditions from early childhood. She worked in her family's Big Boy franchise from age twelve. Later she tended bar and then learned as much as she could about wine, beer, spirits, coffee, and so on—basically anything you can drink, always a passion and a major skill for her. Amanda develops and executes master-level beverage and service training for her staff. With her love for writing and teaching she takes pride in intentionally curated beverage menus for both of her restaurants, which enable her service team to navigate guests through the best experiences in hospitality. After working and opening restaurants in other countries she and her husband settled on Traverse City as the ideal place for their first restaurant, Trattoria Stella, in 2004 in its historic setting in the former hospital complex. Ten years later they followed this with The Franklin, seeded with longtime Stella staffers.

Amanda Danielson, b. August 8, 1975
Interview: July 20, 2016
Trattoria Stella, 1200 West Eleventh Street, Traverse City
The Franklin, 160 East Front Street, Traverse City

When you learn the ability to maintain grace and
dignity under fire . . . you can take that anywhere.

I was born in Detroit in Mount Sinai Hospital, like *really* Detroit, not the suburbs like everybody says, and we actually spent a lot of time when I was a kid in the city there. My grandparents, three of the four of them, were immigrants. My Lebanese grandmother came over very young. She was a baby and would consider herself an American through and through. She was my paternal grandmother. My paternal grandfather was an Irish/German/Detroit native, second generation, and my maternal grandparents were both from Poland and came here during World War II, shortly after the war had ended. They lived in Hamtramck originally, where most of the Polish immigrants in the Detroit area lived, and then eventually got a house in a small suburb called Warren, which is now a much bigger suburb than it was then.

The biggest culinary influence back then was that—even though my Lebanese grandmother was a pretty atrocious cook, believe it or not—my aunts were not. They were extraordinary cooks. And so I grew up with that Middle Eastern tradition of food on one side, and the Polish and Eastern European tradition on the other side. We were at Eastern Market, little markets, bakeries, butchers, three, four, five times a week when I was little. There were no large trips to the grocery store when I was growing up. I'm the oldest on my side of the family, so my mother worked when I was young. She stopped when my next sister was born.

So I was with my grandparents, her parents, the Polish grandparents most days, and that meant cooking and shopping at all these little places. It also meant that in one of those classic postage stamp neighborhoods my grandfather had the entire backyard tilled up to a garden, an organic garden. In a pretty industrial area he had chestnuts and pears and plums and black and red currants, every vegetable you can imagine that he could reasonably grow, and I think he spent the entire 1970s working on the soil, in the late '60s and early '70s, in order to be able to do that.

And then my grandmother did all the canning. I remember her traditional routines. She'd have five pots on her big stove going at once so that the color of the green vegetables wouldn't affect the color of the white vegetables, or the orange vegetables. It was fantastic growing up with those traditional flavors, and not just the flavors but the method of cooking and the concern for every ingredient on both sides was significant. It had a huge influence in my life. It influenced my sisters to some extent, but they are considerably younger than I am, four and nine years younger. It's amazing how being the first, how being so exposed to that has informed the rest of my life, right down to now, how my children are fed. It was a great way to grow up learning to cook everything from scratch, and also learning that the time involved in the cooking of those traditional foods is part of the value as well.

We can go and buy grape leaves. We can go and buy kivi, but the way your hands feel rolling them. . . . Or on the Polish side I guess you can go and buy golumpki or cabbage rolls, but when you are actually making them yourself, it's the process of doing that with your kids that's just so fun. That's the part that you can't trade in when you are doing things a little bit more quickly.

We try to bring some of that now. All these years later that has informed what we do in both of our restaurants, with relationships with farms, and whole animal butchery, and honoring everything we do, recognizing that this is not just simply slinging food to a few hundred people a day. This is a craft. It's a craft that is really important to us.

My family was in restaurants, too. My uncles on that Lebanese side started the Elias Brothers franchise of Big Boy back then and eventually became the international franchise of Big Boy. I had worked there when I was little. I worked as a hostess from the time I was twelve years old and learned other aspects of that business. Short order, breakfast, fast-paced, greasy—no, I wouldn't say the greasy spoon, but close. It was an interesting way to learn how to be organized and how to do things consistently and very well, though I also knew that going back to that more traditional food that I was raised with was more important to me than having that kind of large-scale operation.

I remember my uncle Louis Elias, who passed away a few years ago, and I was probably thirteen, and I was a hostess and I was dressed up to be a hostess. He was sitting in the back just having coffee with a couple of his friends. He asked me to come and sit down with them, and he said, he told me that my life was three things. He said it was one-third work, one-third sleep, and one-third family. And he said a lot of times work will cut into sleep and family. So he said, "Love what you do. Do something you love." And he said, "Buy a goddamn comfortable mattress." That was the other bit of information. And I was, like I said, probably thirteen at the time, and I remember when he said that—he was a funny guy and he didn't have any children of his own so he always had plenty of advice to dispense—I remember that advice, and I have always owned a mattress. I have actually foregone other furniture in my home in order to be able to afford and prioritize a very comfortable bed. And I do, I love what I do.

My first love, I think, is writing and teaching, for sure, but what a great platform. Food, and now, by extension, for me it turned into wine, beer, and spirits, but it's a study of history and geography, geology, certainly, right, it goes so far beyond agriculture and the business of it in what we do. It's amazing. I love, love, love to learn. I read the *New York Times* every day. I read the local paper. I read all the time. I read many trade publications, not just *Wine Spectator* type of trade, but serious books by people who specialize in one very small part of the world. And it isn't just about the current output or the bottle of wine on the table or the leg of lamb that's on the table, but it's about all the other things that have contributed to eventually ending up at your table.

I've always tried to honor that with everything, and it's just been this really neat intellectual pursuit, so through the lens of a restaurant I've been able to continue to teach and continue to write, and continue to really—on a table-to-table basis—give people something that they can't get anywhere else because of myself making it such an intellectual pursuit. I think the other great thing about the business that we have chosen which works, too, with restaurants in general is that anybody can work in a restaurant. Anyone can get a job, and it's a great first job to serve as a dishwasher or a hostess at fifteen, sixteen, seventeen years old.

There's an obligation by the people running those restaurants toward those kids, to give them at a minimum an excellent and a safe first job experience, but even better, give them a foundation that will take them to whatever career they choose or college, or whatever, because the job, no matter what position, it requires organization, it requires successful presentation of yourself, not just in a job interview, but if you are in the front of the house communicating with a diverse group of clientele, as well as a diverse group of employees, people that you see every day. And in the heat of the moment in the summer when you have people at the door and you are telling them that there's a two-and-a-half-hour wait, and you are doing it with grace and poise and they are yelling at you, and you are just happily handing over a business card with the phone numbers so that they can make a reservation next time, but in the meantime, "We'd be happy to put your name on the list, and you can have a drink in the bar."

When you learn the ability to maintain grace and dignity under fire for lack of a better term, you can take that anywhere. This business can teach you to never panic. It can teach you to deal with any amount of pressure. It can certainly teach you, when you really get into it, like our staff has to, especially at Trattoria Stella, with all those Italian wines. I teach master classes at Northwestern Michigan College. People pay me to teach, and I pay my staff to attend because I want them to be able to have a comfort level table-side. When you can have all that in a business that is really inclusive of anybody, you have the opportunity to send hundreds of people into the world with a serious skill set. So we take that seriously. I certainly have, and, as I say, I teach master's level classes to my staff that they are required to attend. And they love it. They really, really love it. We are sending people to restaurants in New York, like Thomas Keller restaurants, one-off hospitality restaurants, like Blackbird on Long Island or in Chicago. Because somebody worked at Trattoria Stella, and that restaurant is known to those other restaurants, they get a job. And there's a lot to be said for that, because those are places that are notoriously difficult to get into as an employee.

That's been so much fun for me in this business, starting with that family history and then figuring out where does it go. You don't really plan your life that way, at least I didn't. I feel like I plan everything, but I didn't necessarily realize what an impact I would have the potential to have on people. And then once I realized it, it was like: "Okay. Let's get serious, because now everybody is really depending on me."

I didn't have any professional culinary training. I loved to cook, but I had never cooked professionally except a little bit in the Big Boy. I had learned how to do that short order, which I think is why I was a very good bartender when I tended bar because it requires so much organization. Even more so now with the craft cocktails and everything. It has come back around. I went to college at Wayne State. Creative writing was my thing. I always wanted to write short fiction. It's my favorite genre. Lately I've been writing a lot of nonfiction essays and fun things for papers or for people or for blogs or whatever. And some poetry, just for some brain activity. But I always really wanted to write short fiction, and I think I'll come back around to that one day. I've thousands of unfinished short stories. But when I was in college I actually worked for TGI Friday. And then Elias Brothers after that. When I worked for TGI Friday I became one of their new store openers, which gave me the opportunity to travel all over the world and insert this really formulaic program for restaurant management. It was all the same drinks, all the same food, everything that you would teach started in the United States. They would come visit you. You would go to whatever country, and then open the restaurants with them as a professional team that would go in.

To make a long story short, there were a lot of openings internationally for TGI Fridays, and then I circled back to Elias Brothers, to my family, my uncles' restaurants, when they started expanding internationally. I helped them build in a similar program. When I was with them I was in Brazil and worked for a company that was opening up some Big Boy restaurants in the malls in São Paulo, Brazil, and got to know the owner of that company very well. In fact, we are still in touch, not often, but his children went to Interlochen a few years ago.

We had to open a steak house in the Israeli district of São Paulo, but this family was Muslim and they didn't drink, so they needed somebody to prepare a beverage program for this steak house in the Israeli district of São Paulo. I started from scratch just building a program in a country I didn't know, and I was just learning the language at that point. I grew up around wine, but I didn't know it well enough to put together a program, so I had no choice but to really, really learn and to learn quickly. But that was the seminal wine moment for me. I know that I can do this. What I realized about wine then, was that the more you learn, the more you will never know because it changes on a dime every year, in a different way in every place, all the grapes and the changes in the technology. Everything just continuously changes, and I loved that about it.

I knew I would never get bored, and I knew I would never be "finished" learning about wine. And that was really important to me, because I do—I think that's why writing appeals to me so much—because it never ends. You just go and go and you find those recesses in your brain that something triggers, and then you come up with something different, and it's infinite, and that's true of wine, beers, spirits, cocktails, mineral water, you name it, tea, coffee. The list goes on. And then forget about food. It never ends. And I loved that about wine, so I kept pursuing it, and pursuing it.

This was before the internet, so it was books, and it was getting the next edition, the next huge volume of the Oxford Companion, and now it's all available online, fortunately. The bags aren't quite as heavy when you are going from place to place, but I knew then that this was a field of study that I could go very deep and very broad and very far with. And I never stopped. I mean right up to being accepted and invited to take the master sommelier exam, which I have yet to pass, but I've been a little busy with two kids and two businesses, but with a 1 percent pass rate I don't feel too bad about having not achieved that yet. We'll see to that yet. We'll see. I guess with all the time, if I'm actually going to take the master sommelier exam again—and the court has been kind enough to grant me a pass; I can take it whenever I'm ready—but I don't know if that's where I want to devote forty hours a week to study when I can devote that time to teaching and writing. I know I'm doing the work at that level, and they know I'm doing the work at that level. I guess my ego isn't such that I need those two letters after my name. I'm happy to have hundreds of people out there that are doing great work because they learned those foundations from me, and that's the greatest reward, I think.

If I were to go back with restaurants in particular, and what I might change about what I do, it wouldn't be anything about the restaurants that I own now. There's always a learning curve in anything. We opened Trattoria Stella in 2004, twelve years this past July, 2004, July 6. I was pregnant—accidentally—with my oldest daughter, Sophia. We opened in July, and she was born in December. And then we celebrated the ten-year anniversary of Trattoria Stella by opening The Franklin downtown.

I always knew I wanted my own restaurant. I had opened enough for other people. I knew that I could do this for myself. When my husband and I met, one of the things that we had in common and still do is a love of the business. We knew that we wanted to open up a restaurant. We had actually moved to Traverse City in early 2000 before we were married. We were married in 2002, but we moved to Traverse City together in early 2000 and bought a house and started working in the industry up here to get the lay of the land.

Back then, as far as fine dining, there was Tapawingo and Windows, and that was it, both good restaurants in their own right. Pete Peterson deserves the world for what he started up here, in my opinion, and he's just a spectacular guy. We used him as inspiration and had an idea of what we wanted. We wanted to do that classic—the term is making me crazy because it is used everywhere, but—farm-to-table—because that's what Italian food is. That isn't my history, but it was my experience and where I grew up, and the neighborhood where my grandparents lived was actually an Italian neighborhood.

So we both moved here, and we were kind of on that five-year plan working in the industry, and the opportunity with the Minervenis over at the Village, Grand Traverse Commons, came about, and we took a look at the space. It was a long shot. We didn't have any money. We didn't have anything. We borrowed $50,000 from my mother-in-law, which we since paid her back with interest, until we could secure a solid bank loan. We could get credit, we just didn't have any money, and we had our house, and we were the first business in the redeveloped part there. There was a coffee shop and some offices in the newer central section. But we were the first business in the redeveloped part of the Village at Grand Traverse Commons, and had quite a large restaurant: 175 seats, 7,000 square feet, a lot of seats for a small kitchen. We just stuck to our guns with everything we wanted to do.

It was difficult staffing back then, for reasons different from staffing now. We quickly realized, too, that there wasn't the kind of experience among the employment pool that was necessary to execute the vision that we had. It was simply, "All right, then we just have to build them. We'll create these people, and we'll make them the people that we need," and the rest really is history. And it continues. The story isn't over yet. That's what we do, and training has been a cornerstone of what we do, a huge investment in training, development, my time, their time. We pay them their wages in addition to requiring them to come in. The materials, the travel. There is so much involved in it. They are really getting a master's level class. If you go to Stella, and you ask them—even the newer ones, because I supplement their education for them—they can speak conversantly, I mean really confidently and fluently about all of the obscure areas of Italy, the great varieties, what wines pair well with what.

And it has been a long time, and we have very little turnover. We've been open twelve years, and I still have people who have been with us since the beginning. We have several who have been with us ten years or more. And the over five-year mark is probably half of the year-round staff at least, which is not common in the restaurant industry. A lot of it has to do with the fact that they make good money. That keeps people where they are, but when you are older professionals in an industry that sometimes doesn't regard you as a professional, you want to stay where you are treated as a professional, if not always by the guests, certainly by the people that are employing you. And we've always done that. It's been nice in the last five, six years—and I'll throw out another word that I loathe—this "foodie" culture has grown up as people are more and more respectful of the profession that it is to serve, to tend bar, to cook, etc., with or without the celebrity. We can say whatever we want about celebrity—some of that has done a good thing, I think, for the public in seeing how the service industry really is, a set of skills that can be acquired by most—but to execute at a high level requires practice, diligence, and a standard to be set by the leadership of whatever operation it is to be very high.

So that's Stella, and Stella continues. It's far less seasonal now than when we first opened twelve years ago. Then it was very seasonal. There were nights when we would have no business in the dining room, but we stuck to our guns and remained open. We've always been open for seven nights. We don't open for lunch on Sunday. So it's seven dinners, six lunches, and those have been our hours since we started. We stuck to our guns, even in those cold winter months when there weren't very many people, and it might have been just me and my chef, Myles. He cooking and me up front. But that was okay, because I think you have to be there for people, right? If you are not consistent, they don't know that they can go there. And we wanted to be that neighborhood place. We are bringing that fine dining, the Italian sensibilities, great service, a diverse wine list, but we're bringing it to people in a way that's inclusive. You can come in after snowshoeing around the Village and grab a beer and a pizza or a glass of wine and a pasta, or just a soup and salad, or just a whiskey to warm yourself up, right? You can do whatever you'd like. You can feel comfortable to come as you are. We wanted that "come as you are," but with all those fine dining standards, and back then that was a little bit of a departure from what people were accustomed to. You had your fine dining, white tablecloth, and then you had your casual eatery, and we really wanted to marry the two, which you see a lot more of now, especially in the Midwest. This was happening on the coasts, but here in Michigan and especially in northern Michigan, at that time, you didn't have this.

Windows and Tapawingo were higher end. You would dress up to go to those restaurants. And we didn't want people to feel like they had to. We've gotten some flak over the years as well on account of the brown paper. We put brown paper over our white linens, and we have white linen napkins, nice heavy china and flatware. But we always wanted that for that reason. When people complained we said, "You can dislike the paper if you want to, but it isn't designed to save the tablecloths. We change them just as frequently. And it isn't designed for any reason, really, except to show people the emblematic of that marriage of that casual 'come as you are' hospitable environment, that true 'third place,' if you are familiar with that concept, and that fine dining, high level of service from well-educated, professional service people. I think we succeeded at that. And whenever we do get people that mention the paper on the tablecloths, I just say, 'Feel free to give them my business card. I'd be glad to chat with them.'"

I did have an interesting phone call the other day from a woman who was very upset. She called up, and she had seen our website, and there's a picture of Myles—and this goes back to the education—a picture of Myles butchering a hog. But all you see is the whole hog. He hasn't yet actually cut into the hog. But we wanted to show people on the website that this is where your food comes from. I teach my children that. If you are going to eat bacon, you need to know that it's a pig. If you are going to eat steak, you need to know that it's a cow. If you are going to eat a chicken, you need to know that it's a chicken. These animals walked the earth. They don't come in a pink Styrofoam tray. That's not where food comes from. You can choose to eat it, or choose not to eat it, but if you are going to eat it, you need to know where it comes from. Part of our whole-animal butchery philosophy is that we honor the entire animal. We don't just harvest choice cuts, pay a premium, charge a premium, and that's what you get. You can get those choice cuts along with a lot of other things.

This woman called and said that she was really looking forward to coming in, and she went onto our website, and they are coming up for their honeymoon, and she had heard that it was the best restaurant in Traverse City, and they were looking into a really high-end experience, they were planning to spend a lot of money. Then she went on our website and she saw this "grotesque" picture of our chef and a pig. She said, "Your chef was on your website slaughtering a pig. Did you know that?"

I said, "I don't recall any pictures of our chef slaughtering a hog. In fact, they come to us having already been slaughtered and treated by the facility that is necessary, but there are likely some photographs of him butchering a hog that had come in, and that's how we handle our meat here."

She said, "Well, I am just offended at that picture. I can't believe that you would advertise that."

I said, "Well, Ma'am, do you eat meat? Are you a vegetarian?"

She said, "Of course I eat meat. I'm not a vegetarian. I eat meat. I just don't want to know where it comes from."

And I explained to her that we believe in honoring the entire animal. We don't just harvest those choice cuts. We have skilled people that butcher beef, pork, chicken, etc., duck. We have skilled people that butcher those. And I'll give you an example. With our last over-three-hundred pound hog, we had fewer than five pounds of unusable material, between charcuterie, stock. That's saying something. Any animal would be proud to die for that. At the end of the day human beings are omnivores. You can make choices for your diet, and that's okay, but if you are going to eat meat, we believe that it should be from an animal that was raised humanely, slaughtered humanely, and butchered to maximize what that animal is giving you. And we've always done that. We agreed to not agree on that particular point, and she probably won't ever come into the restaurant, which is okay. It's fine, right?

You can't please everybody. Even if I'm very open about our mentality where that's concerned, and I think it has helped to educate people up here. And now you see it. Now, it's a thing that you see much more of, and I am thrilled about that.

So Stella is an interesting place, and then we decided we were going to open up The Franklin. My husband and I are partners with our chef, Myles, and Myles and I pretty much hijacked Stella from Paul. He wanted to do something that was a little bit less ambitious in terms of the menu and the wine list because he wanted it to be more inclusive, and Myles and I had just proved that you could be inclusive at a higher level through education and a well-trained staff.

Myles and my husband had worked together. It was his first exec chef position, and my husband's first general manager position at a restaurant in Ann Arbor and they worked together. Myles was doing other things at the time. I think selling food for some company. He had previously been one of the sous chefs under Louis Sharkus at the Townsend in Birmingham. So he had had some skill, obviously, prior to going in and being the sous chef at this restaurant. And then they knew each other and worked together really well. When we were ready to look for chefs we put a short list together, and Myles was at the top of that list. We invited him to come up and we showed him the then still very bombed-out, horrific-looking, terrazzo-chipped-up, raccoon parts everywhere, the basement of the old insane asylum that had been abandoned for twenty-five or thirty years at the time. He stood there and just looked around and said, "So this is going to be my kitchen."

We still had some time, so he went to Winter Harbor, Maine, and opened up a restaurant there just for six months, a seasonal thing, just to wet his feet again in culinary, and actually be a chef at a restaurant. And the rest is history. He's our partner now. He wasn't at the beginning, but about three years in we made him a partner, and that's been great. He's a partner all the way around. So when we opened up The Franklin and decided to do that—Myles and I had hijacked the concept of what Stella became, it was very much what our vision was—and so The Franklin was much more of what my husband wanted, I think, originally. And who knows?

I think it worked out just the way it should have. It's neat. It's ambitious. It's 240 seats when the deck is open, and 140 when the deck is not open with a very large kitchen and a fantastic staff. Here we've been able to do a different level of butchery, because we have the space, so instead of just part servicing large entrées and sauces and whatnot, we have a really ambitious charcuterie program. We're not allowed to cure, and we don't do that—we can do quick cures and things like that—but we don't use pink salts or anything; we don't hang salami. The FDA does not allow us to do that, and neither does the Michigan Department of Agriculture at this point, but hopefully we'll change that. So what we've done is we've worked around those laws in such a way that we can provide a really diverse charcuterie program that gives people the opportunity to taste those items, while still being in line with the Department of Agriculture and all those requirements.

A more casual environment than Stella, to be sure, but still that level of service and training. It's quicker, a quicker pace, so the servers don't necessarily get the opportunity to spend the kind of time with the clientele that they do at Stella, so it's different. We've had to adapt a little bit. But we've put the same amount of education into the staff here. We really focus on training again, mandatory, biweekly wine, beer, and spirits training, plus ongoing daily requirements for the job. There are tests, quizzes, instruction, preshift tasting, everything we can do in a quicker-paced restaurant to still give that level of education to the staff that works for us. There's a lot more seasonal staff that we have to hire here, so it's a little bit different, but there's enough of the seasoned year-round staff including several Stella expats that came here, that I think are able to maintain that level very well. So that's The Franklin. And this is only our third summer here. For a restaurant, many restaurants, that's the end of their life. But with twelve years at Stella I feel good about our ability to carry The Franklin. First star on the left, straight on until morning. I feel like we can do that here. And I love it. The rooftop deck and everything, and being right in the center of downtown.

We talk about coming full circle. My father and my uncle used to own the Beetle Building, which is the building directly across the street from us, and they had the Big Boy that was in the first floor of that for years. A long time ago before I even met my husband, and I was up here with one of my friends—he was a brewer—and he said, "We should really put a brew pub in that place, in your dad's building."

I said, "That would be great, but I don't know anything about brewing beer."

He said, "I can brew beer, and you can focus on the dining room. It would be great."

I said, "It's a great idea, but now is not the time." And then ironically my dad and my uncle sold the building to the founder of Mackinaw Brewing Company, which is still there, no longer our building, but there's a brewery there and a restaurant, and now I have this new building right across the street doing a restaurant that, more so than a brewery, I think, suits my sensibilities.

My husband and I and also our chef have spoken to some of the classes at the Culinary Institute. It's very difficult for me to commit that kind of time for an entire term. So I have done classes for consumers. I've mentored many people that are going through the sommelier program, and as I work into a different role in my restaurants, which I'm working hard to do—I have more and more great people coming up as managers and staff—I always maintain a role. I am one of those people that will never retire. I'll just do it differently. And I'll write more and teach more and be there as that lifeline for the people that work in whatever places I have at the time. I like to teach and I would like to teach more. And I'd love to teach more formally like that—at NMC—but the mentorship that I can give to people I think at this point is far more valuable, and I like to put my energies there for now. Part of it, selfishly, is to work myself out of a job. But the other part is to set them up for success in a way that no hospitality program is going to. Because you can learn a ton of theory, but unless you can really make decisions table-side in the heat of the moment, change on a dime if necessary, all the while maintaining that strong core value system and never compromising what the values of the business are, you really haven't achieved any level of success or professionalism in this business. And no school is going to give you that.

I never had any formal business training, but I run my businesses with my husband. I was working with another group that was trying to acquire something right now. They asked me to consult for them and they gave me the balance sheet of the business that they wanted to acquire, and I sat with my banker, and I said, "Well, banker, Mitchell," his name is Mitchell, "I'm going to run through this balance sheet, and I'm going to give you what I see, my opinion, and I want you to let me know what you think." And I did that, and I walked through three years of financials with my banker sitting next to me, and I handed it to him, and he looked at me and just said, "You nailed it." That was it. And it's twelve years of being in business. It's not the same when you are doing it for someone else.

We had no money when we opened this place. We leveraged our house and everything because we believed in it. We didn't have a bucket of money and we won't have partners or a boss. The partners were Myles, my husband, and I. We don't have financial partners behind us, nor will we ever do that unless it's selling parts of the business to people that work for us so they can then become owners. Those are the only partners I would ever have because I'm never going to have anybody telling me how I have to run things. When it's your money you know every penny, you know every term, you know the implications financial and otherwise of every decision, and there's no better learning than that. I know all the financial terms, right? My father's an attorney, very good at finance. And I just learned. It's my tendency to overintellectualize. So if I'm going to have to write a P and L, profit and loss statement, I'm going to have to know what every single one of those lines means. And that's just my nature. I prefer to overintellectualize the fun stuff, the wine, beer, spirits, etc., but it's a necessity to have smart business knowledge.

In fact, with the whole sommelier thing, too—I see this all the time with people coming up in the business. Everyone wants to be a master sommelier because now they are rock stars, just like the chefs are, right—so people go to culinary school, or they work their tails off to study, study, study for the master sommelier exam, and you have people who are twenty-one, twenty-two taking this test, to become one of two-hundred-some people, and some of them succeeding in the world—but they can't run a beverage program to save their lives. They can tell you all seven subzones of Val d'Aosta. They can tell you what the base grape is in Vin Santo. They can tell you precisely how much aging is required for these obscure natural wines made in Alpen places like Jura and Savoie, but they can't run a business. They can't even put together a smart wine program that takes into consideration the people that are actually going to be walking through their door. So I think to myself: "Wow. There is a disconnect." And you can apply that to culinary school. I see people coming out of culinary school, and they can chop up an onion. They've got some knife skills, but you put them on the line when you just sat sixty people, and you have dishes—each one requires four, five, six steps or more, and it has to be perfect and consistent—and the list goes on, and they are like a deer in headlights. It's amazing. There's no substitute for getting in there and doing it. And doing it the hard way.

Think about a tomato. If you irrigate the hell out of tomatoes, and you just give them every bit of love that they need, and you have them in a sun-drenched area like the Central Valley, they have no character. They are mealy and bland and watery and boring. And who wants a tomato like that? But if you have them in an area with ground like in Michigan, for instance, where the weather varies quite a bit, and those tomatoes actually have to dig deep to get the water that they need and they suffer a little. That suffering is what makes them fantastic. And that's true of anything. It's true of anybody. So without a little bit of suffering and a whole lot of effort I don't think there's any real character. And certainly without that you can't get your chops, so to speak.

I had somebody leave—for a good reason—she left me a couple of years ago to open a restaurant in Detroit. She was great. I wanted her for another year. And I explained to her: "I'm thrilled for you and this opportunity," but I wanted to be able to sharpen her teeth just a little bit more and teach her just a little bit more. Fortunately, the person she went to work for is a dynamite. He's a great guy and I like him a lot, but he's very different, ego-driven in a way that is, I think, productive, but nevertheless ego-driven, which is a different way to work. And she had to work for him and in his way and his plan. She's doing very well there, but it was baptism by fire. Even though she had the training and experience from us, she never managed for me. She was never the one with her finger on the button, so to speak, and I really would have liked to have given her that opportunity before sending her off into the big, wide world. It worked out fine, and I take responsibility for those people who leave, for the best reasons. I want them to spread their wings. I feel fortunate when they boomerang back and want to come back and stay in the business and stay in the business with me. That's what it's about. You want to send people out into the world with a skills set that will contribute to their overall success, and hopefully they take your example and teach others the way that you taught them.

I have a bartender right now at Stella that I hired this late winter or early spring. He had been living in Chicago, and he came to us because I had employed two of his best friends previously, and when he moved back—neither of them work here anymore: one of them is living in Australia right now, and the other is a very successful manager for a small restaurant group on the West Coast, Colorado area, Kansas City, that whole western seaboard area. He's very successful for them right now—he reached out and said, "Hey, I'm moving back to Traverse City, back home, and what do you guys think?" They said, "There's nowhere else for you to work. There's only one place you can go to work." He applied, and came, and we interviewed him, and he's great. He's working for us, and I just adore him. He's a bartender and a server, a real humble service professional, and not a kid. Maybe a kid to us, twenty-nine, thirty, but in the business there are so many really young people that when you have someone who is that age this is a profession to them. It was great. He's here because of these people I've sent out to the world and I think that's sort of the circle of life, at least in this business. And I love that. And I do take very seriously the obligation to create that environment for people, a successful one, at least it gives them the potential to be successful.

It is my nature to be entrepreneurial and to keep building. I have a rule that I will not own or operate anything to which I cannot ride my bike. I live downtown in Slab Town, and that is about a five- to ten-minute bike ride from my home to both restaurants, with about ten minutes between the restaurants themselves, so it would have to be somewhere in that radius for me to do anything. I'm not saying no to expanding or opening another restaurant, but I'm not planning another restaurant at the moment. The Franklin is still young; it's only three.

The Franklin is ten years younger than Stella, and Stella was exactly where it needed to be to allow us to open The Franklin without compromising anything at Stella. The Franklin is getting there but it still needs attention. It still needs love. It's not quite ready to get out of the crib yet.

I still run the beverage program for both, with the assistance of an administrator who manages the inventories and ordering. Here at The Franklin my bar manager and head manager have both been with me for a decade or more. They help with some of the decision-making and the ordering here at The Franklin. The selection is me with them. Stella, I do all of the selection for everything, and I do education for both, assisted again here by the bar manager, Abby, who, as I said, has been with me since she was seriously a kid. She started when she was fifteen as a hostess. I love the team that I have. And it's a process. I'm one of those people . . . I tell everybody everything that I know. I don't keep anything from them. I see no reason for that. I don't mean real secret perspective. I'm a steel trap where that's concerned. But when it comes to what I know business-wise, education-wise, wine-wise, how I do things, money-wise like balance sheets, that kind of thing . . . I want to tell them everything, because I want them to be able to take that information and find their own way. I always tell them: "You don't need to do it the way I do it, but let me show you how I do it. And maybe you'll find a different way. Maybe you will find a better way. Maybe you will just do it my way. That's fine. It's not up to me to dictate how you choose to operate professionally, but I'm going to set the standard, and I'm going to give you every bit of knowledge I can." That has served us well because I think that's what people want. I've never understood people who . . . I've had bosses in the past. They are at their desk, and they are hovering over whatever balance sheet and they are telling you your costs are off or your costs are good, but they are not actually sharing with you what you did.

That doesn't make any sense to me. I say, "Give me everything. Let me look at it my way and then figure out the best way for me, which will ultimately benefit you."

But so much of working for other people is learning what not to do, and I think maybe that's why my husband and I have been successful, because we really pay attention, and have our entire careers, includ-ing to ourselves. When we do something hopeless: "Well, let's not do that again." But that's okay, too. And I think we've learned as much what not to do as what to do. And we give other people the opportunity to learn both the good and the bad from us in an environment that is truly nurturing, and more than just a professional way, too. After all these years we have spent a lot of time together. Everybody is very close. We have Maureen, who worked with my husband in the Detroit area, and with Myles in the Detroit area. She has a daughter who is now almost sixteen. Maureen still works for us at Stella, and her daughter, Grace, just started working here for us at The Franklin as a hostess. That's crazy, right, when you officially have the second generation? And I didn't think I was that old, to be honest, but then I got a call a couple of months ago from somebody that needed a judge for a whiskey competition. And they called me up. I said, "You've got some great beverage professionals down there." They said, "Well, let's face it. There are a lot of hipsters in this business. And there are way too many men. We need a mature woman with street cred to sit on this panel." And I think my initial reaction was an expletive because that's really not something you should say to anybody. But I knew what he meant. And it was well-intended. And I went, and it was fun. It was interesting, especially in a town where I am known, and where I know people. I realized that I really am among the matriarchy of this industry, certainly in Michigan, and maybe anywhere. That's a neat place to be.

Traverse City is beautiful. We saw it almost twenty years ago, and I've been coming here for forty years. My aunt and uncle had a place up here for that long. I love it up here. I love the growth, the smart growth that we've seen. It makes me sad that there's a Starbucks going in on a prominent corner, because I really prefer the independent coffee houses, the independent restaurant operators. And I hope that our county commissioners and the leadership will consider that. It's just a beautiful place, second to none. Having been all over the world, there are few places as beautiful as Traverse City, and now that there is the agricultural community to support the growing restaurant community, I think there is a lot to discover for people who live here now, and for people who will come here and visit in years to come.

Cocktails

AMANDA DANIELSON, TRATTORIA STELLA

1. Savoie Fare—chilled coupe—no garnish

1¼ ounces Mammoth "Old Dam" gin

½ ounce Dolin Blanc vermouth

½ ounce thyme water

1 scant barspoon Merlet Crème de Cassis

Stir all ingredients with ice; strain.

2. The Southview—chilled flute—no garnish

2 ounces Limoncello

½ ounce lemon juice

¼ ounce Fernet Branca

Prosecco

Shake limoncello and lemon juice with ice; strain into Fernet-rinsed flute; top with Prosecco.

3. Perfect Italian—chilled coupe—orange twist

2 ounces Valentine "Liberator Barrel-Aged" gin

½ ounce Contratto Rosso vermouth

½ ounce Contratto Bianco vermouth

2 dashes orange bitters

Stir all ingredients with ice; strain.

Photo by Madeleine Hill Vedel

13

Donna Folgarelli

Donna's Italian parents owned a wholesale food business in Detroit; she grew up in the food business, familiar with both the preparation in her grandma's kitchen for big family meals and the marketing and production in restaurants and stores. When she moved up to Traverse City as an adult she missed the foods she knew and loved. It wasn't long before her parents also moved up and started the store here that celebrated its fortieth year in 2017, Folgarelli's, renowned for its imports and its locally made pastas and sauces. With her son now in the business, the Traverse City store can boast of three generations of the same dedicated family in charge of it and maintaining the standards they set from the beginning.

Donna Folgarelli, b. August 7, 1947
Interview: August 29, 2017
Folgarelli's Market and Wine Shop,
424 West Front Street, Traverse City

Family and food go together. They unite people.

E ven though I was born in Highland Park, I was raised on Seminole [Street] in Indian Village, Detroit, with my grandma and grampa and my aunt and uncle, and my dearest cousin. We all shared a beautiful home there. In that backyard my grampa, coming straight from Italy, had a plentiful garden. When they decided for everybody to buy their own homes, my parents and my aunt, we all went to separate locations. My grandma and grampa moved to East Detroit. Their entire backyard was garden. We had peach trees and fig trees growing against the house, which was unheard of. My grandmother could eat a peach and throw the peach pit out down to the side of the house, and within a year we had a little peach tree.

Amazing. Italians—I don't know—they have the knack I think that makes things just prosper. So since grandma and grampa spoke very little English, we only knew Italian at that point. I was four years old when we moved to our own home. Every Sunday without any discussion in anyone's life you went to church in the morning, and you were at grandma's by ten thirty in the morning. That's where the cooking began. We were in the basement and we were making gnocchi and pasta and learning how to roll the gnocchi and making the home-made sauce.

This memory is horrifying to me to this day. . . . On Saturdays we would go to the Eastern Market to buy live chickens and fresh vegetables. Grandma used to kill the chickens that she brought back. One Saturday I was in the basement with her, and we were going to make chicken soup, and she chopped this chicken's head off, and the thing flew around the basement with NO HEAD!!! and I about screamed my own head off.

But she taught me that that was the way of life, and it was fresh, and it was good, and I learned how to pluck the feathers and get all those little pin feathers off. It made an amazing dinner. Every Sunday all our relatives would come—about eighteen of us all sitting at a long table—and enjoy a seven-course meal. How can you not love food at that point? Realizing that family and food go together. They unite people. I think no matter what business you are in it can't be as tight as sitting around the table with the family. That was the start of my food love.

In the city where my mom and dad lived we owned a wholesale food business called Lombardi Food Company. So I was vested in the food industry early in life and was a treasured part of my dad's business because I was entertained many, many times going to various restaurants throughout the city of Detroit with him while he would take orders. They would let me sit in the kitchen at one of the little tables and give me a butter knife, and thus I learned to chop, chop. And after school I could go with my dad to the warehouse to gather the snails that had escaped from their wicker basket.

I moved from Rochester Hills, Michigan, in 1972 with our two children. I live on Center Road on the peninsula in Old Mission and have resided here for seventeen plus years now.

When we moved to Traverse City I promptly began working in various venues. I soon realized that we were very much in need of what I called real, European Italian food. My dad started sending truckloads of food up to our gourmet food group. They would disperse all of their foods out of my garage, and we would dine pleasantly for the next couple of weeks until the next truck arrived.

Well, my mom and dad having two grandchildren in northern Michigan decided that it was better to live in northern Michigan with them than run a wholesale food business, so they retired and moved to Old Mission. After about a year my dad decided that this region needed an import food market. So we began a small market in 1978 on Gillis Street, which is behind our present location on West Front Street. We stayed there for not quite a year, Mom and I working with customers and Dad working at the register. I had many hours of solitaire with my mom while we waited for customers because no one knew what Italian food was at that point, and I think people were a little suspicious of these Italians moving to town. It was funny.

Anyway, we moved to Front Street, and the store began to thrive. We also opened a Fox wholesale food on Woodmere, which I ran with my husband. We ran that for about seven years, and Dad decided that the store needed to become larger. We closed the wholesale food industry and doubled the size of what is now our West Front Street location. Mom and Dad ran that business until 1985 when they said that they had discussed selling it. I promptly told them that yes, they should sell it, and that would be to me.

While my mom and dad ventured into this new prosperous location I was also playing tennis. I became the head of the USTA, United States Tennis Association, for northern Michigan. Playing many wonderful tournaments and traveling around the Midwest was an excitement for me, but the food industry was always something that lay heavy in my heart. That was the most important thing in my life. I stayed with the United States Tennis Association for about eight years and was really honored to be able to meet many of the champion tennis players of my years. After retiring out of the United States Tennis

Association I became a teaching tennis pro at the Logan Racket Club, which turned into the YMCA.

When my mom and dad decided they didn't want to work part time anymore I took over Folgarelli's full time. At that point my son Darric came to work with me after graduating from Northwood University in Midland. He has been with me ever since then. He is now the third generation with the store, and our grandchildren are also working at the store during the summer and on holidays.

My life has been full. Many people, many different ideas of food. Going into the catering business has given us a treasure of newfound friends who then tell other friends about us, and that in itself has been one of the most wonderful pleasures of my life. Giving someone the opportunity to learn about good food and how to prepare it and enjoy it. And with running the store I also decided that it was time to do some culinary classes so I ventured into that. We did culinary classes here in my home on the peninsula for over ten years, and it was a fabulous ride. Many of the people after learning a little bit about cooking and dining here, of course, ventured off to Italy and France and really got a wonderful taste of what the European world is about.

And with that I continue on into the food business. We are marketing a sauce that I compounded for the house red sauce for Folgarelli's. It's taken off beautifully. We still do many other projects such as my mom's house Italian dressing and little bits and pieces of things that we put together in the food tastings that people truly enjoy. Her dressing is used on many of the sandwiches we serve.

As the city started to grow, more and more people—especially those that had children at Interlochen—found us, and our business then became more widespread throughout the city because these people had of course come from all parts of the world. They knew what European food was. Some of the teaching of the culinary classes and also in-store classes drew in more and more local people that had been perhaps a little bit shy because they didn't quite know what the product was. But once they knew what prosciutto was and what—not parmesan but Parmigiano-Reggiano—is, it was fun, and it still is fun. So more and more people then became very involved in the store. Our older friends' children wanted to work at the store. We have graduated many kids through our store. We are also very vested in the Culinary Institute at Northwestern Michigan College. We do a lot with the Culinary: fund-raising, and donating for their scholarships, and we are very proud of a lot of young men and women that have gone on to many restaurants around the United States and the world that are chefs. That makes us very happy.

Everything is kind of at a wonderful bubble. It just seems to be growing and growing. We like to say that we not only started a new venture in food, but we continue on with that. And since we have been in business now for thirty-eight years, we've noted a lot of other places in Traverse City that, of course, have opened. I always would be a little apprehensive, thinking, "Oh, gosh. What's that going to do to our business?" Well, it actually makes us thrive because not only are we our own Old World market—we're modern to the taste, but we're old in the feel. People love coming in and knowing that we know what we are doing with cheese, and that the meats that we provide are the best that are available throughout the world.

There are other little bits and pieces of course throughout my life that I was lucky enough to do. I modeled as a young girl, just in high school, for Saks Fifth Avenue. I carried on modeling for a wonderful store that opened in Traverse City that was called Bagatelle. They are a wonderful French family. I modeled for them for over five years. The food, the modeling, learning how to understand people in many different ways, it just has been a true honor for me.

I took many classes in France and Italy to learn more about products there. I learned that their products are organic, as we labeled them. They don't do what the United States had done to food to prosper it, to make it grow faster and larger, so when we brought the foods from Europe here, they already were a natural type food that hadn't been embellished by adding anything to it. The people that learned about that type of food understood that it didn't have to be grown differently in order to be real or natural.

And so we sit hand in hand with organic foods that luckily now we are doing so much with in the United States. Long overdue that we know that what we feed our bodies is what we are. People aren't naive anymore. They have good knowledge of what foods are, and when they come in to buy something, they know that it's the most natural thing that they can get. From the olives to the olive oil to cheese to the meats. I think that's what has made us so sustainable.

Then with that, of course, I have to back up a little and say that when Mom and Dad started the store we had exactly five sandwiches. We somehow have translated that into forty-eight sandwiches. I love the bewildered look of customers when they walk in and look at the three boards and they go, "How do you decide?"

And that is fun. It's really fun to get them in a little avenue of: "Okay, it's okay. Is it something that you want your taste buds to just go crazy over? Or do you want one of our famous Godfather's? It's an award winner."

And they'll go, "What is coppicola?" (or "copacala" as they call it).

"Coppicola is an Italian ham that has paprika on it."

"Oh, that sounds good."

"It's not hot. It just has a lot of flavor."

So little by little they come in. We have customers that have been good customers for thirty years. They'll go: "Okay. I'm on number 30. Now I've gone back to 13, but now I'm going to go to 31. I'm going to venture out of my box." It's fun, watching them explore.

The standards for importing have changed quite a bit. The United States really didn't know that much about importing foods from Europe, so it was a learning curve for them as well as for the entire food industry. Our biggest problem for many years was that they would hold a product because they didn't know what it was, and it would deteriorate. So we would order a half a pallet of something and never receive it because they didn't know what it was, how to process it. So it wasn't available. Now, luckily, education has caught up with most of us. We're in a good way now. Taxation is tough. They like to tax everything that is coming in big time. When somebody says that they can go to: "Oh, I was just in Milan. You only pay $12 a pound for prosciutto da Parma."

"Well, I know, but to bring that little pig all the way across the big water, and pay for it at the border, and then get it here, it's a little bit more." But they don't complain. They truly don't complain. In Piedmont when I went truffle hunting with the tartufo king and went to all these Asti places, I was buying amazing Asti Spumantes for $2 and

$3 a bottle. But that's okay. That's what you go there for. And to know that now we have it here, I think that's something that everyone can treasure because not everyone has the accessibility to go to Europe. So we bring Europe to them.

So with that said, I guess my life just carries on. Watching our family business grow now through my children and grandchildren is wonderful. We are rich in many ways.

Pasta with Broccoli and Gorgonzola

DONNA FOLGARELLI

Serves 4

1 bunch broccoli broken into florets

1½ cups heavy cream

¼ pound Gorgonzola, crumbled

½ cup Parmesan, grated

salt and pepper to taste

12 ounces al dente pasta

Boil broccoli for 5 minutes until cooked but slightly crunchy. Drain and cut into ½-inch pieces.

Reduce cream in skillet over medium heat for about 1 minute. Add Gorgonzola. Cook pasta. Keep sauce simmering over low heat until pasta is cooked.

Add broccoli to pasta and pour sauce over the pasta.

V

WRITERS AND TEACHERS

The Joy of Sharing

14

Patty LaNoue Stearns

Patty LaNoue Stearns found her way into the food world through journalism. High school was not a happy place for her except for the good luck of encountering a gifted journalism teacher. Her luck then continued because her mother was a journalist and helped Patty at a young seventeen to get her start in the newspaper world in Detroit. This in turn led to writing about food and eventually becoming a restaurant critic. When she and her husband moved to Traverse City, Patty continued writing about restaurants, working on different area publications, and publishing several books. They have recently moved back to Detroit but stay in close touch with friends in Traverse City and its food world.

Patty LaNoue Stearns, b. August 25, 1950
Interview: January 12, 2018
Detroit; formerly South Twin Lake, Traverse City

My mother was a stone soup cook who would
pull a rabbit out of a hat every night.

I was born in Detroit, Michigan, at Henry Ford Hospital. I am the fourth of four daughters with three younger brothers. My big family, when I was born, lived in Allen Park, Michigan. Both of my parents were educated in Detroit. My dad was a mechanical engineer. My mom was a homemaker at first, but she had studied journalism at Wayne State University, and when my youngest brother was ten, she returned to a writing career at age forty. My father studied at Lawrence Tech and other places. He was a World War II vet, and the need for engineers brought us to the Detroit area. Allen Park is a downriver suburb of Detroit. It was near the Ford Motor Company where my father worked at the time.

I was brought up sort of in a Wonder Bread, Space-Age kind of eating existence. Everything was modern, and my mother was very much a stone soup cook who would pull a rabbit out of a hat every night, and we'd eat it. I'm kidding, but meat pies, Velveeta cheese, Appian Way boxed pizza mixes, or anything that my mom could economize on that was on sale at the A&P supermarket, would be on our dinner plate. She wasn't really very experimental, but we were always well fed.

Before there were McDonald's restaurants there were Big Boy restaurants. As a junior high kid, that was one of the places that I loved to go if I had any extra money. I figured out how to make that Big Boy sauce, which was absolutely an achievement because I had never cooked that much. I was never that interested in cooking until I started tasting food that was not on my Wonder Bread table.

As our lives moved along, my mom went to work as a columnist for a chain of local newspapers, and, remarkably, a year later, at seventeen and a senior at Allen Park High School, I started working at the same group of papers, the Mellus Newspapers, based in Lincoln Park, as a copy girl/society reporter.

I was a terrible high school student. And before that a horrible junior high student. I just had raging hormones. I was—I would call it maladjusted—and all of my classes bored me. All the teachers bored me. I really had no idea that I would have any kind of career until I took a journalism class and fell in love with the written and reported word. And I was in love with the teacher, Mr. DesHarnais, too.

Somehow because of that journalism class, and the fact that my mother was working at the paper as a columnist, I got the job, and I was never bored again. Between the cultural revolution of the '60s and the fact that Watergate was happening it was really an interesting time in journalism.

I luckily was hired by the *Detroit Free Press* about six months later. Some people who worked with me at the Mellus Newspapers had been on strike during that time for the *Free Press*, and they liked what I did, and they endorsed me as a good candidate for a copy girl when they returned after the strike. And there I was, at age eighteen, working in downtown Detroit at one of the country's top ten newspapers.

I've spent fifty years at this business, and during that time I would say half of it was spent one way or another in the food world. I really liked the people in the food world a lot better than any other topic that I covered. I think that food people are very experimental. They are very creative. They paint a plate with great artistry, and they understand the chemistry of it all. I mean, they are scientists and they are artists at the same time, which is really amazing.

I have done journalism in many ways, starting as a society reporter, an auto writer and editor, then managing editor for *Detroit Monthly* magazine, working at the *Free Press* twice ... once in the beginning as a copy girl, and in the end as a feature writer, a food critic and restaurant columnist, and after that as a full-time freelancer for publications all over the country.

What's remarkable about all of that is that when I was a teenager I was so shy that I could not even look at anyone. I kept my head down, eyes averted, and when people talked to me I couldn't look them in the eye. It was just so anxiety-ridden to be who I was.

Somehow over the years I overcame that shyness and was able to start interviewing people. I think one of the things was to be able to move it all over and ask people questions so that I wasn't put on the spot with anyone asking me questions, which made me really nervous. It changed my whole life and allowed me to have the same profession for all those fifty years.

I've always had a love interest in food, restaurants particularly, because they bring the whole equation together, the communal aspect of eating, and that so appeals to me. The décor always appealed to me in restaurants, which is not really a food thing, but the whole ambiance makes the dining experience come together.

I wrote about restaurants and other subjects while working at *Detroit Monthly* magazine in the 1980s and early 1990s, then went back to the *Detroit Free Press* around 1992 as food columnist and feature writer, then later became a restaurant critic there. So what happened to me over the years is that it brought together the skills that I needed to go on to great things, and be able to interview so many different people, from celebrity chefs to fabulous home cooks, who then made me even more interested in all aspects of the culinary field.

Over the years as a food critic I received lots of letters that would say, for example, that they loved what I wrote, but I also got a few from restaurant owners who really, literally, wanted to kill me because I did some reviews that were really harsh—even after three visits, which was required at the *Free Press* if it was a negative review—I had to write what was going on there. I actually was threatened by a guy who had ties to the Mob. He wanted me to talk to his brother, and I kept thinking, "Wait a minute. This is the guy that has the cement shoes, right?"

And so, after that, I left the business. I left the Detroit area in 1999. It's sort of a weird thing, but I got a little scared. During the time that I was writing there we'd had a really nasty strike at the paper about five years earlier. People were still upset. It was the beginning of the end of the *Detroit Free Press* as the paper I knew and loved. It was a very sad time. I decided that I'd had enough. My mom had just passed away, I loved her dearly, and I felt like the world of journalism was collapsing not only in the Detroit area but everywhere.

We decided to move up to Traverse City to a house on a lake. It was an amazing house. We felt like we had our own lake, South Twin Lake. I started doing freelance writing up there for the *Record Eagle* and for the *Traverse* magazine that I eventually worked for as senior editor. But to be honest, I was kind of afraid being up there at first. Here I had lived in the city of Detroit proper, and yet I was more scared being up there on a little lake with nobody around and no city lights than to be in the big city. I don't know if I was afraid of the animals, a bear or whatever. But I soon got over that and it became very comfortable living there and a joy to be on that little lake.

We made beautiful friends in the food industry, and I observed and wrote about the beginning of the revolution of sustainability as a concept. It just kept going. It grew and grew. It was wonderful to see how a relatively small town in a far-flung area embraced the farm-to-table movement that had already taken hold out West. One of the things that was really tough in the beginning was transportation. For the farmers to get their product to the restaurants was difficult because there were just two-lane highways to deliver food to all of the places in northern Michigan that have good restaurants—all of the little towns and burgs. But then that actually started happening. There were more delivery vehicles and a place where produce could be centralized for delivery, and people started being able to transport their fresh food as it was being produced. I think that really changed the whole nature of the sustainability movement there.

There were some cool things in my life and career. After my horrible years at Allen Park High, I was named to the Allen Park Hall of Fame for my contributions to the field of journalism. I couldn't believe it. So my plaque is sitting up there somewhere in Allen Park High School along with a lot of other very notable people. It was shocking that they would award me such an honor when I had been such a bad student.

A journalism class changed my life. It was with a wonderful teacher named Gerald O. DesHarnais. We called him Jerry. He was the most motivational, hilarious, different teacher that I'd ever had in any of my classes. He had this real zest for news, and was very patient, as far as having us put together stories and figure out topics to write about. It was in the age of Watergate. I think everyone wanted to be working at a newspaper.

I never actually got on the school yearbook or anything. I was too shy even to apply. And I had this mad crush on Mr. DesHarnais. He was just so appealing as a human being. He later, afterward, went to the AP in New York, and I visited him there once. And I still had the mad crush on him. He was very helpful and happy to see me. We went to an off-Broadway play, the *Fantasticks*. That was my first time in New York, too, so that was exciting. I was twenty years old. Nope, we never dated.

At that time I was working at the *Detroit Free Press* as a copy girl. I was still shy and green and all of that. But that changed once I started interviewing. I started writing these little—we called them "Heroes" at the *Detroit Free Press*. I was in business news, and it was a column about all the people who got promoted, and so we just jokingly called them the "Heroes." I would have to interview company presidents and other bigwigs, and I was stupid in those days as far as my interviewing. But little by little, that's where I learned those skills.

Many years later, when I returned to the *Free Press* in 1992 and became the food writer—at the time it was food writer and feature writer, pre restaurant critic—I had always had the dream of going to France since that is my father's nationality, and I studied French in school. I loved everything about France. My sister Nancy and I talked about, "Well, maybe we could go and take some cooking classes." Since I was already working at the *Free Press* as a food writer, I pitched the story to my editor, and he said, "Yeah, if you want to write about that, that would be great."

So we looked and we found that Le Cordon Bleu—which was our huge dream—was having their centennial celebration, and they were offering all kinds of cooking classes. The ones that I took were basically for homemakers who wanted to make fancy food, but the first class was a whole tour of all of the markets of Paris. We had a chef who took us around, and we went to various markets where we could buy exotic fruits. I remember the first strawberries of the season had come in, and they were like little raspberries. They tasted so good! They were the best strawberries I've ever tasted before or since. We went to several markets, all within Paris, and then went back and cooked our meal. Everything was fresh and delicious.

The next day we did a cooking class with another chef who taught us how to make a whole dinner. It was a chicken roulade with a tarragon cream sauce that we put in a bag and had to force into the chicken breasts. We cooked tiny green beans that were from the fresh market. And little cherry tomatoes. We made a dessert that was this big creamy, fabulous thing. It was like a giant cream puff. It was eye-opening to be in Paris, and where Audrey Hepburn had been in *Sabrina Fair*. We walked probably ten miles a day and ate fantastic food. I've been back there five times since then. I did one story called "Pastry Quest 2000," when we went to all the top pastry houses in Paris. I just love Paris. Let's put it this way. I want to die in Paris.

I've also written several books. The first was the *Detroit Free Press Restaurant Guide*. I was the main reviewer. We had a couple more who helped out on that book. It was published in 1998. Then after I moved up north I was doing restaurant reviews for the *Traverse City Record Eagle*, and I compiled a book based on all of those reviews. I visited all of the good restaurants in the area and wrote about them. What I like to do when I write a review is really get into the people who are creating the food. I felt up north that a lot of the restaurants were real, the authentic kind of restaurant that you'd find around the countryside in Europe where they were doing this not as a giant venture to make piles of money, but just doing it out of love. That's the kind of restaurant that I adore. There are a lot of them in the Detroit area that are like that. You could call them mom and pop restaurants, but it's way more than that. It's an extension of who these people are. It's almost like they are inviting you into their kitchen and letting you be part of their dining experience. That's the kind of restaurant that I love.

Tapawingo was like that, up north, and La Bécasse, still there and still wonderful. I'm delighted that those old standards, many of them are still around, and certainly a lot of the people who were part of those restaurants made it so rich and cozy and delicious. I enjoyed doing that guidebook, based on all of those visits that I made to restaurants. It's called: *Good Taste: A Guide to Northern Michigan Cuisine.* I also included recipes in that book.

The other book that I did is called *Cherry Home Companion.* It's all cherry recipes, breakfast, lunch, dinner, drinks. A lot of the recipes were contributed by the fine chefs in the Traverse City and Petoskey region as well as some food writers around the country who were friends of mine. I belonged to the Association of Food Journalists at the time. That book was very successful. It was reviewed all over the place. I did that book because a lot of people love cherries, and certainly the Traverse City region is known for its cherries.

We moved back to the Detroit area in 2015. I'm happy about my life. I'm happy that I can still write. I'm not doing as much food writing right now, more about lifestyle and design, but the memoir that I'm writing—that I've been working on for years—will include many recipes, many food memories, and many things about food that I love. It's a lot about growing up in Detroit and how Detroit has changed over the years and is rebounding now. It's a happy story.

Grandma Mitscha's Hungarian Goulash adapted by Patty LaNoue Stearns

PATTY LANOUE STEARNS

Serves 6

This recipe employs the braising method—quickly browning meats and vegetables in hot fat, then slowly simmering them over low heat in a small amount of liquid for 2 to 3 hours. If you don't own a Doufeu or Le Creuset Dutch (French) oven, any heavy pot with a tight-fitting lid will do; pots made specifically for braising will have points on the inside of the lid from which liquids will drip back onto the food as it cooks. Check the liquid periodically and add more if needed.

1¼ cups yellow onion, finely chopped

1 sweet green pepper, cored, seeded, finely chopped

3 tablespoons olive or vegetable oil, divided

1 tablespoon butter, divided

2 pounds beef chuck, trimmed of fat, in 1½-inch cubes

1½ tablespoons flour

2 tablespoons Hungarian Sweet Rose paprika

1½ teaspoons salt

¼ teaspoon pepper, freshly ground

1 teaspoon cider vinegar

2 cups beef stock, broth, or water

16 ounces extra-wide egg noodles (I like Essenhaus Homestyle)

Over moderate heat in a Doufeu pot or other heavy enameled cast-iron pot, sauté onion and green pepper in half of the oil and butter until pale and golden; remove from the pan and drain on a paper towel.

Heat the remaining oil and butter over moderately high heat. Lightly dredge beef cubes in the flour. Add the meat in batches so it browns evenly, turn heat to low and stir in paprika for 1 to 2 minutes. Return the drained onions and green peppers to the pot, add salt, pepper, cider vinegar, and beef stock, cover and simmer 3 hours or until meat is tender.

If using a Doufeu pot, fill the cover with ice and, as it dissipates, add more throughout the duration of your cooking, stirring occasionally. Otherwise, check covered pot, stir occasionally, and add liquid as needed.

Boil egg noodles halfway according to directions; drain, then add to the pot until thoroughly cooked.

Photo by Madeleine Hill Vedel

15

Barb Tholin

Barb grew up in Illinois and didn't come to Traverse City until 2007. Her grandparents had a farm, and her mother told her many stories about life on the farm. After earning a degree in agronomy, Barb worked on several farms including an organic vegetable farm and a farm in Tennessee with draft horses. For almost two decades she managed a food co-op in Minnesota. All along she wanted to help educate people about food, where it comes from, how it's grown, how it's made. When she discovered the *Edible* magazine that was beginning in different parts of the country she was eager to bring the publication to this region that she knew from visiting her mother-in-law, who had an orchard here. In 2018 Barb celebrated the fiftieth issue of her magazine. She relies on a committed team of writers and photographers to craft the feature articles on local growers, producers, restaurateurs, and more.

Barb Tholin, b. April 28, 1961
Interview: August 5, 2016
Edible Grande Traverse, Cochlin Street, Traverse City

We have two months of summer, six weeks of spring,
a couple months of fall, and a lot of winter.

I was born in New York City. My parents were there while my father was getting a doctorate in theology, so I lived in New York City for two years and then we moved to Naperville, Illinois, which is where I was raised until high school. Then we moved to Evanston, Illinois; both were suburbs of Chicago, the big city. My father was from the

Chicago area. My mother was from a farm in Lake Odessa, Michigan, which is down between Grand Rapids and Lansing.

Growing up in Chicago we were pretty much city kids, but we did go to my mother's family farm a couple times a year. That's where I was introduced to farms. Grampa by then was starting to rent out more and more of his farm, but it was the family farm that was settled in 1850 when the family moved over from Germany. It's a very solidly German community. My grampa was ninety-five when he died. He was born in 1906, but he was the last native German speaker in the county. He was very proud of that—it's kind of poignant—but he was definitely proud. And it was a centennial farm, always in our family until he died.

My mother for most of her life thought she would take the farm when he died. But basically she was too old by then or she felt too old. She still considered it when he died, but then decided to pass it along. She and her sisters sold the estate, and that farm just went away. It became contracted out to ever more corn fields. The house remained on a little couple-acre parcel surrounded by corn fields, contracted to the big farmers there. My mother had really fond memories, not all good memories, but she was very attached to her upbringing there and proud of the farm heritage.

It was a typical general farm with all kinds of animals, bees, maple syrup, canning, and the wood stove. I was raised with lots of stories about what that was like. How her mother and grandmother and all the women made food for the men in the field. How they had potatoes three times a day. They would cook them once a day, and then had them for all three meals. How in strawberry season they would just have dinners of strawberry shortcake. Big platters of it. How they would slaughter the pigs and preserve them, big crocks down in the cellar. I enjoyed going to the farm and hearing all those stories. And some of them must have stuck.

I was raised more or less in the city, the suburbs of the city. I was a bright kid, and I went through most of high school at an accelerated pace until I hit the wall, and really wanted to do something different. There was an alternative program for seniors at my school. It was kind of a school within a school. One thing they had was a farm out in Wisconsin, a dairy farm. And so, instead of working in classrooms, we worked in sessions. In the spring and the fall there were two- and three-week sessions out to the farm. That's where we had environmental education and also various kinds of farming, slaughtering chickens, and doing the dairy chores, things like that.

I fell in love with farming. That's what I wanted to do my senior year. When I told my mother that she was shocked. She had no idea where it came from. Even though she loved her farm on account of her father's personality and some of the lifestyle stuff there, she couldn't wait to leave. She moved to the city, and she was surprised that I would want to be a farmer. She didn't understand. But I did. That was my big passion.

I found a school in northern Vermont that had a one-year farming program: Environmental Education and Agriculture. It's called Sterling College. It's still there. At the time they just had a one-year program. But while I was there they were adding a second-year program and an associate of arts degree. So I stayed for that. I finished up school eventually at UVM in Burlington and got a plant and soil science degree, agronomy. All of this was toward wanting to be a farmer myself.

After my two years at Sterling I took an internship nearby at an organic vegetable farm before "organic" was actually a certified thing, but they called themselves organic. This was in 1982. There was the start of certification, the New England or the Northeast Organic. There was an organization, but I think certification was still a little ways down the road. At any rate, the farmer ran it as a little bit of a commune-y thing. He had inclinations that way.

There were four apprentices, and we worked six days a week, really six and a half days a week, long days for room and board and something like $50 a week. I loved it. I got to know some farms in the area, sheep farms, dairy farms. I ended up staying there past the growing season and staying a full year through the Vermont winter. We heated with wood so there was a lot of woodcutting to do. The winter work there was in the woods and then eventually maple-sugaring. And while we were maple-sugaring we were also planting seedlings for the coming growing season.

I stayed for a full cycle. I had plans to work on a sheep farm and I had actually been contracted with to work the sheep farm down the road while the owner did a trip to Europe. But unfortunately I got sick with botulism, food-poisoning, so that interrupted my plans. It's a paralysis, a nerve thing. I didn't have any strength. I had to go back to my parents and recuperate for some months.

That kind of broke my heart because sheep farming was what I was getting really drawn toward. That was one of those things that changes your path. When I signed up to go to UVM I decided instead of the farming gigs I should finish up a bachelor's degree and I got a bachelor's degree in plant science.

From northern Vermont I had gotten involved with a guy back in Chicago, so I went back to Chicago for what I thought was just a brief stint and then I'd move back to Vermont, but I never made it back to Vermont. I was working at a macrobiotic and vegetarian restaurant that I had worked at in high school. They were growing and expanding. I worked there for a couple of years, working my way up in management and the front. I was running the front of the house by the time I left, learning about service. It was quite a popular place. Macrobiotics was especially big at that time. I learned a lot about natural foods and different diets there.

I still wanted to farm, and my boyfriend at the time was catching the bug. We went to a horse farm in Tennessee, a draft horse farm. We wanted to learn how to raise draft horses and work with them. There was a farm in Tennessee that raised Suffolk Punch draft horses. They are a British breed, bred to work and never bred to be big tall carriage horses, but they maintained their work status. We apprenticed there for a year and a half and learned how to work the big horses. But we missed the north, so from there we moved to Minnesota. Neither of us wanted to go back to Chicago, and we had heard that the Twin Cities was a great place to live and that food co-ops were really big there, that the whole consumer co-op movement was really strong there. So based on that we up and went there. We didn't know anybody. I applied for work and got hired by a food co-op to run the produce department, and I stayed there for nineteen years.

It felt perfectly fitting for me to do that—from my agronomy degree to go into retail—I loved it. And the reason it was a real fit for me was that I just loved farming so much, and I loved everything about it, and I knew that a lot of people didn't know much about it, didn't know where their food came from. This wouldn't happen at a big grocery store, but at a food co-op, that's what you are there for. You are there because the shoppers are the owners, and they want good food, and they want to know about it. It's all about sourcing, and it's all about quality, and the qualities of the food. I knew that was a great fit. As the produce buyer and the produce manager I was working with local farmers. We were contracting and bringing in their produce, planning ahead on quantities and types. We were also bringing in lots of organic produce from all over the country and from all over the world. It was an exciting time.

I started there in 1989. And, for example, I remember somewhere early—a couple of years later, I think—the New Zealand apples became available. That didn't exist before that, to have fresh apples available in April. It never had happened before. That was really exciting.

My first job in high school had been at a little neighborhood grocery store, D and D Finer Foods. A couple of Greek brothers owned it. I still remember Granny Smiths. I still remember the produce that hit the market as brand-new things while I was there, and one of them was Granny Smith apples. Until then we pretty much had Macintosh and Delicious, but suddenly there were green apples coming in. I remember bean sprouts hitting the market. We didn't have those before. So my grocery history actually goes fairly far back.

The New Zealand apples came in the '90s, and then we expanded our store. I remember when a couple of other new things came on the market from the conventional suppliers. One of them was baby peeled carrots. I brought them in, and some of my coworkers and some of my customers were aghast. They couldn't believe it was a product. It just didn't seem natural enough. It wasn't long until it was the single top money-making item in our produce department. The other item at the same time was baby spring mix, baby mixed lettuce, and nobody could believe that we had to charge about $10 a pound for it. Nobody was going to buy that. So on the sign we always broke it down to the ounce price. After that, clementines, then tangerines. It was a big time. There were local markets expanding in produce. Seasonality was disappearing. I was excited by it. I loved learning about figs from California. We were in northern Minnesota. I loved learning about figs and about the Spanish clementines and produce that came from South America or from Asia.

What we were all about was having as much variety as we could and having as much selection as we could so that we could be people's destination produce store and then also provide as much organic at the best prices as we could, so that we could convert them with some stealth and some planning. Definitely our mission was to sell more natural foods, to sell more organic foods. The way we felt we could do that best was to still provide conventional foods as well, always give people choices, and hopefully they would more and more choose the organic. Nobody at the time, and still, bought 100 percent organic. Everybody made some choices.

I also managed the meat department, and, once again, I was working directly with farmers. The only kind of meat we sold for a long time was bought directly from farmers, so at times we were buying whole hogs and working with them as to how we wanted them cut for our retail. We were working early on with chicken farmers who were doing rotational and free-range poultries. A lot of this was before there were organic standards for meat. There had been organic standards for produce for a long time. Meat was a tricky one, and so for a long time organic meats were sold without the benefit of certification, which meant that they developed their own marketing and marketing terms and customer base, so that when organic came along with meats, this other whole marketing thing had come alongside of it, so organic wasn't so important with meats when it finally came along.

But again I was working directly with the farmers. The consumers who wanted natural meats learned about what that meant. It's different from going to the big supermarket and just picking out the parts you want. Things weren't always available. We didn't always have enough bacon, for example, or pork loin, since we were buying whole animals and needed to sell everything. Sometimes we ran out of those choice parts. I was always interested in teaching the consumers more about the food they shopped for and the food they eat.

That was at Mississippi Market Food Co-op. While working there, in Saint Paul, Minnesota, in 1993 I had married my boyfriend at the time. We bought a farm out in Wisconsin, a so-called hobby farm, eighty acres, about an hour's drive from the co-op. I continued to work there, and I commuted all the time. That was like the next stage in my plan, in my dream. We bought the eighty acres, started in basically a big garden, some animals, some chickens, got a couple of young steers we were going to train for oxen, thinking about horses, because we were trained in horses. I got some sheep, just a few sheep from a nearby sheep dairy farm, Dorset ewes, older ewes that were bred. So we kind of started down that path. However, my husband decided it wasn't for him after all. We had the farm for four years, and then we closed up shop and sold the farm, and also, at that point, we divorced. I was living back in Minneapolis and still working at the co-op.

While working at the co-op something led into the next phase. A magazine network, *Edible*, Edible communities, appeared because we had a publisher in town. *Edible Twin Cities* was publishing about the local foods in our area and stories about the farmers and the chefs, the food artisans, the gardeners. Local businesses were advertisers, and our co-op was one of them. That's how we got to know the Edible concept.

I think it started about in 2003 with one magazine, not a chain of any kind. But somebody saw it and wanted to do another on the other coast. It started with *Ojai, California*. So rather than just copying it, they contacted the owners and asked, "How could we do one of these ourselves?" and they worked out a plan, a way to do that, and then realized they could keep on doing that. More and more people could do these in their own communities. It grew kind of organically as people saw it. It wasn't like sold. They weren't going into new markets and trying to find publishers. It grew as people saw it and liked it. *Edible Twin Cities* was about the thirteenth or fourteenth title, so that was in the early days. My partner at the time, Charlie—and then we were married—he was in marketing as a career, and he had also been working at Mississippi Market, as the marketing director there. He also became very familiar with the *Edible Twin Cities* and the network. And then, Charlie was from Traverse City.

At that time we were coming to Traverse City frequently to visit his mother and his family that have a farm out on Old Mission. That's where Charlie was raised. His family are apple and cherry growers. We were coming out here frequently, at least a couple of times a year for visits. His mother was aging. Like a lot of people we were thinking, "Hey, this would be a nice place to live."

Charlie was interested in giving it a try. He had left here after college. We had had a son in the meantime, too, in 2001, and we decided when he was ready to enter grade school would be a good time to move here, so that's what we did. We moved here in 2007 and we had already negotiated a purchase of the *Edible Grande Traverse* title, and a territory here for us to run our own magazine.

It's not technically a franchise. It's a network. We are independent publishers with more freedom than typical franchises. Franchises are more product-related, like cookie-cutter product. As owners of our own magazine we own the license to publish, the trademark from Edible communities. There are now just about eighty titles in the network, and we cooperate in various ways, and we help each other out. We have an annual meeting and conference for training purposes, but we are all independent.

So in 2007 we arrived with our license ready to publish an *Edible Grande Traverse* here. We first had the concept in 2005. Things were quite different here. The region was starting to change. There were some wineries. There weren't many new restaurants at that point, but there were some wineries starting up, for sure. Good Harbor was producing, and Château Grand Traverse, which was a neighbor of the Wunsch Farm of my in-laws. Peninsula Cellars had started up.

We were watching the wineries closely as a good indicator. "Taste the local difference," the part of the Michigan Land Use Institute that was running a food program, a farming program, an educational program, and marketing . . . they were already here, so we were watching them. We were watching the wineries and some of the food trends. We knew that it's a small market for this business, and at first we thought it was too small, but we took a plunge, and it worked, and of course we're still doing it now. It felt risky because of the size of the market, but there was just enough evidence that this was becoming a food place, and it was what we wanted to do. It was a great crossroads again. Charlie had the farming and marketing background. I as always had this love of farming and food and this real interest in telling people's stories and helping consumers learn more about their food, where it comes from, how it's made, what goes into it, all of that.

I felt like it was a natural progression from working at the food co-op. We are co-owners now. We have divorced along the way, but we're still working together on the magazine. I have always been the editor of the magazine, and my partner focusing more on the ad sales. We distribute it for free, largely at our advertisers' locations as an added value for their customers and as a draw. Best-case scenario, people see it as a draw. And it's free. The advertisers are supporters. They advertise because they like the concept and also because they know that they are getting in front of a readership that really cares about food.

We use a printer out in New Hampshire. When we moved here and launched we did publish with a local printer. But there is a printer in New Hampshire—not the exclusive printer for the Edible community's network—but they print a large amount of them. Paper is the crazy expense in the business. And we use high-quality paper. Everybody in the network uses similar paper, definitely high quality. So this printer, by getting so many of our accounts, can do so at a price that makes a big difference. And since we are giving the magazines away—and a lot of that is because it's mission-driven—we want to get the stories out, we want to get the magazine out in the community to as many people as we can. So having a printer that we can afford makes that possible and makes it possible to get more copies out.

We use an uncoated paper that's rarely seen in the printing world now, at least in periodicals. And from the start, I still remember especially at the start when we came out with our first magazine, and we talked to people, handing them some. They were always feeling them, rubbing them. The covers have a style that's simple, uncomplicated photography, just photo-based without a lot of exclamation points and sensationalist text. It's just a photo. And then the paper. People would really rub the paper, especially at first when they hadn't seen it around. They'd say, "Wow! This is really great." And they'd open it up and touch the paper again, and touch the pictures. That was something else. People really appreciated that and they still do.

The magazines are printed to be kept as well, with the high-quality paper, and hopefully the content and the recipes. I love people saying they have every copy, and we're up to forty-four. It's five times a year. The original concept with the Edible community was a quarterly magazine. We launched with four in mind, a quarterly for each season, but pretty much right away we started looking at that schedule, and we wanted to add another one. Some of that is simply about the seasons. When you are this far north the seasons actually aren't that long. To publish summer, spring, fall, winter on a quarterly basis, that's not how the seasons happen. We have two months of summer, six weeks of spring, a couple months of fall, and a lot of winter. So we made two winter issues. We made a holiday and a winter issue and then spring, summer, and fall. We print from 13,000 to 18,000 depending on the season.

I'm the editor in chief. I work with copyeditors so I don't do all the copyediting myself. And I've learned on the job. People ask me that a lot. I've learned on the job from my cohorts in the Edible community. I've learned from the copyeditors that I've hired and contracted with. I've learned from my writers and photographers. We get a certain amount of training at our conferences with workshops and things. I learned from Charlie. Both of us came from academic families. My mother was an English major, never quite employed in that capacity, but she and my father became book dealers. They were academics and linguists and good with the language. That didn't hurt. Charlie's father was an English professor at NMC, and his mother was also an academic in art. So our backgrounds helped us. Charlie and I worked on the editorial in the early days a lot more closely. As we got busier, we needed to turn away from that. We needed to specialize more.

We look for stories that have a sustainable leaning, about farmers that tend toward organic or sustainable. We want our readers out there in the more environmentally friendly agriculture that's around here and in the natural foods that are around here. But we're not exclusively that. I think that partly patterns after what I was talking about with the produce department that we ran. You need to welcome everybody in. That's kind of a first. At least, that's our approach. Everybody's working hard. You talk about farmers, agriculture, restaurateurs. Everybody's working hard doing a great job.

Farming is really hard to do organically and especially in our area. Fruit farming is especially hard to do. We are not a heavy organic farming community. We don't dis that. We want to tell positive stories about the food that's being produced in our area. We have a great and strong fruit-farming culture here. It's wonderful. So we look for stories that are about sustainability and organics, more closed-loop systems. That's part of the sustainability, but that's not exclusively what we do.

The restaurants can get great-quality foods from the local farmers: fruits, vegetables, produce, cheese, meats. A lot of restaurants support that. The restaurants have a lot of challenges, though. It's called "winter." It's called menus. So if you want to provide chicken breasts on your menu and have it as a regular item, that's like the pork loin. Those are the parts that are really expensive for a local natural producer. The average customer is not used to paying that much for chicken breasts. So there are very real challenges for restaurateurs. That's another good reason to tell more stories so that our readers start becoming more educated about what that's like and why restaurant prices are as they are, why sourcing doesn't always seem as ideal as they'd like. They are feeding a hungry tourist town. It's not always easy to get the supplies locally.

With the "farm-to-table" trend or interest they rely more on changing menus. They don't have set menus. A lot of those restaurants have daily or weekly changes. That way they can buy from the locals and stay fresh.

When I meet with the Edible community I see that what's unique to this area is the fruits. The fruits are big. Not all areas are blessed with great orchards. All of the Edible magazines reach out to their community. Our community is pretty small compared to urban areas. I think we have really good participation in story writing. We have contributors who are more food enthusiasts than they are writers or journalists. And yet they write great stories.

We are all freelance, so I don't have a staff I can just assign to. But we have worked with a lot of regular contributors along the way, and once we've worked with somebody a few times, and I get to know them, if I have story ideas I'd like to land somewhere, I like to pair up a story idea with a writer I think would like to do it and would do a good job. So there's kind of pitching stories both directions. I definitely encourage our contributors to pitch me ideas.

Photographers are also freelance. We have a couple of regular freelancers that we love and work with almost every issue. Those are assignments more often than not. But we also have journalists or contributors who are contributing both. They are writing stories and taking the photos for them. I learned some photography when I started this, and I take many fewer now than I used to. I call myself the backup photographer. Food photography is an art. There's a lot to it to make it so beautiful. I can come up with stuff that works, but I love working with our contributing photographers. They all do marvelous stuff, getting the people right and getting the food right.

In this foodie town they have even included foodie films in the Michael Moore film festival starting in 2015. They incorporate the food movies with the local chefs who were doing appetizers and local foods to pass out after the films, plus a panel of local food people to talk about the movie afterward. I was included in one of those panels last year, and that was fun. The film was about a Danish biodynamic cattle farmer. It was a marvelous movie, and I was able to talk about it afterward with Angela Macke from Light of Day Organics—she's a biodynamic tea grower—and with Jess Piskor of Bareknuckle Farm. I mentioned "Taste the local difference" earlier, with LMUI, which is now Groundworks Center. They have a goal of 20 percent local foods by 2020, to get the local food economy to be 20 percent local foods by 2020 through marketing programs and consumer awareness and actual logistics to connect farmers to markets.

After a couple of years of getting the magazine started I took on a part-time job with Cherry Capital Foods, which is our local food distribution. I spent three years there as a produce buyer while they were in their building years. They have since moved to a brand-new facility and have expanded statewide. They are all about Michigan foods for Michigan markets and providing the wheels for that to happen. I learned a lot behind the scenes there about just how the devil is in the details. There is a lot of expense and there are a lot of complications.

My impression is that CSAs are holding their own. I don't know that they are expanding. The model has become more flexible and it's become more year-round. There are a lot of CSAs that can run right through the winter because of hoop houses and because of stored crops, and a little change in expectations or just in what they offer. Some CSAs have expanded to meats so there are various local farmers who put together packages. It's like a subscription.

CSA is interesting. Early on it really was this kind of pure thing, paying ahead of time for a share, an undetermined portion of whatever was available, whether it was bounty or whether it was lean. Over time it has involved to more of a sense of paying up front—that's usually still involved—but for a certain portion. A lot of farms will have both. They will have shares, and they'll have market garden. So they are always offering the same amount, but along with that it's almost always paying up front. That's where meat producers might come in. They offer package deals on a regular basis.

For example, I buy from a farm that does poultry shares. I do a six-month poultry share and I pay up front. I get two chickens a month, and I get a turkey at Thanksgiving. From that same farm I could buy an egg subscription and get a dozen eggs every week. I also buy a rabbit subscription so I get a rabbit a month. That concept of buying a subscription of a share from the farmer and buying ahead of time for monthly supplies seems to be expanding.

I also personally enjoy cooking, but running my own business cuts into that time. I don't cook at home as much as I used to. That's been a challenge. It's really interesting raising a child in this environment. As much as I try to influence him, now that he's a teenager, he does not eat as much local foods as I would like, unless the local stuff at 7-Eleven counts.

The support from friends and neighbors in this community has been amazing. This magazine has been well received and supported. I've made a lot of amazing acquaintances and friendships through it. We get so much support from contributors, certainly from advertisers and distribution places. And even more than that, when we distribute the magazine, to be able to—that's one of my favorite parts—it's difficult, because we still do it from our cars. It's important to us for our model to do that in person. And in turn it becomes one of the best parts of the job because we are out there. I get to drive around Leelanau County. That's my main delivery area. It's beautiful and farm-y, and I get to stop in to all these great restaurants and farm markets and see people. Every year, every issue, it's wonderful. People are so grateful for the magazine, and they are supportive and happy to see it, each new issue. That makes it feel like a community that we are serving and that we are a part of.

Photo by Madeleine Hill Vedel

16

Carol Worsley

Carol always loved to cook. Growing up on the Upper Peninsula with a French grandfather and a Finnish mother, she watched as her mother prepared huge breakfasts for her dad and others working in the copper mines. Years later she tried to serve comparably huge but inappropriate breakfasts to her own husband, until he protested. She took cooking classes wherever they lived from California to Yokohama to Glen Arbor. In Glen Arbor a woman offered to introduce her to Julia Child and Simone Beck, and this led to a long collaboration and to teaching with Julia and Simca in France and in this country. She later opened Thyme Out and then Thyme Inn, a B&B, in Glen Arbor, teaching classes and preparing extraordinary meals. Martha Ryan and Susi McConnell both worked with her there.

Carol Worsley, b. November 3, 1937
Interview: September 1, 2016
Thyme Inn, 6362 West Western Avenue, Glen Arbor

How would you like to go to France in the fall?

I was born in a little town on the Upper Peninsula called Luriam, Michigan, named after an Indian tribe, I guess, at least that's what I was told. I lived there until I was about eighteen.

I come from an interesting background, a European background, really, because I am Finnish and French. My father's father was from France, and they settled in Quebec. He raised horses, and the horses were being quarantined at the border before allowing them into the United States because a lot of times prize race horses would contract something from the lesser horses or sick horses. He came to this country and he looked around. He was told that on the Upper Peninsula you can get property for practically nothing, and that's what he did. That's why I'm from the Upper Peninsula.

My mother's parents both came from Finland very young. My grandfather came to work in the copper mines because things were very bad in Finland in those days. They were farmers, and things were not going well. He met my beautiful redheaded grandmother. She had Titian-colored hair, that's what they called it. She had come over when she was eighteen years old, and she brought a huge loom with her. She was a weaver. She had been trained as a girl to be a weaver. So they shipped this enormous loom, which is still up in the Upper Peninsula with my grandmother so she could earn a living. It's one thing to pack a suitcase, but quite different to pack a loom. They met, and later my father and mother met in the UP.

My husband and I lived in Birmingham, Michigan, not the Upper Peninsula. When I met Don I was eighteen years old. He was in graduate school. He had an engineering degree, and he was in Wayne State University Law School. I was working. I had planned to go to the University of Michigan, really because of a young man I met. I was heading there, but then I met Don. Our first date was May 5. By May 7 he had proposed. We agreed that we should wait for a year because I was only eighteen, and then I could go to school, and then we would get married.

What happened was this. We were engaged, and I was taking some classes at Wayne State University, and then he was called into the service. In those days the army was hot on your track. He wanted to be a pilot in the navy. His father had airplanes, and he used to fly with his dad or his stepfather. He was going to be drafted into the army and so he had to leave and go to Officer Candidate School in Newport, Rhode Island, to be in the navy. We found out that we had to be married if I was going to go to his next duty station. Whoa! It was going to be Southern California, San Francisco, and then Japan for three years. If he had been in the army we would not have been able to be together.

We got married in Newport so I could go with him. Then we went to Southern California, the Ventura area. He was stationed at a place called Point Hueneme, and I fell in love with it. I was blown away by California. We lived in navy housing that had been a motel and then it became housing for fliers. There was an air base across the street.

I'd go down to the beach, and it was the first time I had ever had an avocado. I met a woman who was writing a book. She would write down on the beach. I would walk up and down, and one day she just said hello to me. I didn't know anybody, so I thought this was very nice of her. We started to talk, and she said, "Would you like to sit down?" She was on a blanket on the sand. She said, "I'm about to have lunch. Would you like to join me?" And she had an avocado. I had never seen or had an avocado. Believe me, in the Upper Peninsula, especially in the winter, you are lucky if you get fresh oranges, anyway in those days. It's different now. So I would meet her down there from time to time. I would also go to the beautiful fresh fruit market that was across the street from the little hovel that we were living in, full of ants. Every morning I would get up and go over to the Japanese food market, and they would see me coming, and they would have a melon ready.

I always had a passion for cooking from the time I was a little girl. My mother was a very good cook. You could call her a gourmet cook because everything she made was so delicious. There were five of us in the family, and you didn't have to call us for dinner. We'd be sitting there with knife and fork in hand. We would ask: "Mom, what are we having for dinner tonight?" We knew there was always going to be a treat.

Anyway, in California, I would make breakfasts for my poor husband like he was a lumberjack. My mother always made a big breakfast because there were five of us, three brothers and a sister. The girls didn't eat that much, but the boys ate a lot. She always had oatmeal, plus eggs or pancakes—or eggs and pancakes—always oatmeal because my father got up at a quarter to five in the morning, and he had oatmeal every day. But in California, poor Donald, I would make these fruit plates, bake the oatmeal, ask: "What kind of eggs would you like?" He told me that he was so miserable when he would go off to work. He was very slim. I think he had a smaller waist than I did, like a twenty-nine-inch waist. And he said that he'd be logy all morning from all that food, but he never wanted to tell me because I got so much joy out of it. Getting up at the crack of dawn, really.

That's how I've always been about food. I didn't cook with my mom, but I did a lot of cooking in that kitchen. We had a homey kitchen, nothing like what I have now. My girlfriends and I used to cook. Mom's kitchen was always available. In fact, when I had an apartment in Detroit when I was working in Detroit before I was hopefully going off to college, I did the cooking. They said, "You do the cooking, and we'll do the cleaning." Well, I ended up doing the cooking and the cleaning, too, because I'm Finnish. We have that innate urge to clean everything. And they never did a good job. They'd do the bathroom, and then I'd go in and redo the bathroom.

So when did I become so interested in food? I really give my mother the credit. Everything she made was delicious. She made the most beautiful cakes and tortes. I remember during World War II when eggs were hard to get—everything was going to the war effort in the Upper Peninsula—and mother would get together with her friends. They would save up their eggs until they had twelve eggs, and then they would come to our house. If somebody was having a shower or a wedding or something, they would pool the twelve eggs, and they would separate them very carefully, and they'd make a sponge cake with twelve yolks and an angel food cake with twelve whites. They were heavenly. Mother used to do a white angel food cake where she would cut out the top, hollow out the inside, and then she did this wonderful whipped-cream chocolate with toasted almond, and I've made that for my daughter's birthday parties over the years. My whole family loves it. After you put the top back on you frosted it with this wonderful chocolate whipped cream and put the shaved toasted almonds all over it. I think I'll have to make one shortly!

Then we went to Japan. I was supposed to be in school, but we were 650 miles from any university that I could go to that would teach any classes in English. But I taught at a school. I got a job—I can't really call it a job although they called it a job. It paid so little that I didn't really take anything. It was a Japanese school, and I taught twelfth grade English. My husband was a great help with that because he was a grammarian. I said, "If I'd known that before I met you, I would never have dared . . ." My mother said, "No dee's, dem's, dat's, or dose." I would have been a little more careful with my English grammar.

But at any rate we were in Japan. I came from the Upper Peninsula, and we really didn't do a lot of traveling when I was a child. My father had his own business. There were a lot of us. We did have nice little excursions, but nothing big. Here I went from Newport, Rhode Island, to San Francisco to Japan. It was like living a dream. But then I met these navy wives. I was very young. I was nineteen years old, and I was so impressed with these navy wives who had lived all over the world, all over Europe: Italy, France, wherever the navy was, wherever the ships came into port. They entertained so beautifully that I was just stymied. Of course I didn't get to take my wedding gifts along with us because we got married in Newport, and they were all in the Upper Peninsula, but mother started sending them to me so I could set a nice table.

We moved to Yokohama our last year, and I met some young wives whose husbands were at the embassy. The chefs at the embassies would teach classes. So I got to go to the French embassy and take classes. It was wonderful. I guess I've always had a natural affinity for cooking because when I get a recipe—unless it's one of my mother's recipes or somebody that I know is a really good cook—I make it two or three times before I would ever do it for a cooking class.

When we came back to the United States Donald's business took off like a shot. That man worked so hard! I worked with him. We had a little townhouse, quite similar to the one I'm living in now but not quite as large. We bought a desk. We had $300. We went out and bought a big desk because he had to have something to use as a drafting table. He needed a big desk that he could roll his blueprints out on.

We had an eight-month-old baby when we came back. The only place that was big enough for the desk was our bedroom. We had a big bedroom on the second floor. So we lugged it up there, and he would work. I'd put the baby down after dinner. I'd spread a big sheet out on the bed, and I'd take all these little cheerios and things for him to eat, and little toys to play with. Don worked on the desk, and I typed on the ironing board.

After my husband's business took off—and he had three very successful businesses; no man ever worked harder than he did—we laughed about those days. But it was so much fun. I'd say, "Time for a break," and he knew it was dessert time. I always made dessert because my mother always made dessert, and I liked doing it.

I was from Luriam. I've always loved being up north in the copper country. I think it's one of the most beautiful spots in the whole world. We've traveled a lot, but I always said, "You know, Don, I know they've got the mountains, but you remember those beautiful cliffs in the UP?" We were looking for a cottage. Actually, we were looking for a ski place. We wanted to ski at Boyne. We were looking around Walloon and Torch Lakes, and an architect client of ours—I say "our" because I was working for Don ever since we got married—one of the architects had been up here.

We had never heard about Glen Lake. We had stayed on Crystal. Nobody had ever mentioned Glen Lake, and I made this horrible statement which Don could never let me forget. I said, "Honey, we've looked at every lake in the area. It must be some mud-hole." I was thinking about the fishing lakes in the UP where people don't have cottages because they are "mara lakes," soft bottom lakes.

So we came up here, and we found our property on Glen Lake—which I would love to show you—the view is spectacular. I was expecting a baby, and I had two little boys, and our friends all said, "Why did you buy a property high up on a hill?" One of the first things Don and I put in, the two of us, was this long, windy path. In later years, when we could afford it, we put in a lift. But our little boys thought that path was magic. The lake was magic. This whole area to us became so important. We always called it our happy place. So that's how we came to northwest Michigan.

Don said to Mr. Foreman: "Is there any place to stay in Glen Arbor?" He said, "Really not. There's a small motel, but it's no good." We had our two little boys with us. He said, "I think we can find you a place at Leelanau School because the students aren't here right now, and they have the cabins." So he called over to Leelanau School. It was before they had any commercial properties over there or condominiums. They put us up in this little cabin, and our boys were excited because it had the river on one side and the lake on the other.

Mr. Foreman said, "Do you want to look at more properties?" Don said, "No, I'm going to buy this one." He wanted to be here long enough to arrange with a bank, because he wanted to make a down payment to make sure we had it. We bought 327 feet on the lake, and five acres. We still have 227 feet. We sold 100 feet to a wonderful family—she was a pianist. She played all the time; it was marvelous—to help finance the cottage. Our cottage cost $29,000 and I spent $19,000 on furnishings. Don thought that we were in the poorhouse. I had nothing to put in there. While we were in Japan all my sisters and brothers got married and they got all the family stuff. That was fine with us, but I didn't have even a tea towel to put in there. So I did everything from blueprints with an interior designer in Birmingham, and when we moved in, in January 1966, everything was up here. We had the place cleaned, everything moved in, had our little boys, and we had a baby girl. I put her to bed, and the little boys got to stay up all night with us while we put everything in place, all the things for their bedrooms. Probably the most exciting night of our life.

So, down the road, here we go into the culinary part of it, how I got to know Julia Child, Simone Beck, and have a cooking school in Napa Valley with two chefs from San Francisco. It was all because of a lady called Aileen Martin from Tulsa, Oklahoma, who owned a farmhouse across from us in Glen Arbor, across the road. She had a beautiful peachy-colored house. I thought nobody in Michigan would ever paint anything peachy color. Her house was on the walk, and I was taking tennis lessons, and I had a sitter who would come, because Don was a great tennis player and I was lousy. So I was taking tennis lessons at the Homestead, and I had a sitter who came every Thursday morning. That was the day of Aileen's cooking classes. But when I went through her house—and we still laugh about that—(and I'll be seeing her in Palm Beach later this winter and stay with her), we still laugh about how I came, and I had my tennis clothes on. Remember those days when we wore the little frilly tennis clothes? Anyway, my hair in what we called "buffies." I had long blond hair, and I had two elastics because I was playing tennis. She said I bounced in.

She had a hex sign on her barn, on her garage. It was painted a really wonderful barn red with a hex sign. And she had "Red Barn Cooking School" on it as her sign. I looked at the place and I fell in love with it. They had a porcelain fireplace, free-standing. And everything was from France. Much like what I have here. I fell in love with the house. I fell in love with the furniture. And actually fell in love with Aileen because I said to her: "Do you teach cooking?"

And she said, "Yes."

I said, "Pennsylvania Dutch?"

She said, "Heavens, no! French."

And I went, "Oh, good," because that's what I was interested in, coming from a French background. My father was truly a gourmet. He loved fine food. And I have that in my blood. So I said, "Could I take your classes?"

Now this is a funny story. She thought I was the Swedish au pair for the Lampierres, who are from Indiana. They have a big estate on Glen Lake. They were our neighbors. Their huge estate is still there, with boat houses, tennis courts, everything. They had hired a Swedish girl to be an au pair with their grandchildren that summer, and to help with the cooking. She liked to cook. So at any rate that's who they thought I was. And I had to get back after the class. Aileen had clients. I couldn't talk to her in her open house. She thought I couldn't afford the classes, which I think in those days were all of $12 a class. Now she charges over $100.

But at any rate, so she said that yes, I could. She asked, "Do you know how to cook?" And I said, "I know how to cook."

So she said, "Sure, she knows how to cook." So I came on Thursday morning and she said, "Bring an apron."

So I said, "Well, okay." And I had received as a gift an apron from somebody who went to the Cordon Bleu. So I wore my Cordon Bleu apron. Also, when I married Donald and started having children, he wanted me to have a very safe car, so I had a Mercedes, a chocolate brown Mercedes.

Well, Aileen thought I was driving Mrs. Lampierre's car, because I wouldn't have a car as an au pair from Sweden and had borrowed Mrs. Lampierre's apron. So I was in the back. I was chopping and getting things ready. She'd say, "Give me the butter. Get me this out of the refrigerator. Chop this, do this." And I was working as fast as I could. So she really liked the work I did. But afterward, I was waiting to talk to her. Actually, I was going to say to her: "Don't I owe you something?" or whatever, but she was talking to all her friends. So I just said, "Can I come again?" And she said, "Next Thursday."

I show up next Thursday, same apron, same car, and they still think I'm an au pair. And afterward I had to bounce off because I had a babysitter. I had given up my tennis to do the cooking, and I had a babysitter. So I just went out and: "Next Thursday?" She said, "Fine," but she looked at me, and I worried. Maybe she doesn't like what I'm doing. Maybe I'm not doing it right. And I just worried about it, but I thought no, I did everything right, or I think I did.

And then I got there on Thursday, and she and her husband are sitting in the living room, and they said, "Who are you?" I wondered, what did I do?

And I said, "My name is Carol Worsley."

She said, "You are Swedish, aren't you?"

I said, "Oh, no! Where did you ever hear that? I'm Finnish."

She said, "You're Finnish?" And I thought, why is she so surprised? What difference does it make?

So they said, "We know you are Carol."

I said, "Yes, I'm Carol Worsley."

"Where do you live? Do you work at the Lampierres'?"

I said, "No. I live down the road."

"Where?" Well, they wanted to see that darling little cottage. There were old cottages that I wish we'd been able to buy. Ours was new and fresh and wonderful and done by one of our architects. She said, "Oh, we've been wanting to see that."

So we laughed, and they said, "We thought you were the Lampierres' au pair."

"Well," I said, "I can see the resemblance, blond hair, blue eyes." I was all of thirty, I think, or maybe thirty-two, but she was a lot younger than me, probably a teenager.

That's how we met and got to know each other. I helped her for the rest of the summer. And then the next summer. And the next summer she said to me—and I found out that she knew Julia Child and she knew Simone Beck—she said, "How would you like to come to France this fall?"

And I said, "Oh, no," because my daughter was so little. She was probably about three. So I said: "I'm sorry, my children are much too little for me to leave."

She said, "Well, that's too bad, because I was going to introduce you to Simone Beck and Julia Child."

Well, let me tell you . . . they were my heroes, along with James Beard, Craig Claiborne from New York, the list goes on and on. I said, "Oh, wait, let me talk to Don about it."

I told Don about it and he said, "You've got to go. Call your mom."

So I called my mom and I said, "Mom, do you think you could come around the beginning of September?"

She said, "Of course, honey. Dad won't be able to come, but he'll come down if I need him." And my dad did that, because he wanted to spend every minute he could with the grandkids. I had a wonderful black maid who had worked for me for years and years. She always called herself my black sister, Martha. Martha was going to be there, and I also had an Irish babysitter, Doritty, who would help my mom. It was a glorious time for my mother, no cleaning, cooking, just to be with my family and really get to know my kids.

So that started my career going. I met Simone Beck and fell in love with her. She was the same age as my mother. It seems strange to say that from this perspective. And Julia was around the same age. My mother was born in 1913. It just started a love affair. And Donald always had a guilt complex because I didn't get to go to the University of Michigan.

I would go to France for short periods of time. When I went to the Cordon Bleu I took three-week increments over a number of years to get through the Cordon Bleu. And then I went to La Varenne in Paris, which was sponsored by James Beard, Simone Beck, and Julia. But I did that kind of like a spy. Anne Willan was running it, this wonderful English woman. It's kind of tough to deal with the French sometimes financially, and the figures weren't working out right. They trusted Anne; they knew it wasn't Anne, but they knew something wasn't right. Well, I'll tell you what happened. These American kids were coming over there and working for free living in little garrets. That was all they could afford, to room together and work for free. But they were helping themselves out of the larder big time. One of them I caught when I went downstairs one day to go to the larder to get something for one of the chefs. She was eating a truffle, a whole truffle. Now we all know that a truffle is a fungus. You can eat a whole mushroom, but you don't eat a whole truffle. It's a little bit like eating a car tire because of the consistency.

Well, I came back from that trip, and Julia—Simca always stayed with me—but Julia always preferred to stay in the Michigan Inn or a hotel because Paul was with her, and Paul didn't like to stay with people. She always traveled with this bright red wok. She would make their breakfast, in the bathroom, there in the hotel. They always had little refrigerators in the rooms. Anyway, she called me, and she said, "I know you've been to La Varenne and you found there were some problems." She said, "I'd like to talk to you." I invited her for lunch, but she said, "No, I have to stay here. Paul is here. Would you come down to the Michigan Inn?"

There was a fellow called Harlan Peterson, Pete Peterson, who had the restaurant Tapawingo in Elsworth, and now he has a new restaurant called Alliance, right there by Indigo in Traverse City. I heard that he had been there. He was still an executive for Ford Motor Company, but he was so interested in cooking that he'd gone to La Varenne and then spoken glowingly about it. So I called him. It was in the morning. And I said, "Are you free for lunch today?" Julia had said to come down, and she would make a little lunch, and she did, right there in the hotel.

And Pete said, "Oh, Carol, I can't. You know, I'm at work. Could we do this some other day?"

And I said, "Oh, too bad, because I was going to introduce you to Julia Child."

He said, "Where? When? I'll be there."

So when I was in Alliance this summer just before going to California, I saw Pete and I said, "Do you remember me? Carol Worsley? Every time I went to Tapawingo you weren't there. I would ask for you, but it was just your night off, I guess." I only went about two or three times. I said, "Do you remember me?"

"Of course I do. You are the woman that introduced me to Julia Child, and that woman changed my life."

I felt so good about that. Julia made such an impression on him. I had to leave because again I had children coming home from school, but Pete stayed longer. I invited another gal who was a cooking teacher from Birmingham who was kind of on the cusp about it. The instructors at La Varenne were good. It was taught all in French. She thought they could have done a better job by having somebody interpret, not trying to stumble along with what French we had or they had.

Then I started teaching. Donald built this wonderful home for us on the ravine and river right in the heart of Birmingham. And he built the kitchen so I could teach. Otherwise, I was traveling with Simca. I went to Seattle with Julia. She was doing a thing at the Pike Street Market. It was thrilling. I was part of the crew, but I was unpaid crew. I wouldn't have dreamed of asking for anything. I was just thrilled to do it.

While we were there they had a cocktail party for Julia in their aquarium. And because she liked oysters, they had oysters on all the different levels. I followed her around all night, just trying what she was trying, and listening to what she was saying. It seems like a large number, but I think they said they had twenty-seven different kinds. I didn't know there were twenty-seven different kinds, but I love oysters. Anyway, I learned to love oysters.

Then Simca would travel. She came to Birmingham twice to a club that I belong to—a very lovely women's club in a beautiful setting—to teach cooking. And then when she would teach in Tulsa at the Petroleum Club—because the Martins were from Tulsa—I would go down there and assist her. And then at the Women's Athletic Club or Women's City Club in Chicago. I just became her girl. She didn't have children, you know. Her husband was a prisoner of war for six years, the whole stretch of the Germans, and they couldn't have children after that.

She and Julia were very open. That book and movie where they said she wouldn't have liked, *Julie & Julia*. I knew that wasn't true. I think they did it to add sensationalism. Maybe they were told that; I don't know. But I know it was not true, and I didn't like that at all.

Simca was very tall and statuesque. She was born in a château in Normandy. Her father was a French industrialist. She had an English nanny from the time she was born. She spoke impeccable English with just the trace of an accent. It was perfect. I used to tease her. I said, "Gee, Simca, I'd become as famous as you if I had that accent." And of course Julia's voice . . . At any rate, they were more than open.

When we were down in Saint Louis—where I took my French boards; I mean my chef boards years and years ago—my son had challenged me. I said, "I'll do it out of town," because I was going to be in that area. I had so much fun. Julia and I and Marguerite Mondavi went off one night. For some reason Marguerite was driving. I don't know why; she had flown there. She was driving a station wagon. Maybe she had borrowed it, because it wasn't a rental car.

We wanted to put Julia in the front seat. The other people who were invited to go with us were all dressed up in high heels and hose, and they had to crawl into the back of the station wagon. We wanted Ethiopian food. We'd never had Ethiopian food. We took Julia for Ethiopian food.

Michael James was the protégé of Simone Beck. I traveled with Michael and Simca. His partner was this redheaded guy called Billy Cross. I went to Europe with Michael and Billy, and we went to southwest France, outside of Pau, near Lourdes, and the Roquefort caves. We had a cooking school in Napa, and chefs would come to Napa, like Michel Guérard, whose parents owned the spa called Eugénie les Bains near Pau. Michel Guérard came to Napa to teach at the cooking school. We were partners with Billy and Michael, because my husband was backing us, along with Alayne Martin and many other people.

I went out for the French chefs and the Italian chefs. Of course Julia and Simca kicked it off. They were there first, and they were wonderful. All the vintners came, because that was before the French Laundry. There really wasn't even a good restaurant in Napa at the time. There was no cooking school. So the vintners were thrilled to have us, and in truth, we never bought a bottle of wine. We had cases of wine from Schramberg, Beringer's, Mondavi—he was our main supporter with the wine.

Alice Waters came, but she was not there in the spring and the fall, and I could only go in the spring and the fall. I could go in the spring before the children got out of school, and I could go in the fall when they were back in school. My kids were getting older. Mother always came to stay with the kids, and Martha and Dorrity. Don was there. Then he'd come out afterward so we'd have a little vacation together. I was just recently in Chez Panisse. I've never had a bucket list, but when I was out there I said to my friend, Kay Hendry, who lives near Sausalito: "I guess I have a bucket list, because this is on my bucket list."

But I never got to meet Alice Waters. She came at least twice, I think, to the cooking school, but I wasn't able to come then. But Chez

Panisse was my dream. We had the most wonderful dinner. They just do the one menu. We were in the restaurant downstairs. Upstairs is the à la carte café, but I was taking them for dinner, and I wanted them to have the prix fixe menu. So that's what we did. I had in my mind what Chez Panisse was going to look like. It didn't look anything like that. It looked very Frank Lloyd Wright. The ceilings and the woodwork and the art deco-ish looking wall sconces were gorgeous. I felt like a kid in a candy store.

So, to bring it back here to Glen Arbor, we had our cottage on Glen Lake and I always looked at this house. The house was very plain, no gardens to speak of, but the backyard was all lawn and fruit trees. It was very attractive. I would look at this place and say, "Honey, that house needs a porch. And it needs a stone wall." Jill Ball lived here. She had an antique store. We came over several times and I bought a few things from her, a few primitives for the cottage. I loved this setting. I could show you a picture of what it used to look like because it was in a magazine, *Country Living*, a number of years ago. Jill gave me the copy. But it was very plain.

One Sunday we were heading back to Birmingham when Donald said, "Let's stop by the Balls to see Jill."

I said, "Oh, honey, let's not do this to her again. We're not buying the house and we don't need any more antiques."

He said, "Well, let's just stop by and see her."

He and Jill loved to talk. It was an interesting combination because she's an ultraliberal and Don's an ultraconservative, but Don liked to talk to everybody, and she liked talking to him. So they were having a wonderful conversation and I'm looking at antiques and having a wonderful time, and then I walked into the kitchen thinking it's time to get on the road. So I walk into the kitchen, and Jill's got this big smile on her face. I thought: "Oh, what's going on here?"

I said, "What's up?"

And she said, "You just bought a house."

I was weak at the knees. "This house?!?"

She said, "Well, what else?"

This is really funny because she didn't have any formal paper in the house. So they got out a piece of scratch paper, and Don wrote a little contract. He had his checkbook with him, and he wrote her a down payment. He wanted to sew it up. It had been on the market for four years and had come down to a very reasonable price. This was in 1997. So all the way back to Birmingham I am just stunned. Don loved to surprise you. He surprised me many times with many things. He was just the most wonderful man in the world. Really. I realize how indulged I was, how kind and wonderful he was to me.

I always worked with him. I was told I was the best unpaid secretary. He had a secretary for thirty years. Four years ago Marilyn passed away, and that's when I gave up the little shop, the Thyme Out shop, so I could work for Don because he needed me. I'm glad I did, because now I more or less know what I'm doing. We were just finishing Indigo Hotel in Traverse City. I have to hang in there until it's finished.

Don said, "Well, I thought we'd have fun restoring that house. I know you like to decorate. I'll do the practical stuff." He did all the plumbing and new wiring and got all that done. All this furniture is from my Birmingham house. We didn't know we were going to sell the Birmingham house, but after we bought this I said to him one night: "Donald, what do you think about me having a B&B?" He said, "I thought you'd get around to that."

"What do you think?"

He said, "It's completely up to you. It's your house." And it is my house. I mean, I've put it into the trust now, but everything is in my name here. He said, "Are you sure you want to do that?"

And I said, "Well, let me try it. It's not like going to prison. If it doesn't work for us I won't do it, or if you don't like me doing it, I won't do it." And I said, "Promise me that in the summer you won't be gone more than a couple of days."

He said, "Okay, three days, four at the most." He wanted to go on with his business. He wanted to give up the contracting, and as soon as we finish Indigo and another retirement village at Grosse Pointe, contracting is out of our lives. But he was going to go on with his designing and with the design consultancy. I think he wanted to keep me busy.

So that's what I'm doing now. I decided to have a B&B. I've had it now for about twelve years. I love it. The people who come here are the nicest people. I've only had one person in all these years—a young man who came to a wedding—that I would not have in my house again. But that's it. I love what I do, and really I do see the Lord's hand in this.

Don and I both have very deep faith. I can see how everything happened, how it worked out.

I don't teach classes here. I teach cooking classes in Birmingham at a club or I teach in my friends' kitchens. Or I teach in other people's kitchens when they want to have a cooking class. But in the last four years since I've been working for Don I haven't done any of that. But then this winter again I'll be back teaching cooking.

It certainly wasn't my plan. I never had a plan. After I found out I wasn't going to the University of Michigan I didn't have a plan in my whole life. I was just going to go on with whatever life handed me. My mother would say, "Fat, dumb, and happy, Carol." But I had a wonderful man who took care of me, my husband. And now I have this. It's quite different without him, but . . .

RECIPE

Simca's Scotch Whiskey Chocolate Cake

RECIPE ADAPTED BY CAROL WORSLEY

¼ cup raisins

¼ cup scotch whiskey

7 ounces German's Sweet Chocolate (chopped)

½ cup unsalted butter

3 eggs separated

⅔ cup white sugar

4½ tablespoons cake flour

⅔ cup finely ground almonds

Macerate raisins in scotch. Place chocolate in double boiler with 3 tablespoons water and stir until smooth. Remove from heat. Stir in butter one tablespoon at a time, incorporating each piece thoroughly. Beat egg yolks adding sugar gradually until pale yellow. Cool chocolate slightly and add to egg mixture beating constantly. Add flour mixed with the ground almonds, then stir in the macerated raisins. Beat egg whites with the salt until stiff but not dry. Stir ⅓ of whites into chocolate to lighten then fold in the rest.

Butter an 8½-inch cake pan well and dust with flour and add batter. Preheat oven to 375 degrees and place cake on middle level. Bake for 20–25 minutes. Center should be moist and outside firm. Cool cake for 15 minutes and unmold on cake rack and cool overnight.

Icing recipe

6 ounces German's Sweet Chocolate

6 tablespoons confectioner's sugar

6 tablespoons unsalted butter

Place chocolate in double boiler and add 2½ tablespoons water. Melt until smooth and add butter one tablespoon at a time. Sift sugar into chocolate gradually and blend well and spread on cake.

Photo by Tyler Shumway

17

Nancy Krcek Allen

Chef-educator Nancy Krcek Allen's mother was Ukrainian, her father Czech. This fueled her passion for international cuisines. She has traveled around the world to study them. Nancy has worked in kitchens and classrooms since 1985. She graduated from the California Culinary Academy in San Francisco. While working in New York City, she taught recreational and professional cooking for the Institute of Culinary Education (ICE) and the Natural Gourmet Institute in Manhattan, and in Viareggio, Italy. Allen has owned a restaurant, cooking school, and catering business, and has worked as a freelance writer for various publications. She taught for a decade at Château Chantal Winery Cooking School on Old Mission Peninsula and at Northwestern Michigan College, both in Traverse City. She is the author of the culinary textbook *Discovering Global Cuisines: Traditional Flavors and Techniques.* She currently volunteers at an organic farm and works as a freelance writer.

Nancy Krcek Allen, b. March 31, 1951
Interview: August 25, 2015
West School Lake Road, Maple City

Writing is still my favorite thing,
to be able to express myself in words.

I was born in Centerline, Michigan. My mother used to call it "the hole of the doughnut" of Warren, Michigan. My dad was in the auto industry. He worked for GM Fisher Body. My life was very much an immigrant community. My parents were from Ukraine and Czechoslovakia. My dad came over from Czechoslovakia with his brothers when he was about ten, so he spoke English and went to school here. He was pretty young and so he wasn't as deeply embedded in his culture as my mother was. She was seventeen when she came to this country, and she had left a full, rich life. She loved to sing and dance and she had a lot of friends. So when she came to this country I think she felt pretty forlorn even though she came to an auntie she knew well, and she went directly to their farm outside of Detroit. The only thing she really knew how to do because she was the youngest in a family of four was to cook. Her mother had always put her in the kitchen when they went out in the field all day to work. They had a small farm.

So my mom knew how to cook. And that was something that stayed with her for her entire life, a love of cooking. And when she was at my grandparents'—I called them my grandparents, but it was really my great-aunt and my great-uncle—at their farm outside of Detroit, they had animals, they had all kinds of vegetables in a big garden. So I grew up with all of that. As I aged I was really interested in art and drawing horses, animals and those things. I loved food, but my mother would never let me in the kitchen. I had to watch a lot.

She would hand-make everything. She made pierogi, she made borscht. She would make cakes. She had a neighbor who was Italian. The Italian neighbor came over and taught her how to make lasagna and pasta and what have you, and my mom would go over there and show this lady how to make chicken soup and pierogis and stuffed cabbage. My food life was really pretty rich as a child. I had homemade bread every week. My mom never bought anything in the store if she could help it. She had a big garden in the backyard. I can still remember her digging up beets out of that rich, dark clay that they have in the Detroit area.

Ukrainians love to sing. My mom was in choirs. I was in a choir with her, but I also had this love of food. It kind of came out in an art way, but I don't think I really understood what it was.

I went to Michigan State, took art, but it didn't move me enough. I went to Europe for a year and traveled around, and, again, there came the food. I lived on Crete with some friends for a year. We lived in a small village, and I met people who later became well known in the food industry. We would just get food. I'd walk along the beach, and somebody would throw an octopus at me, so I learned how to cook octopus. We traveled around to a lot of different countries. I really learned different foods. We stayed for several weeks in the south of France where one of the people traveling with us had an aunt and uncle. I had my first salade niçoise there. It was a great trip and very influential in my life. I felt like I was going back to my roots in Europe.

I kind of bummed around after this trip and then went back to school thinking I would finish my art degree, but I never did. I was trying to find something to do and ended up cutting hair, another creative pursuit. I went to barber's school. It was wonderful to work with my hands. I made a lot of money and worked at that job for eighteen years off and on. I had my own salon in Traverse City, eventually. I worked in Detroit first and then moved up here. But if you go into a salon you probably know for yourself that there are two things that we always talk about in salons: exercise and food, diet and food.

I started to get really revved up about food again. I had moved to California when I was married for a couple of years, and then I moved back here. And when I moved back I had the salon but I couldn't get California out of my mind. I had lived in the Bay Area. I devised a plan to lease my salon to the gal who worked with me and to go out to California and go to culinary school, which I did. I went to the California Culinary Academy in San Francisco for a two-year program. I met many people and I learned a lot. I lived in Berkeley, and that was exciting. I had a chance to go to the Culinary Institute of America in New York—but the food scene there wasn't as exciting to me as San Francisco. California's food is just phenomenal. I went to the culinary school in '85 and graduated in '87.

After that I came back here to the Traverse City area, and I worked at Hattie's, which was in Suttons Bay at that time, for Jim Milliman, for almost two years. I was teaching a little bit, but I just felt frustrated. At this point I am married already to my artist husband, and he's wanting to go to New York. So eventually he went to New York for a month and stayed at the Art Students League, and when he came back he said, "I'd really like to move to New York for a year."

I said, "Oh, really? Okay, I could dig that. There's culinary schools there that I would like to visit, and see if I could get a job."

I was terrified. I was screaming terrified, out of my wits. And Glen Wolf, who is an artist, had lived there, and I was cutting his hair one day—because I still cut hair on the side—and he said, "You know, Nancy, in New York, you are head and shoulders above everybody else if you just show up and do what you say you are going to do." He said, "Most people just don't come through." So I thought: "Well, I can do that. I'm really reliable."

My husband found a studio in Brooklyn under a bridge, an area called DUMBO: District under the Brooklyn-Manhattan Bridge Overpass. The studio was a really scary-looking place. It looked like a place where they would shoot *The X-Files*. My husband was firmly ensconced there, and I found a place for us to live, where we lived for about a year or two. What was supposed to be one year ended up being five. You can never go to Manhattan or New York and live for just one year. It's not enough. You are just beginning to taste it. Over those five years I worked at the Institute for Culinary Education. It was called Peter Kump's at that time. I worked full time for them even though I didn't have a contract. I was freelance. I also worked for the Natural Gourmet Institute. Luckily, these two schools were about a block apart in midtown Manhattan.

They always say that you retain about 50 percent of what you do hands-on, but you retain 75 to 80 percent of what you teach. I thought teaching was one of the best learning techniques I'd ever encountered. It was really an eye-opening experience. I met a lot of people, and I worked on curriculum for the program at ICE. I did their entire Asian and Indian section for their professional program, and I wanted to keep writing. At that point I had been writing some pieces for Anne Stanton. I'd written some restaurant reviews for her, and when I moved to New York she tracked me down. She was working for *Forward* magazine and asked if I would like to do some cookbook reviews. I said, "Sure." They don't pay very much, but it was way fun, and I got a lot of free books. Writing was something I was trying to develop.

For the Asian curriculum I had traveled some, but it was really more just through studying that I developed an expertise. I was smitten with Japanese food and Chinese food. And I had lived in San Francisco. I ate in every sushi bar and Chinese restaurant I could. But it was mostly home study.

I took a lot of writing classes here before I moved to New York because I was frustrated that I really didn't know how to write. I took Writing Down the Bones, a class run by Duncan Spratt and Mary Knight. That really freed me up. I took classes through NMC, creative writing, and then eventually I did a week at Omega with William Least Heat-Moon. That was phenomenal. "Writing is re-writing." I think that was the title of it. So my writing skills were really starting to come into play when I got offered this opportunity to write curriculum at PK's, or ICE, as they call it now.

My husband's mother was ill at this point, and we were starting to get ready to come home. Both of us really wanted to come back. New York was exciting but it was also a real drain on us. I had already turned fifty or was close to fifty, and everybody was ten to fifteen years younger than we were. We were exhausted by New York City. We had a great apartment. We were in Brooklyn, a first-floor apartment with a garden and everything, but it just wasn't home.

My husband moved home first. He was back here for six months caring for his mother. Eventually I couldn't stand it anymore and I came back, too. I got a lot of flak from the people at ICE. My boss was mad at me because they had invested a lot of money in me. They had sent me to China, actually, before I did this curriculum, for two weeks with Barbara Tropp. It was an amazing trip. It was eye-opening for me. It was like an affirmation of all the things I had studied when I saw them in real life. I saw how close to it I really was. I am a reader, and you can learn so much from good cookbooks, and the *Time-Life* series.

We moved back here. I had purchased a building two years prior to moving back with the thought that I would open a restaurant, and I was leasing it out. When we moved back I turned it into a restaurant. I gutted the downstairs and put in a commercial kitchen. It was so much fun. Putting together the restaurant, the people; everything was great, except the staffing. I was no good at that. I should have had somebody running it and me be just the chef so I didn't have to deal with the people part. I was a wreck. And eventually, that stress, after a couple of years, just broke me down. I closed the restaurant portion, but I remained doing catering, food carryout. I also had cooking classes there, which is what I wanted to do to begin with. I really only had the restaurant portion of it in order to have cooking classes.

I continued to teach, and then about a year after I closed the restaurant I was approached by Liz Berger, one of the people at Château Chantal. She asked me if I'd be willing to put in a cooking school there. That really got me excited. At this point I'm writing for the *Record Eagle*, too, an article every other week. They are paying me really well for them. I got to do research for each of these articles—the food section—and they let me write whatever I wanted. They didn't edit heavily. I would usually make the food, and then a photographer would come and take photos of it.

The cooking school was hard work because they were five-hour classes as I had taught in New York. Eventually I got the proper staffing, they set up tables for me, and we got everything right and tight. I stayed there ten years, and then things just kind of fell apart. I was having a lot of problems with rheumatoid arthritis in my hands, a lot of pain. My sidekick, Lynne Brach, who became my coteacher, helped me a lot with things I couldn't do. She would do some of the demos when my hands were really bad. But eventually I had to let go of it. It wasn't working for me anymore.

While it lasted, all those classes were phenomenal. We would do twelve dishes. Usually we would do European food: Italian, French, soup classes. "I like meat" was a really popular one. We'd have a butcher come in and talk about the primal cuts and all of that. It was really fun. I taught a lot until the teaching became too hard for me.

Château Chantal had sent me to a North American Travel Journalists conference where someone had invited me to speak. They actually paid for my plane fare to Cleveland. I got to speak, and I met all these wonderful people, and one of them had told me she had just finished a textbook on career changing and midlife.

I thought: "How cool is that?" and I said to her, "I really want to write a textbook."

And she said, "Well, let me hook you up with my editor at Pearson."

And I said, "Really?"

And she said, "Yeah. If you've got a good idea they will take it."

So a week later I had a phone conversation with her editor, and he said, "I like what I'm hearing." I was pitching him an international cuisines book that was technique-driven, and he liked that. He didn't have anything in his lineup that was like that. He turned out to be a really cool guy. I just love him. I loved my editor there at Pearson. The book took five years. I had thought it was going to take only two. In the middle of it I went to India for a month. It was a labor of love. Huge. I don't know how we did it. I look back at it, and it was just this enormous passion I had inside of me that I had to get out.

Being an artist, my husband works every day. But me, it's like I just spit this whole thing out. I worked at it for five years, and now I'm doing small things. I don't know if I'd ever have the energy to do an enormous project like that again. It was really time-consuming; it consumed me. For five years I pretty much only did that. I taught a little bit here and there. Also when I moved back from New York I started working on Fridays at Meadowlark Farm, which is an organic farm in Lake Leelanau, a CSA, and eventually they asked me instead of picking kale and picking bugs off of stuff, weeding, if I would like to cook for them on Fridays for lunch. And I said, "Hallelujah! Yeah. Love to." So over the years—that's probably been about seven years now—I cooked every Friday for them.

We started off with a two-burner gas stove that only had "high" and "off." Eventually, I persuaded them to get me a four-burner stove, and then countertops. There was a sink in there, thank goodness, and so now it's like "Whoa! A real kitchen, a full country kitchen." I continue to go there every Friday from June 1 until October 15. And I get a box of this amazing, wonderful food. Jenny Tutlis and Jon Watts run Meadowlark. They've been hugely instrumental in my life, a big influence, because I have a source of really fresh food. And what chef wouldn't get excited about being in this environment at least once a week and being able to just say, "Bring me this; bring me that." Every Monday I text Jenny and I say, "Okay, what's up this week?"

This week it's artichokes, tomatoes, and squash blossoms. So I'm going to do a tomato-mozzarella salad. With basil. They have lots of basil. I'm going to do stuffed squash blossoms. I like to bake them because they get really luscious. I stuff them with rice and vegetables. And then I'll do a black bean chili for them, because it's cold this week, which will use their tomatoes and onions. And then stuffed artichokes, or maybe steamed artichokes with tarragon butter. I don't know. It's really fun to think up menus. At this point I have so much crowding my head that it's really fun and easy to be impromptu like that.

What's also developed is that I teach there. People come and want to work with me. They'll sign up for the entire summer. I have two women right now who are dedicated to coming every week so I have helpers. I don't have to do everything, which would be hard. Usually I feed between fifteen and twenty. This year it's been more like twenty to twenty-five but now it's starting to dissipate. That's really been key to my life. I tested a lot of recipes for my textbook there.

I was a hairdresser for about eighteen years, so that was an artistic influence, too. My husband is a sculptor, and that was another influence. I had wanted to do more plating and working in restaurants, but it just never happened. That's such a male-dominated career. It's hard for women. The hours are tough, but I wish I could have done more of that. One of the experiences that I had in culinary school—I was doing an apprenticeship concurrently with the last term of culinary school—I went into Fleur de Lis, and the chef there was French, Hubert Keller. He's famous and he's now on TV. Hubert was kind of running the restaurant. He wasn't in the kitchen a lot. The sous chef was pretty much running the kitchen, so here I come in, I'm an apprentice. At this point I was paying probably $100 a week for parking, and I'm not getting paid—this is of course an unpaid apprenticeship—but I'm the first woman who has ever been in this kitchen and probably their first apprentice as well. There was a Japanese man on the garde-manger, and he was nice to me, always giving me Japanese things because he knew I loved Japanese food. But Rick, the sous chef, had me chopping parsley every day. I'd come in and there'd be a load of parsley waiting for me. One day he walked by me after I had been there for like two weeks chopping parsley, and he said, "How are you doing, Nance?" and I said, "Not so well."

And he said, "Why?"

And I said, "Because after two weeks I'm still here chopping parsley."

And he looked at me, and he just walked away, and that night I was on the hot line, which is what you come there for, to get experience on the hot line. I had been on the garde-manger line, which was great—it's the cold station with all the salads and the meat and everything. I enjoyed that, but I wanted to get on the hot line before my apprenticeship was over. After that, I didn't have to be mean or angry—it was really a revelation—that I could just ask for what I wanted.

That was great. I went on to do a couple more apprenticeships with two other chefs. One was at a vegetarian restaurant in Marin County. But it was always hard being a woman. The guys in the kitchen hung together, and they had this guy-club and treated me as a doofy young woman. I had just gone through culinary school but that didn't mean I had skills. I knew what I knew, but I hadn't used it and really solidified it. They made fun of me a lot, but I just kept plugging along. That's one thing I have: determination. I don't give up. I never give up.

That's how I could write a book that took five years. It's enormous. It's like nine hundred pages, a textbook, twenty cuisines. I love to do research and I had many people who helped me out, too, over the years, with support. The first instructor—the head of instruction at ICE—gave me the opportunity. He sent me to China and gave me the opportunity to write a curriculum. When I came home to Michigan, Jenny from Meadowlark would drop produce off to me. I had friends always coming in, and if I wasn't there and I needed something done, and they lived in town, they would run in for me.

The community is huge here. That's what's so beautiful about living here. There's an enormous community. When I was in the food industry really heavily here, there weren't many women in it yet that were like me, who were educated women who knew what they were up to, or had their own, like Martha, but now there are. I wish that I were starting a restaurant now with some of these women like Madeleine Vedel and Martha Ryan and Rose Hollander. It's a great community with a lot of talent.

Of all these things that I've done, probably the writing is my favorite accomplishment. I think I'm an accomplished cook. I have very good taste buds and a good eye for fresh food. I have a deep knowledge of technique from having worked all those years in New York, which honed my technique and my knowledge about food. And I'm always open to new things. But I love to write.

I met a young German man here, Christopher Melz—I was a little nervous working with him, a young man, a chef now, and he's in that guys-club kind of thing—but we talked about putting together a book on oils. We worked together in the kitchen. It was fun and it reinforced the fact that I do have the skills. As the woman in that French movie—it's during the war and she's sent to Norway—*Babette's Feast*. At the end she says, "You know, they can take away everything from me, but they can't take away my art."

I don't feel like anybody is trying to take away anything from me, maybe just aging and life does that, but I feel that the knowledge I have gained and the skills I've gained are always going to be with me. Writing is still my favorite thing, to be able to express myself in words. Maybe someday I'll do something else with writing. I'm working on another cookbook, but that's safe. My husband keeps saying, "You should think about writing a novel." I don't know. I took many classes at NMC and through Grand Valley about creative writing. I even took a class on writing a novel, but I don't seem to be really sparked for it although it would be fun to write something outside of the food realm. But that's what I know, and they always say to write about what you know. Food is what I know.

My hands are painful. I have already had surgery on one wrist, and I'm going to have surgery on the left wrist. I don't have the dexterity I used to have, especially with chopping and twisting things and lifting things. I have to have other people lift for me. But even though that has slowed me down, it hasn't stopped me. I just plow right through it. If you have a passion, even though you might have some sort of a disability, you can push through it. That's what this disability has taught me. I still have this passion deep inside.

The local and organic food movement has changed everything. I've lived up here forty years, and in 1976 when I first moved up here there was nothing. I mean, you could get corn and potatoes and beets and cabbage locally. There were a few people who were beginning to grow some organic things, but it was very few and far between. It was hard to find. And everybody was still eating lake fish. I ate my share of it. Perch was wonderful, walleye. But there really wasn't much of a local movement other than fruit, cherries, all sprayed, of course, heavily. There was no farmers market. And I wasn't as aware of how bad that was. My parents never used chemicals. They were pretty aware. My dad used a spray on the lawn, but never in the garden. So I was kind of aware of it, and I was a health foodie. But I don't think we knew the extent of the chemicals at that time.

Sonny Swanson had a stand on M-22 probably about the time I moved here, which has been about twenty-six years. I don't remember what year the farmers market started, but it wasn't very long ago. I don't think the farmers market in Traverse City has been there more than about ten or fifteen years. It just kind of slowly blossomed with a few people, and then Jenny and Jon were the first CSA in Leelanau County. That really shifted everything. I think the year I went to New York, which was 1996, that may have been the year they started their CSA.

So it's been a long time, almost twenty years. The local food thing has just blossomed in the last twenty years. Now we have food trucks. I was in a small restaurant a couple of days ago with a friend, the Harvest, near Union Street Station, on that alley at the back, and I felt like I was in New York or Toronto or somewhere. My girlfriend kept saying, "Nancy, introduce yourself to them. Tell them who you are." I said, "No, I don't really want to." You know, that old thing about that male dominance thing. I didn't want to go up there and make myself vulnerable. Finally she goes up to the chef and says hi to him, and she says, "This is my friend. She's a chef." He said, "What do you do?" And I said, "Well, I wrote a textbook. I'm not really working in a restaurant anymore." And he didn't ask about it. He didn't care. I've come across that so often, particularly with men in restaurants, this really kind of snooty attitude, and it makes me feel sad that there can't be more camaraderie. I think many of us in the food industry are really insecure. I guess every industry has its insecurities. So I don't usually reveal who I am.

But by the same token I was at the farmers market, and the same friend had introduced me to an older woman friend of hers, and she said, "Oh, I didn't catch your name. What's your name?" And Margie says, "This is Nancy Allen," and she exclaims, "Nancy Allen! I read your column every week. Can I touch you?" So I laughed and I said, "You are terribly kind." So there it is. Both ways. I still write for the *Record Eagle*, biweekly, every other week. It's really fun. I chose not to get paid this time because I want to keep the rights to my columns. If I give them the rights, they are gone, and they can publish them anywhere, and I don't get paid. In any case I would only get a pittance, and I said, "I'm not giving away my columns for a pittance. You can have them, but can't republish."

I'm still doing that. I spend a lot of time at home relaxing and reading. I read a lot about food. I try to stay current with it, but this CSA cookbook right now and cooking for Meadowlark and writing for the newspaper are the three main things I do right now. The recipes for the CSA book are things that are simpler but elegant, and make really good use of the foods that come throughout the season. I like always to give people options to change things. For instance, I included a really simple zucchini soup—puréed zucchini soup—which just has onions, zucchini, thyme, and chicken stock. I tell them: "If you don't have enough zucchini, use carrots or turnips." When you have produce that comes in a box you don't get to choose it. Whatever is fresh that week is what you have. "Kale? Okay, cook that, purée that." I want to give people the confidence to do that. I'm hoping the CSA book will do that.

When I had the last surgery on this wrist, I was unable to use it for six to eight weeks. My right hand was in a cast. So various girlfriends jumped in and said, "Can I come over? Just tell me what to do, and I'll chop for you or whatever." There was a lineup of helpers for eight weeks. One friend a week came, and I would choose something I wanted to test. They would get half, and we would keep half. That was way fun. It was like private teaching. I continue to keep my hand in with teaching. Teaching and mentoring are a natural part of me now.

Lynne Brach is probably my biggest success in mentoring. When I was teaching professionally in New York I retained all of the curriculum. When I came back here Lynne knew that I'd taught professionally. She got several women together and once a week for I don't know how many months, through a whole winter, we went through, systematically, the first three or four of the modules, each of which had five five-week lessons, and each of the classes was five hours. Essentially they had a miniculinary school experience. It was really great. I'd love to be able to do that again.

I also taught at NMC briefly in the summer. Fred Laughlin, director of the Culinary Institute at NMC, and I have always had a friendship. We put together a comprehensive summer class. Even though we had a low turnout, we still ran it. I like teaching technique. I want to free people from recipes. I want them to get into the taste of the food, and the colors, and the textures of the dishes. If they have maybe five or six good techniques: how to make a stew, how to make a soup, how to sauté, they can really make simple meals that are very good. But it takes practice. You've got to burn a lot of onions before you learn how to caramelize. Or burn sugar. I can remember the first time when I was learning to caramelize sugar in culinary school, my instructor said, "Now whatever you do, don't stick your finger in." So here you are, looking at it, and they tell you not to touch it, you are swirling it around, and then you forget. And you put your finger in there and you burn it, and then you put your finger in your mouth to cool it off, and you burn your tongue. Everybody has to do that at least once. And then you don't forget. You just have to make mistakes. That's the one thing I tell everybody. You've got to make mistakes if you are going to learn.

In the kitchen I prefer somebody who is educated but ignorant about food. I can teach them anything. I suppose it's the same thing as having an empty mind. That's preferable to trying to teach somebody right out of culinary school who is really cocky and thinks they know everything. They have skills, but they will not pay attention. The people who don't have the skills tend to pay closer attention. I always tell people that cooking is not necessarily about getting everything right; it's about learning to pay attention to the smell, the sound, the sight, and the taste of food. You've got to get yourself immersed in it. Too many people are stuck on a recipe. Their face is always in that recipe and they are not in their food.

Nancy Allen's City Kitchen Thai Coconut Curry Base

NANCY ALLEN

Yields 3 to 4 quarts, enough for 15 to 18 six-ounce servings

Tweak this to your own tastes and needs. Add a combo of three to four ingredients like broccoli, red bell pepper, shiitake mushrooms, and chicken. Makrut lime leaves (a.k.a. Kaffir lime leaves) give an indescribable, important aroma to the curry. They are available from Asian markets and may be frozen at least a year. A key ingredient is Aroy-D 100% Coconut Milk. It is the best, pure coconut milk available; it will make your curry a star. The best-quality fish sauce is Red Boat Vietnamese Fish Sauce. Refrigerate after opening; keep up to one year.

3 large shallots, peeled and diced

2 small bunches cilantro stems, chopped

¼ cup peeled, chopped ginger root

Zest of 2 lemons and 1 lime

⅓ cup coconut oil

3 tablespoons commercial red or green Thai curry paste

3 liters pure coconut milk (never "low fat"!)

10 to 15 Makrut (Kaffir) lime leaves, crushed/twisted

3 lemongrass stalks, tops removed and bottom 3 inches smashed

¼ to ⅓ cup fish sauce, to taste

3 to 4 tablespoons palm sugar or maple syrup, to taste

Optional: fresh lime juice to taste

Optional: Sliced red or green bird's eye or serrano chilies

Grind shallots, cilantro stems, ginger root, and citrus zest in food processor or wet grinder until smooth. Add a little of the fish sauce or water to facilitate grinding.

Heat coconut oil in 8- to 10-quart heavy pot over medium-low heat. Stir in paste from food processor and commercial Thai curry paste. Cook pastes slowly until fragrant and fat begins to separate out from the mass, 5 to 7 minutes.

Stir in coconut milk, lime leaves, and lemongrass. Simmer base 15 to 20 minutes. Season to taste with fish sauce, sweetener, and optional lime juice. Cool. Pour into 24- to 32-ounce freezer containers. Freeze up to 3 months, or refrigerate up to 5 days.

To use: Scoop 6 ounces of base into small saucepan per person. Bring to a simmer and stir in peeled and de-veined shrimp or finely sliced chicken. Add presteamed vegetables like green beans, broccoli, squash, or whatever simple combo you've chosen. Finally, stir in quick-cooking items like snow peas or diced raw fish, and roasted or grilled shredded meats. Cook or heat through. Garnish with sliced red or green chilies, basil or cilantro.

Prepare a Thai Coconut Curry Base from a Favorite Recipe

Find a recipe you like and use it for guidance for ingredients and proportions. Look at how much liquid each recipe requires and what it yields or how many does it serve. Generally, a 6-ounce portion of the curry base is one serving.

Heat coconut oil and fry extra aromatics like ground or finely diced shallots, minced cilantro stems, minced ginger, minced fresh turmeric, and spices until soft. Stir in a commercial curry paste, pressing the paste against the bottom of the pan to infuse the oil with flavor and toast paste to deepen flavor.

Pour in coconut milk, a little stock, if desired, lemongrass and aromatic Makrut lime (a.k.a. Kaffir) leaves. Simmer, don't boil, to infuse flavor. Season with fish sauce, palm sugar, lime juice. Cool base and freeze in batches.

When ready to use, heat a batch of coconut curry base over medium heat. First simmer long-cooking ingredients like cubed winter squash or green beans until almost cooked through. Stir in quick-cooking ingredients, like shrimp, finely sliced chicken, fish, or snow peas. Add roasted or grilled meats last, just long enough to heat through. Pre-steam vegetables to crisp-tender, grill, roast, or stir-fry meats and seafood, and simmer them in the curry base just long enough to heat through.

Finish curry by seasoning, to taste, with fish sauce, palm sugar or maple syrup, lime juice, finely sliced chilies, salt, and torn basil leaves and cilantro. Allow curry to steep 10 minutes before serving. It should not be thick and goopy, but instead, soup-like and herbaceous, with each ingredient perfectly cooked. Always serve curries with fluffy jasmine rice.

Photo by Eric Gerstner

18

Rose Hollander

Rose's father came to the Bronx from Germany after World War II, and her mother from Austria. They both went into the food business, her father at Ehring's, her mother at Stella d'Oro, two well-known establishments in the Bronx, the latter the subject of a *New Yorker* feature by Ian Frazier a few years ago. From age twelve Rose was working with food wherever they lived, Woodstock, California, Hong Kong with her husband, and then Suttons Bay where they moved in 1989. After living in Asia Rose was stunned by the absence of ethnic cuisine and the ingredients she needed to prepare it herself for catering and for her own family. Cooking for Rose always meant educating herself and sharing that knowledge with others. Bareknuckle Farm, Idyll Farm, the Montessori School, her legal background, and her passion for good farm-to-table cuisine led her to supporting the public policy program of the local Groundwork Center for Resilient Communities to put better food in front of the children in local schools and to assisting the development of a kitchen classroom at the Montessori Children's House in Traverse City. Rose is currently a food columnist for the *Record Eagle*. The theme of her "At the Table" column is how to build community by gathering people together for food.

Rose Hollander, b. February 21, 1957
Interview: August 24, 2016
West Broadway, Suttons Bay

What we are fed as children really fuels the rest of our lives.

I was born in New York, in Yonkers, and then lived in the Bronx as a first-generation American. My parents are both German. They came to this country in their mid-twenties. My father and mother both had relatives who had moved here after World War II. My father had very little in terms of a skills set, other than having grown up on a farm, as did my mother. Both were swept up in the food business right away. My father became a cook at a German restaurant, a corner restaurant in the Bronx, Ehring's, and my mother worked for Stella d'Oro bakery, which had an operation in the Bronx. So I grew up in a household where food was quite a focal point for us.

We walked to our school but came home for our lunches instead of participating in the school lunch program, because lunch was always going to be better in our home. In the German tradition lunch was always a time when the family got together, particularly with a father who worked evenings. That was our family time. I remember those lunches fondly. We lived in the ground-floor apartment with access to the garden outside. My mother was always at the window where everyone went to after school to get a snack. My mother was happily passing over fried dough and different treats at the end of the day, so the giving and sharing of food was always a big part of my life.

When I was twelve my family moved up to Woodstock, New York. There was a better cooking opportunity and my father really didn't like living in the city. He wanted to move his family of four children to the countryside. He built a house in the woods at Woodstock and worked for an Italian restaurant. Woodstock is quite a tourist destination for those who live in New York City, so restaurants are busy seasonally. It fit his lifestyle of being able to garden in the morning, hunt and fish, and then work in the evenings.

When I was old enough—and I think I was twelve or thirteen—I started working in the restaurant. I would work on Saturdays with the old Italian grandmother who was still in the kitchen. It was she and her husband who had started the restaurant. We would bake. She taught me how to bake Italian pastries. And when I was old enough, or deemed old enough, I was given the job of serving those desserts, cutting them up during service time for the restaurant. Over the years I worked into different food stations there with my father as the chef in charge of the kitchen at that time.

When I went to college I definitely wanted to have a profession. I didn't view cooking as a profession. I didn't think the lifestyle suited my idea of having a family, which was a goal of mine. I had missed having my father participate in my school life and many other things because of the profession he chose, so I steered away from it in a big way. I studied social work in college. Then I had an opportunity to live in London. I did a year abroad and was enamored with the idea of moving back to a city. I liked the idea of a small city.

I found my way to San Francisco with a college roommate and promptly ended up working for a five-star hotel, the Stanford Court Hotel, which at the time in the early '80s was really a part of the whole California cuisine movement, which fostered the new American cuisine movement and then the farm-to-table movement. Chez Panisse was still young but had gained a reputation before I got there for their farm-to-table way of cooking. The Stanford Court Hotel had a French chef who was very classically trained, but James Beard was a frequent guest, and the American regional cooking became a focus point of their restaurant, Forno Ovens.

Everything was new there. I worked on the office staff as a personnel director, but often we were asked to participate in luncheons to fill seats because people didn't quite get what we were doing. I had some amazing experiences. I remember this woman named Shirley Sarvis, who was doing the whole "break the rules" about what wine you drink with which foods. No one would come to her seminars, so we would come. The staff would sit there along with a few other folks who did know what they were doing and eat the most wonderful food and taste different wines with it. I got quite an education there.

The old French chef whose name was Marcel Dragon developed Parkinson's disease and so was asked to retire. I gathered a group of people who worked in the office because I knew he was lonely. His wife had passed away. He lived in Marin County just outside San Francisco, and we organized a once-a-month cooking class at his home. That's where I got my first taste of true cooking school experience because he was a wonderfully classically trained cook. He loved having this gaggle of office women there. He had a pool so of course we had to bring our bathing suits. He was a very French man and wanted to see us in our suits. We would prepare food and while it was cooking or during pauses we would swim and drink, and then we would share this meal together. A wonderful, wonderful man.

My other California food experiences involved going to various oyster farms. The seafood there was eye-opening for me, and of course Asian food was a big part of life in San Francisco. I had my first taste of the different regional Chinese foods. Thai food was just becoming popular at that point as well. Wood-fired ovens for pizza making—all the things we know now and think of as commonplace even here in Traverse City—were brand-new out there and something I got very accustomed to.

I had a chance to live in Hong Kong for a couple of years. I was married by then, and my husband was an attorney. He was sent overseas during the time the Chinese government and the British were negotiating their lease, and of course money was flying out of Hong Kong. I took a number of cooking classes while I was in Hong Kong because I was not able to work. I did not get a visa to work. We didn't know how long we would be there. It was meant to be a short stay but we stayed for two years. I took some incredible classes.

Entertaining and socializing was a big part of life there. We gave dinner parties all the time. Probably the most memorable was when I wanted to do Thanksgiving overseas, but I wanted to do a Chinese twist, so we did a Peking turkey complete with pancakes and plum sauce. We entertained our non-American friends in our Thanksgiving traditions. We belonged to a wine club while we were there, and I think my education to French and European wines was begun at that point. The focus in California had been on California wines.

We moved back from Hong Kong to San Francisco again for a few years and then started having children. At this point I had a husband who had the profession, and I was the lesser of the bread-winning pair in terms of the salary, so we determined that I would stay home, or at least be more available for my children. I worked part time with a community program out of church, and yet participated in food to the extent that we still gave great dinner parties and still went to wineries.

And then we determined that we should move out of San Francisco and have the children grow up in another community, and that was Traverse City. My husband had lived here for a while and wanted to come back when we had children. I moved here sight unseen. I remember the first thing I noticed about the culinary scene—I was appalled—that half-and-half came in little plastic tubs at your table. It was horrifying to me. The lack of ethnic cuisine—this was 1989—was still pretty poor. Only a few restaurants did any work in that.

I promptly developed a lifeline to an Asian market in Grand Rapids. A fellow shopkeeper in Suttons Bay—we moved to Suttons Bay—would travel to Grand Rapids with my list. I felt like he was my drug runner in a way. He'd call me and say, "I'm heading down to Grand Rapids," and I would say, "Great. Here's the list." He would bring me back foods from an Asian market there. Or Stuart, my husband, and I would travel down when we needed to. We had some markets here that were slowly starting to gather ingredients or start selling, especially Asian food. It must have just been that time lag. By the mid-'90s we were starting to see things in our regular grocery stores, so we could cook Asian food.

But the notion of local foods and celebrating wasn't on my radar yet. I didn't go to farmers markets to the degree that I do now. They weren't in Suttons Bay, and the Traverse City market wasn't a place that I would travel to. It was too far to go. I did rely on a market outside of Suttons Bay. Wagon Wheel at that time had some great produce seasonally and certainly all the fruit farms. We were great friends with some of the orchardists, and we always had great fruit. I had a little kitchen garden outside my house. I started a catering company on the side, just to have something to do while raising small children. Catherine was eighteen months and Ian was three when we first moved here, so they were quite young.

The catering business focused on those things from California that I thought would be appealing to people here. That included a lot of ethnic foods, and that's what I became known for. I became the woman who would do a Thai curry dinner, and I would be the woman who would do Chinese food. We know wraps now as wraps, but at that point they were Lavash sandwiches that you rolled and sliced into pinwheels. They were novel then, which is funny to think of now when they are so commonplace. Caesar salads weren't ubiquitous. A Caesar salad was a true Caesar salad. Those were the things that I shared with people through the catering business. I did mostly weddings and events where people just couldn't manage the forty to 120 people that they were inviting.

We got in deep, head over heels, a partner and I, Donna Popke from Suttons Bay, and later another partner, Trish Van Dusen. We got so busy that I was doing exactly what I had said I wouldn't do with my life, which was to be unavailable in the evenings, because that's where the catering life takes you.

In the meantime my husband's business, his law firm business in Suttons Bay, was growing. I have an aptitude for writing and research, and he convinced me to help him out in the office, which I did sort of kicking and screaming at first. But then I found that he was very respectful of my need for autonomy and could teach me, and did, and allowed me to step back and work with clients directly. I morphed into a life that took me away from food as a business and back into it as an avocation.

Stuart and I wrote a book together. We dealt with a lot of families, and the estate law practice that we had, and we wrote a book about family cottages and passing them on. That was a two-year project that took a lot of our time, but was a great working relationship. Our children were starting college or finishing high school.

When Stuart passed away I finally read the acknowledgments in the book, which said something to the effect of my putting my aspirations on hold. He wrote that, and I realized that probably the aspiration he was talking about was this idea, this notion, that I was a chef at heart, or a cook at heart, and that the avocation was really the thing that fueled us. We could spend hours happily planning the menu for any dinner party, hours talking about food, figuring out what restaurant to go to next. We had our own restaurant-critic commentary notebook that we kept in our car that we would fill in every time we went out to eat. It was a big part of our lives. I decided to look into the idea of going to a culinary school, not with the notion that I would ever run a restaurant, but just that I would learn those skills.

I had been working at a wonderful farm, Bareknuckle Farm, which I think was one of the first in the region where a young person started off in the farming business with the notion that people are ready for a wide variety of vegetables that can be grown locally, and wanted to introduce them to vegetables that we didn't see normally. The chef-owner, Abra Berens, asked me to help with some of her farm dinners. I asked her where she learned to cook, and the next thing I knew I was signed up for a program in Ireland at the Ballymaloe Cookery School in County Cork. That cooking school has been around for twenty-five years. Darina Allen is the chef who started the school. She was part of a family that owns a family estate in Ireland that also runs a bed-and-breakfast and has wonderful grounds and an organic garden. That has been her focus from day one twenty-five years ago.

She and Alice Waters at Chez Panisse are great friends. Alice Waters spends every birthday with Darina, either in California or at this farm in Ireland. They have a very close connection. I went in January, which is probably not the time one would think of for farming, but they had these wonderful glass houses, and of course the climate in County Cork is very temperate. It is their bread basket. It's in the southeast corner of Ireland. I was there, and I happened to have wonderful weather. It was an unusually mild winter for rain so we had great access to the herb gardens and the formal gardens and the vegetable gardens.

The process in the cooking school was to get up every morning and do your farm chore, participate by cooking in the kitchens the recipes you were shown the day before, and then eat them, those that lunched together. The teachers would demonstrate the next series of twenty or twenty-four different recipes. You and a partner were given six of those to reproduce the next day under the tutelage of these older Irish cooks who ran the teaching kitchens and who were wonderful. You alternated partners every week, so in my twelve weeks I had twelve different partners. They were people from all over the world, all ages. I had a wonderful experience, saw a lot of the growth of the food market there, the farmers market, organic foods.

I came back to working part time in the law firm as my stable paycheck, and then did a stint at Idyll Farms, a new goat farm operation in Northport, for two summers, through a friend of mine. The head cheese maker, Madeleine Vedel, invited me to come and help make food with their cheese and help feed their staff, to use their kitchen garden and to help see how we could augment the cheese-making and selling. It was a wonderful experience for a couple of years.

At my current stage of life I am looking forward to leaving my law firm work next year and pursuing more of this idea that there's still a lot for me to learn. When I was working as a caterer I also worked at a Montessori School once a week as a Great Books leader, something I've done for almost thirty years now. When they moved to their latest location in Traverse City they bought an old nursery, so they had greenhouses, and they wanted to place a kitchen classroom as part of the curriculum. I helped write the grant for that and we got a grant from the Kellogg Foundation. They have a full-time chef now, but at one point I was helping plan the menus and working with the cooks there to integrate the students into the making of the food for other students in the classrooms.

I can see doing more of that and being involved in public policy. I'm really interested in what we do early in life. I can certainly see it shaping my food choices. What we are fed as children really fuels the rest of our lives and shapes our relationship with food. I think the schools are the place to start. I don't think we are ever too old to start anything. I can see getting more involved in that and working with Groundworks, which has a great program food coordinator, Diane Conners. I'm talking about working with her, so I envision next year as taking more cooking classes. I'm certainly traveling a lot more. Wherever I go I take a cooking class. I want to help make sure that our children have that early experience of food in a really healthy way. That will create a healthy community for all of us.

I think because we have all this agriculture in this region, and we have tourism, the tourism has fueled a more open-minded community to some of these ideas. And as our tourism has grown, and maybe those cities that tourists are coming from—cities might be more in the forefront of change than a rural community—that has sped up what's going on here, so we have the template of great growing land, and we have people with a desire or an understanding of good food, and of certain types of food. This gave the opportunity to restaurants who were looking for that opportunity to do something a little different. I think the local townships have also done a great job of recognizing that the agricultural community and landscape is what fuels the tourism as well, and so, rather than lose it to developers, those programs that have encouraged the farms to stay farms have really helped.

The move from cherries to wineries and now beer, craft beer, has been a good response to a market for cherries that wasn't sustainable. The wine is, or seems to be, and certainly the beer is. The beer is almost a no-brainer. It shows no sign of stopping. I think there's more general appeal. The wine industry has a tougher sell in terms of selling to a particular palate that might not be as sophisticated. Beer can play a lot more with flavors and be all things to all people in a way that wine maybe just takes a little longer to get there. Along with that I think we have had the movement of super chefs, or celebrity chefs, but it also morphed into the farmers. The younger people now that are becoming farmers are given more of an opportunity than they might have been earlier before that awareness of farmers as an important part of the culinary piece of the restaurant world.

The Food on Film as a part of the annual Michael Moore film festival in Traverse City came into being last year with my son, who works for Tribeca. After seeing a number of food films, and knowing my interests, he asked if I could help push the idea that we could do a "food on film" series here in Traverse City. The food on film series brings documentary films about farmers or chefs and pairs them with a panel of local chefs or producers who discuss the film with the audience. The audience then samples food made by these chefs as they leave the theater. It worked really well last year so of course we did it again this year. One of my food heroes from San Francisco days actually came. The film was about Jeremiah Tower, who was one of the first chefs at Chez Panisse, and who then opened up a restaurant called Stars in San Francisco. We got him to come, which was amazing. I got to shake his hand. I knew his reputation from San Francisco. He knew the Stanford Court where I had worked. He had eaten there a couple of times, but I hadn't met him. He was a wonderful man. His book talks about—and the movie does too—the evolution of how California cuisine affected American cuisine.

He's very good friends with Mario Batali. I worked at the Four Seasons Hotel when I came back from Hong Kong. Mario Batali was one of the line cooks at that point. So I remembered him with his red ponytail. He was only there a short time. He became an influence here, and I think he's a great supporter. Jeremiah Tower went right from our screening to Mario's house for dinner afterward. Susi (Mario's wife) went to U of M and one of her roommates had property up here. I think Mario dated Susi in college, and Susi still came to her friend's here and would travel up here on a regular basis. It was a destination for

Susi every year. I think she brought Mario along as their relationship developed, and he eventually bought property here.

Our Epicurean classic festival started around 2002. It was held first at the Hagerty Center and then at the Culinary Institute. It would bring in cookbook chefs. The cookbook chefs would be assigned a restaurant and would help the restaurateurs do the menus. They also did cooking classes, and that grew significantly. But then it got too big for the school to manage, and the school wanted it at a different time of year, and that didn't work for the publishing schedule or for the chefs. It ended up moving downstate. That was also something that put Traverse City on the map. The culinary movement here, or the food movement here, is a product of the reputation that Traverse City gained. I think on its own it would have taken a lot longer to get us here.

If I have a small piece in it, it's to contribute to local charities by giving dinners. Most of the people who buy my dinner know my reputation as a caterer and that I do certain foods, that I have that avenue to play in. But I hope I open people's minds. I did some cooking classes, and I know that when we nudged our local supermarket, Hansen's, in Suttons Bay, he was wonderful and he said, "Anything you want, I'll put on the shelf. Just let me know what it might be." So I could direct people and say, "He's going to have rice paper wrappers so you can make these spring rolls if you go to Hansen's." There was great support by people in the industry to help those of us who wanted to see certain things happen here.

The food on film series this year—while the film festival was all about women directors and producers, and the person who produced the Jeremiah Tower movie was a woman—when Amanda Danielson, who was in charge of finding the chefs, and she and I were thinking about the chefs, it was really hard to find women. There certainly aren't as many, certainly not downtown. I think that's still a function of the world of food being a difficult one from a life-balance standpoint. I think women are smarter than guys. I don't think it's just because guys don't care. I think we have figured out that it's not a lifestyle—even if you didn't have a family—that's an easy one to sustain. That's also true of farming. It's a seven-days-a-week commitment. That's a place I won't go.

I have had the experience of participating in the all-woman butchery weekend a couple of years ago. One of the other things I did when I moved here, though not right away, is to hunt during hunting season, something I would never have imagined myself doing. But when you become part of this community you realize that if you are going to eat meat you should understand that it comes from an animal that was killed for that meat. I have a friend who is very supportive, and I knew I could ask him to show me how to hunt. He has property that was close to our house, so I do go hunting. I like the ritual of it. I don't go out long hours. Opening day is sort of my day to go, and then I might go a couple of days. Half the time I will shoot a deer, and many times I don't, and that's okay. And I've just gotten into fishing.

So while I might not farm, I do have my little kitchen farming operation outside my door, and I do like to hunt. The butchery was an interesting process to go through, especially since it was all women, and it was very intense. We were hauling huge hogs on a pulley system to hang them so we could cut them. And then we had to skin them. She did things not necessarily in the 1910 era, but the meats were set for curing. We had a woman who had studied butchery and who was a butcher in Kansas City, and then in Chicago, and had moved here and hoped to open her own business someday, and she was great. She really knew what she was doing. And we had two veterinarians who were friends of the woman who owned the pigs, and they were great. They knew all the animal parts. I learned so much that weekend. And in our Traverse City home we have chickens, so I do own a little kitchen garden, but I'm not milking cows or goats. That's my life.

Shrimp and Avocado with Tamarind Sauce

ROSE HOLLANDER

Serves 4

¼ cup vegetable oil

1 large shallot, thinly sliced and separated into rings

¼ cup tamarind pulp (from a pliable block) OR 2 tablespoons tamarind concentrate

½ cup boiling-hot water

2 tablespoons sugar

1 tablespoon soy sauce

1 tablespoon Asian fish sauce

3 tablespoons fresh lime juice

2 firm-ripe California avocados

1 tablespoon minced peeled fresh ginger

1 garlic clove, minced

2 fresh Thai chilies or 1 serrano, stemmed and minced (including seeds)

¼ teaspoon salt

1 pound large shrimp, peeled and deveined

⅓ cup roasted salted peanuts, chopped

Accompaniment: jasmine rice

Garnish: fresh cilantro sprigs

Fry shallot and make tamarind sauce:

Heat oil in a 1-quart heavy saucepan over moderate heat until hot but not smoking, then fry shallot, stirring, until golden brown, about

2 minutes. Transfer with a slotted spoon to paper towels to drain (shallots will crisp as they cool). Reserve oil.

Soak tamarind pulp in boiling-hot water in a small bowl until softened, about 5 minutes. Force pulp through a sieve into a bowl, discarding solids. Add sugar, soy sauce, fish sauce, and 1½ tablespoons lime juice and stir until sugar is dissolved.

Cut avocados and cook shrimp:

Halve, pit, and peel avocados. Cut into 1½-inch chunks and toss with remaining 1½ tablespoons lime juice in a bowl.

Transfer reserved oil to a 12-inch heavy skillet and heat over moderately high heat until hot but not smoking, then sauté ginger, garlic, chilies, and salt, stirring constantly, until fragrant, about 30 seconds. Add shrimp and sauté, turning over once, 2 minutes total. Stir in tamarind mixture and simmer until shrimp are just cooked through, about 2 minutes more.

Spoon shrimp and avocado over rice, then sprinkle with peanuts and fried shallot.

VI

TWO HOMESTEADS

Preserve the Past and

Celebrate the Future

Photo courtesy of Susan Odom

19

Susan Odom

Susan did not grow up on a farm but in a Detroit suburb. She discovered cooking and baking in her home economics class in seventh grade. After college she tried city planning as a career but found it draining rather than exhilarating. It wasn't until she worked as a historical interpreter at Greenfield Village in Dearborn, a living history farm re-creating life in 1885—a job she held for seven years—that "a light went on." She had found her passion and her life's work. She created her own historic farm in 2011, Hillside Homestead, and now welcomes visitors who want to reconnect with the land as it was experienced in earlier less-mechanized times, to eat food grown and prepared in traditional ways, cooked on period equipment, following vintage recipes. With overnight guests Susan does have electricity rather than kerosene lamps or candles, also indoor plumbing, but she makes few other concessions to modernity. She sees them coming to her Homestead because they are seeking to reconnect with the land. They had a connection but it's gone, and they want it back.

Susan Odom, b. November 10, 1964
Interview: July 9, 2017
Hillside Homestead, 3400 Setterbo Road, Suttons Bay

*The reason I love all those old cookbooks is that I
love solving puzzles, and they are puzzles.*

I was born in Wheaton, Illinois, which is near Chicago. My parents lived there for a couple of years until we moved to the Detroit area, Detroit, Michigan, and that's where I grew up. I grew up in the suburbs.

People said I should have either been a lawyer or married a lawyer, but I didn't do either of those things.

I went to college in a couple of different places, first to Earlham College in Richmond, Indiana, and then to the University of Montana at Missoula. I got pregnant along the line, and I came home back to Michigan as a single mother. My son now is going to be thirty-one years old next month. That was obviously a big change in my life. I came home when my son was about a year old, and I went back to school to Eastern Michigan. I had only about two semesters to finish to get my degree.

I always had trouble finding a major because I loved all my courses. I've always loved learning. I've been a very curious person. I ended up in the Geography Department, which is a well-rounded kind of school. I thought I would work in city planning. That was the only thing I could figure out. Well, I did that for a while, and I did not like it. I didn't like being staff although I liked the idea of city planning. I decided I wanted to be a planning commissioner someday. I knew I would land somewhere where I loved, where I lived, and now I'm on the planning commission here. In fact I'm the chairman of the planning commission for Suttons Bay Township.

I had a lot of jobs after I left the city planning. I did all this soul-searching at one point. I was utterly dissatisfied with everything in my life. I was twenty-eight years old. I was struggling being a parent with a difficult child to raise by myself. My work left me utterly empty. I was completely dissatisfied with my work. I did all this soul-searching, and then I figured out that I liked visiting museums and nature centers. Maybe I could get a job at a museum. A lot of people get jobs at museums. So I went and applied for a job at a big museum I knew about at Dearborn and ended up working at their living history farm, Firestone Farm. It's based in the year 1885.

When I started working there, a little light bulb went off in my head. "Oh, my God! This is what I was supposed to do." They were the first ones to put a historic cookbook in my hands. We had a coal-burning stove. I now have a wood-burning stove. I loved the historic cooking that we did. My training in cooking is all self-taught. The reason I love all those old cookbooks is that I love solving puzzles, and they are puzzles. They are mysteries. And it's just been forgotten in two generations. It hasn't been that long ago that people understood this stuff.

I get email questions all the time. Someone emailed me this week. She didn't understand. She's been writing down, transcribing her grandmother's diary. She gave me one quote. She said this is every year in January, and she included the quote. Her grandmother wrote down: "Fried out seven and a half pounds of sausage." Or it was seven and a half gallons of sausage. She didn't understand what that meant. And I did. I explained it to her. It was a butchering thing. The grandmother was preserving it in crocks with the lard topper, and so she was frying it out to cook it. This was an old preservation method. It's kind of funny how I've come to the point where I understand that, and I could help her with the context for that.

Greenfield Village was an amazing place to work, and I worked at that farm for seven full seasons. The whole time I worked at that farm I had the opportunity to do a lot of work both outside of the farmhouse and inside. I learned how to milk cows and use draft horses and harness horses, and we sheared sheep. We took care of sheep, chickens, pigs, and now at my own farm I have all of the above except I don't have any horses or cows. I added in ducks and geese because I am really fascinated with them.

The milk cow is my dream. I haven't got there yet. I am still trying to figure out how to work a milk cow into my plan. I know how much work a milk cow takes from my years of working at Greenfield Village. That's why I haven't taken that step. There are a lot of things in my life. I figure I'm halfway, and I'll just go ahead and jump in. But the milk cow, I have refused to allow myself to do that because I know what's involved. I am already working too many hours. I have a young woman who is full time in summer, also a part timer in summer, and we are all already working a lot of hours.

At Greenfield I learned a lot about the history of Ag, which is fascinating to me because I've always been curious and especially curious about farming. Even when I look back at my suburban life I can see me as a child wondering about these things. I tried to start a garden in the twelfth grade. I didn't have any support. I planted my garden under some maple trees, not realizing that the maple trees would leaf out later, and that would kill everything in my garden.

We did all the outside stuff at Greenfield Village, and in the farm-house we prepared a meal every day that the staff would sit down and eat at noon, a dinner meal. I learned all kinds of things about historic cooking and historic food preservation. We'd be sitting at the table. The staff would be eating a meal and we'd all be in period costume, and the guests would keep coming in. One of two reactions would happen. One would be like: "Oh, we don't mean to interrupt." It seemed like such a family eating that they didn't want to . . . "No, no, come in." And then their next reaction would be: "Wow. That looks really good. May I have some?" And they couldn't with the health rules and all of that. And of course we could never have made enough food for 1,500 people every day on a wood stove.

Greenfield Village was what helped me decide: "I want to have my own farm, a farm where people can come and sit down and eat." What I've done at Hillside Homestead is a Farm Stay. Farm Stay seems to be a word that nobody in the United States of America knows what it is, but I trudge ahead. On a good day I explain what it is, and on a bad day I just gloss over it. Everybody calls me a bed-and-breakfast. There is nothing wrong with a bed-and-breakfast, but I am more than that. A very large portion of the food that I serve my guests we have actually raised here.

After my years at Greenfield Village I wanted to create a farm where people could come and visit and have a really connected experience to a farm. I thought most of the guests we had at the Village had a good time. But there was always a group of visitors who wanted more than what they were getting there. You could see that by the way they asked questions. Or they came back time and time again. I would see them often. I created this farm so they could do that.

I keep sheep and pigs and ducks, chickens, geese, and have a pretty large garden, and fruit trees. I'm trying to create what a farm might have looked like at the turn of the last century. Guests can come here and stay the night. I serve breakfast in the morning, cooked on the wood stove, and I follow old recipes. Some of the things I serve for breakfast include venison steaks, fried potatoes, and wilted lettuce. I will serve a very typical nineteenth-century breakfast, which is very atypical to a twenty-first-century person. I get some mixed reviews on that sometimes. Mostly people like it.

I teach some classes. I do farm dinners by reservation. Field trips for kids. I've done some field trips just for families. I've decided some families just want to come and visit, just kind of come for a farm experience, like coming to Greenfield Village, just for an afternoon visit, so I've started to do something like that, too.

Looking back, I didn't notice cooking or think about cooking much until I was in the seventh grade when I had Mrs. Szilagyi for Home Economics. My mom cooked meals for us all the time, but she didn't invite us to help her. My brother and I washed dishes. I washed a lot of dishes. I washed and he dried even though he was older because he found the dishwater kind of "squirmish." He didn't like it when there was food in the dishwater. That never bothered me. Those old Home Ec rooms had like eight kitchens in them, and they were really organized. I'm a very organized person, and I can remember immediately being enamored of all kinds of labeled jars because I have labeled jars today. Mrs. Szilagyi had a very systematic approach to cooking, and we learned a lot about cooking.

She taught us how to bake bread, and I baked bread in seventh grade for Thanksgiving for the family. But there was a typo in the recipe I followed, which was in one of my mom's cookbooks. It wasn't even from Mrs. Szilagyi's recipe; it was from one of mom's cookbooks. It called for a tablespoon of salt for two loaves. It was so salty that none of us could eat it, but it did have a nice rise. I remember that. It was just kind of amazing because salt can actually be—now that I understand things better—salt can actually be an inhibitor to the action of yeast. So Mrs. Szilagyi helped me learn to cook.

I was also greatly affected by *The Little House on the Prairie* books by Laura Ingalls Wilder. I loved reading them. My sister and I would play Little House on the Prairie. Joyce, my sister, is six years younger than I am. I think I was bossy to my little sister. We would play downstairs in the basement. We had all the play kitchen furniture, a stove and a sink. There was even a baby crib.

I would go out hunting, and I would bring back every time six deer and six bears. I would bring them back and then Joyce and I would proceed to tell each other how we were going to butcher these animals, which is just a crack-up. I would never have thought of butchering an animal in suburban Plymouth, Michigan, where meat is served on a tray. But downstairs in the basement we were butchering bears. I can remember coming home and having them over my shoulder. I'd be pretending I had these six deer and six bears. I haven't asked my sister lately if she remembers this. I would press her into service. We would chop up meat, pretending ourselves away.

I have this other memory. I don't know when—it was sometime in high school or in continuing ed classes that I took some type of personal inventory, an assignment somebody had given to all the students in whatever class it was—it was a personal interest inventory or something like that. I kept coming up with kind of farmy agricultural things. I still have that inventory upstairs. I reread it a little bit. I already had this idea where I someday would be sitting under my apple tree working on something. This cracks me up now, because I do have some apple trees, and I have occasionally sat under one of them, but it was mostly when I was trying to do something or when there was a problem with the sheep. I don't know how that came to be, how I had that idea way back then. It certainly wasn't through my parents. They were not farmers.

When I started working at Firestone Farm I would come back once in a while with things I had learned, and my grandmother, my maternal grandmother, thought that was just crazy. My family's from South Carolina. When I came back and I told Granny, "Granny, I've learned how to milk a cow. I'm getting good at it, Granny." She said, "Well now, Susan, that's something I never did, is put my hands on an old cow teat." She was outraged that I would do that.

She was the youngest of twelve or fifteen children. My granny was an aunt before she was born. Her oldest brother was about twenty-one years older than her. She was one of the few kids in that family who didn't grow up on a farm because they had moved to town. And so she's a part of that generation, my grandmother, just two generations ago. They got away from that. She couldn't believe that her granddaughter, who had been sent to college, would want to milk a cow. She truly was shocked. And my hands were in bad shape that day, and she said, "Look at your hands! They look terrible." It was so funny because I am fifty-two, so this is within my lifetime that somebody said this to me. It's almost like people have rediscovered agriculture today. But it's still within the memory. Granny would have been like 110 now if she was still alive. In her mind this was definitely not something I should be doing.

Industry took this from us or relieved us of that, and the mega-farms took over. It was around 1910, 1920, 1930 that Ag starts getting big. Things are more mechanized. You don't need as many people. There's a shift in the economy. Labor starts to become more expensive, and stuff becomes cheap. Whereas in 1850 labor is cheap but stuff is expensive. The industrial revolution switched that around.

What I do here is expensive. Having a small farm like this I am not operating on the scale of economies like I learned about in college in Economics 101. I'm flying contrary to that, and so I work too many hours. I work too hard. I can't have a cow. Having a cow is too expensive. A person from 1850 would be like, "You're crazy. How can you not have a cow? How can you not have milk and butter? And a cow eats grass!" In an 1850 mind a cow creates wealth. A cow eats grass, produces milk, butter, cheese, beef, manure that enriches the soil, which perpetuates the whole thing. But not in 2017. It's not the way the world works today. It's funny how that has changed. And so trying to go backward and show that always brings up the conversation as to why people can't or won't or don't do things in general today the way I do them here. It's interesting.

When I was in Plymouth, Michigan, I had a house and it was paid for. I sold my house, and I had that chunk of money. That was almost enough, maybe 75 percent enough to buy this property, and then my family has helped me finance the things that I couldn't. I've kind of been getting my inheritance early. My parents have been very generous to me and to my two siblings. I couldn't have done it without their financial assistance. That's wonderful, and they are due for a visit, too, very soon. I'm very excited about that. They always knew that there was something kind of different about me. They realized that this is important to me. They have been utterly pleased and happy to be able to help me do this crazy farm thing, even though they know it's a really different sort of thing from what they expected. I want to cry thinking about how good they have been to me, helping me do this.

I am re-creating the sort of little nineteenth-century farm and trying to do things the way they used to be done on a small scale. I think I'm particularly good at explaining that to guests and visitors. That's what I learned at Greenfield Village. At Greenfield Village the name of my position was an interpreter. An interpreter was the person at Greenfield Village that was between the artifact and the visitor. You literally interpret the artifact to the visitor. At the farm where I worked lots of times what we were interpreting was the process. We even had a name for it: Process demonstration. We would take an artifact and say, "This is a plow. This is how a plow looked." When you are actually using a plow you can talk to somebody about the land and the furrow and all these different things. I found out that I'm good at that. There is limited use for that in life. Being a good interpreter. In museums, yes, but sadly the thing is that nobody ever makes much money in museums. So I'm right at home on a farm because you don't make much money on a farm either.

It's funny because it was a problem one hundred years ago, and it's a problem today. It always depends on the kind of farm you have. Of course in the late nineteenth century people made money on farms with grain in Ohio and Indiana and Illinois and other places with that deep, deep soil, which leads to the big farming. The first mechanization of farming in this country was all about small grains, planting wheat. And wheat is the lesser of the big crops nowadays, corn and soybeans being the big commodity crops, but the mass production of wheat is what really drove mechanization, which is what really changed farming, which is what led to the industrialization of the food system, which leaves people unsatisfied.

So who comes here? Who comes to Hillside Homestead? Why would you come to the farm? Some of my neighbors, old-timey neighbors . . . this is an old community, very tight-knit, even in the 1980s, one of them said to me: "Why would anybody want to come to a farmhouse?" This little community has been so into itself for a while that they are really not too much part of that whole mechanization. They are, and they aren't. So anyway, why would people want to come to this farmhouse?

I can divide all my visitors into two basic groups. We'll call them the twenty to forty somethings and forty to eighty somethings. Twenty to forty somethings have something missing in their life. They feel this twang or something. They want to know where food comes from. They are concerned about eating organic. They are lacking this connection to the soil. They come here because they want to know how food is grown, and they want to see the basic way it is prepared. The older group, forty to eighty somethings, they visited grandma's farm. They grew up on a farm. They went to their uncle's farm one day, or something. They had a connection, but it's gone and they want it back.

So they both actually want the same thing. It's been fascinating to see that. And they can have the whole huge gamut of social, economic, political, religious, cultural differences that are across the spectrum. You can be Muslim, Christian, Far Right, Far Left, poor, rich, it's fascinating. But they come, everybody comes here because there's a connection that they are missing. They want to be reconnected. Through the mechanization, the self-reaping—what do they call those reapers we had? The raking reapers we had? Introduced by McCormick in 1880—that leads to all of that. We were alleviated of all that work so finally it gets to the point where we are so alleviated of the work—and the work was exhausting, absolutely exhausting—but I think the absence of that work is also exhausting and the absence of the connection is dehumanizing.

I can see it in so many of my visitors. They have no idea where food comes from. Some do, but some people sit at this table, and they are amazed. We are having eggs, and of course my eggs have bright yellow yolks, they are rich and dark in color, completely different looking than grocery store yolks, and my guests are taken aback. They don't understand. It's immediately something somebody comments on. They've never eaten an egg from a chicken who got to eat a blade of grass. Grass is great. Plants have photosynthesized. People don't understand the concept of plants that photosynthesize in the sun, how the animals eat them, and we can eat the animals, and that can be returned to the ground, and how that's like a whole cycle. And when you take something out of that cycle, something gets diminished.

Chickens are diminished when you take them out of that, and you raise them in a barn, and you only feed them dry grain, and they don't ever get to eat any grass or bugs. I need to plant some more grass outside. Instead of tilling that all up, I'm going to fence this area around and put my chickens on it. They'll scratch it all to pieces in just a few days if I keep the area small, and then I can plant the grass. So they can do that little bit of work. A smidgen of work and a lot of fertilizer in just a few days. I can make that a whole circle again, the way a small farm was, and yet I live in the modern world. I can see both sides of the coin.

More than half of my customers return two and three and four times. I think the lasting effect is that they think about it more. Lots of them follow me on Facebook, which is whatever it is. They come back and they ask questions about what I'm doing. They stop and think. I talk to my visitors all the time about the farming that goes on around me. I'm surrounded right now by my neighbors' cherry and apple orchard, which is managed in a very modern, mechanized way. This is a very successful fruit-growing valley. Of course they do things differently than I do. I can understand what they do, and they understand what I do. We get along with each other just fine. I have the opportunity to help people see the food system depending on where they are, how much they want to hear. Part of my being a good interpreter is knowing when somebody needs more information, and when they need me just to get them another cup of coffee. I can also do that. I pour a lot of coffee.

This is a very conventional farming area. There's a little bit of organic farming on the Leelanau Peninsula, but for the most part, most of the cherries and apples that are grown here, 99 percent of the cherries and apples are conventional, spraying, all kinds of things to get a big crop. This year they are using a lot of fungicide because it's been such a wet June, which is always kind of crappy. Fungicide is one of the most general spectrums of the things they spray. But honestly I think they are better about it now than they were in the 1970s and '80s. The science has gotten better, and they spray a lot less. They've gotten better at the timing and understanding the weather. There's even a weather station out in this field. They watch closely the amount of leaf wetness, whether it's a good time to spray or not. Sometimes they spray at one o'clock or two o'clock in the morning when it's the most still outside because then you get zero drift, which is great for me. That way they lose less product. They use less and lose less. So they've gotten better about it. It's helpful, I think, for people just to understand the gamut of different ways of farming, how we used to do it, how we do it today, why I'm doing it the way I'm doing it. A lot of people never considered any of those things.

I've always thought of my farm as an authentic place. And then I realized that the word "authentic" is being used as a buzzword or something. It's kind of funny. But yes, this is a very authentic place. It's funny because that word means something in the culture today. With my museum background, knowing that something is accurate and authentic has always been very important to me to the point where I've had departure from my museum colleagues. When we worked at the Firestone Farm we wore our period dress all the time. We made sure we did everything that way. We hid the fact that we had a refrigerator two floors up where we kept things, because we weren't actually living there all day every day, and so we kept some things cold.

But now I've found that what people really like is that I truly am living here. When I first started here people would ask the question: "Well, do you live here?" because when they were visitors they were really confused. They said, "Wow, you guys seem like a family." Somebody asked me that once when I started opening my business. And I just chuckled to myself and said, "I do. I live here. I do. My room is upstairs in the back of the house. It's real." Oh, my God, it's so real, some days it's incredibly real.

So now I've come to the conclusion with my museum background where I should use all authentic pots and pans, all authentic recipes, all authentic clothing, is that I wear my period dress when I make a proper meal. That's the way I think about it. When we're using the wood stove and we're cooking historic recipes with all our homegrown food, I follow that. But as the day goes on I choose overalls for my outside work because I really have to run up to the grocery store because I don't have a cow. Ninety percent of what I buy at the grocery store are dairy products. I'm not going to wear my historic dress up to that grocery store. A lot of my colleagues have always loved wearing period clothing. I never have. To me it's always been a necessary evil. I'm not going up to the grocery store dressed like that. They already think I'm weird. But authentic is something people are looking for. They truly are. Without knowing it I'm becoming more and more authentic, like never leaving the house and working so hard.

Most of our food used to be processed in some way because it's raw or bulk to start with. We sometimes slaughter our own pigs depending on the amount of time we have and the time of year. My neighbors have helped in the past to slaughter them. What I like about that is that you have ultimate control over how the carcass is carved up. What we do sometimes depending on whether I'm going to sell the meat, there's a USDA processor in Buckley that we use called Triple R. We can have him process the meat for me. He'll slaughter the meat. I can get it back from him as a carcass, so that I come back with two halves. He doesn't save all the inside parts that I might want to have saved, whereas when I butcher it myself you can save whatever parts you want because it's your pig. That's been a big change. It's been fun to learn about using all the different parts of an animal. Even the tail. That's a little taster bit, a tasty bit.

The bladder was used as a balloon and a ball. We've tried that. Bladders are also used as jar covers. I don't think they talk about that in *Little House on the Prairie*. It's like Saran Wrap. You take the bladder. It's very stretchy of course. You take the bladder and you cut it open. First thing after you butcher it you have to make sure it's empty. It's hard to empty the bladder after the pig is dead. You soak it in very salty water. You can cut it open and stretch it over a crock. It can be a big gallon crock full of sausage. You can stretch it out really big, much thinner than a dinner plate. You can cut it in pieces. You might be able to get four small crocks covered from one bladder. And then you tie it over that crock, and when it dries it's tight as a drum. And when you go to take it off it pries right off in one solid chunk, and then you can soak it in salty water and use it again. It's like reusable Saran Wrap. Not USDA approved. Old farmer approved. Not USDA. Bladders are stretchy. They have to be.

My son, James, was born in 1986, and I moved here in 2008, so he never lived here with me. It might have helped him. He had no farm experience. In the future, who knows? My son has wandered, or had difficulty in finding direction, which I would say I also did. I think he would like this sort of thing. It's funny. He's really picky about what he eats now. He likes to eat meat and vegetables and very locally grown things. When he talks about what he likes to eat, I'm thinking to myself, "Dude, I've got a freezer full of that kind of meat. Come see with me. I have all kinds of meat. What do you need? There's chicken, there's venison out there. You like venison? My God, I've got so much venison."

I have found direction here. What I know about myself—and I learned this at Greenfield Village—is that I can't work at something without putting my whole self in it, which can easily lead to an unbalanced life. Whatever you do you have to do it all. I had to struggle to find balance. But at least when it's your own business you are doing something that is all yours. I would work too hard at Greenfield Village and put too much of myself into it, and I would run up against a wall because I was never a supervisor. I was never in a position to say: "Hey, that is not the way I want to do it. We are going to do it this way." So now I can make that decision. I know that about myself, that I work too hard and I put too much of myself into something. But at least it's my own. It's hard when you are an employee. I think I would make a terrible employee now. I really would. I would feel sorry for any boss of mine because I can be very ornery. I would say: "That's really nice, but we should do it like this." And I would already have started to do it contrary to the way I was told. That's totally what I would do.

This house was owned before with a barn—the big timber-framed barn next to an acreage that divided off from this house in 1965—by a woman who was also ornery and wouldn't let go. All the neighbors tell me how they—her name was Edith—how they wanted Edith Ann to sell and buy a house in the village of Suttons Bay. She didn't want to. She had been widowed for a while and she loved the farm. She never had much help. She wasn't able to make much of a go of it. She found a buyer for the barn and for the acreage and kept the house and the two acres. She lived here from 1965 to 1986. That's a long time, and she lived on that money that whole time. I don't think she ever made much, and she had lots of jobs off the farm. People tell me stories about her. It's funny when I think about it, that it went from one ornery independent woman who clung onto it probably to another one who will cling.

But I do think about it, who will take it over. I hope to maybe expand someday if any of the adjacent property were ever to come available. I would hope that with some family finances I might be able to acquire that property. Mom and Dad even talked about it. It would be nice if they could build a house close by. I'd love to have them close by. They are already eighty. I'd love to have them close by as they get older. They don't like the snow, though, so I don't know. They live in a little town in South Carolina called Lake City where they grew up. It's south of Florence and about an hour and a half from Charleston. It's a nowhere little place, just this little town.

My dad retired from Ford Motor Credit Company. Ford is what got him to Michigan. Most of my family still lives in South Carolina, although I have a cousin that lives in Connecticut. And one more branch moved to Wilmington, North Carolina. That's the thing about most South Carolinians, they don't leave. Southerners are like that. People in the rest of the country tend to move all over, but a lot of southern families, they stay put. When I told my cousins I was buying a house up north—I shouldn't have used that phrase because they didn't understand it; in Michigan we all called it up north—my one cousin said, "Well, Susan, you already live up north. Where are you going?" She has been here to visit, though. She thought it was the end of the world. I like living at the end of the world. It's nice and quiet out here. I like my little bubble.

Right now with my Farm Stay guests I'm doing three nights a week, overnights on Thursdays, Fridays, and Saturdays. I had one group that stayed five days because they had made that reservation a year ago, and really, that's too much. I'm happy with my Thursday, Friday, Saturday schedule because with all the other things I'm doing I have to have a schedule. I find that I can't get my work done. That's such a Victorian concept. At Greenfield Village we learned about the Victorian work week. Each day of the week was a different job. I get that. I totally do. I have implemented it in my own life in many ways because otherwise I cannot get all this work done.

My favorite quote from my favorite cookbook was the dedication to this *Buckeye Cookery and Practical Housekeeping*, first published in 1876, last published in 1905. The dedication is like this: "To the pucky housewives who master the work instead of allowing it to master them, this book is dedicated." We used to laugh about that at Greenfield Village. Now I look at it and say: "Dude, if at the end of the day I could honestly say to myself that I mastered my work and it didn't master me...." Some days I can say that, and some days I have to say that I am whipped.

There has to be a schedule. I decided that overnight guests ... it's a whole different set of work to have overnight guests versus people who might be coming for a class or a dinner or a field trip and then they go away. It's a lot of work to have people in your home and be entertaining a lot. So I limit that to Thursdays, Fridays, Saturdays. That's what works for me. And most people want to come for weekends anyway.

I love having kids here. I love to be able to show children things. Children still have that curiosity, and they usually haven't yet learned any bias of any kind. They are still blank slates. And they love animals. They love seeing animals and touching animals, and if they don't understand that animals are used for Ag meat, this is a good, gentle place to explain some of those things, for them to see the way they live and understand. They can touch a chicken and touch a lamb and touch a sheep. Sheep are particularly friendly. The children can put a little grain in their hand, and the sheep will come up and eat the grain out of their hand. They can touch the sheep and they can feel the lanolin. We talk about how clothes used to be made out of lanolin. I had an interesting realization about language the other day. The word "fleece." Those are jackets today, fleece jackets, but they are made out of polyester. We have totally stolen that word. A fleece is the raw wool product that comes off a sheep. It's processed into wool. A fleece was a commodity product back in the day. I was explaining and talking about a fleece, and this little kid looked at me and said, "Like a jacket?" "No." "Yes." "No." Oh, my God! We stole that word.

We have tools and implements hanging on the walls. There was a kid here once who was really into astronomy. I have a hand-dipper, a water dipper. He was into astronomy and he was only eight years old. He was showing me all these things. I don't know much about astronomy or constellations. He pointed out the Little Dipper and the Big Dipper, and I thought: "I wonder if this kid really knows." He didn't know what a dipper was. He didn't know why the constellation was called a Big Dipper or a Little Dipper. And so I got the dipper out and a bucket of water. We scooped out water with the dipper. He showed me things, and I showed him things. That was pretty cool. Little things are cool. Most of us know what a dipper is. We have this idea of what it is even though we might not have actually ever gone to a store where they served water from a dipper, but that little boy had no idea why it was called a dipper. That sense of discovery has happened on several occasions and it's amazing when it happens.

People don't always understand the ingredients or the equipment, how things have evolved, how they were in the past. When you went into a store one hundred years ago there would always be one of these dippers by a bucket, and everybody drank out of it. It's all changed. That moment with the little boy with the dipper was a high spot.

I can think of funny faces people have made when they realize they just ate duck eggs. It's old farmers who have a concept, who think duck eggs are bad, and then they realize I just made them eat a custard pie that was made with duck eggs. It's small little things, it's little interactions with people that happen. I find great satisfaction in those little connections. I show them, and they see, and that little light bulb goes off, and I think, "Oh, they understood that little thing." It might pass so quickly, but that is the satisfaction I take from my work.

The other big satisfaction I take from my work is solving the little mysteries. Understanding, like the crock and the sausage. "My grandmother, what is she talking about? Seven and a half gallons of sausage. They couldn't possibly have eaten that that day." I call it "the great forgetting." We have forgotten things. As a society we have forgotten why anybody would fry up seven gallons of sausage one day in January. One hundred years ago, well, of course, she's got to put it into the crocks with lard on top. You've got to have something to eat later.

I like when I can figure out those mysteries. You try it and you fail. Try it and fail. Then you try it this other way. After all those failures you should keep making those observations. You try it with this one new technique. And it works, and you go, "Oh, of course. It had air-pockets in it that way." The little light bulbs and the continual trials. I love the puzzles and figuring things out and persevering. I fail a lot. Lots of mistakes. If you don't make mistakes you don't learn anything. You truly don't. I can tell that. That's the truth. That's me.

RECIPE

Asparagus and Eggs (Adapted from *Buckeye Cookery and Practical Housekeeping*, published in 1880)

SUSAN ODOM, HILLSIDE HOMESTEAD

Asparagus, 2–3 stalks per person

Eggs, 1–2 per person

Butter, about a tablespoon

Salt and Pepper

Fill a saucepot halfway with water and bring it to a boil. Cut the asparagus stalks into bite-size pieces. Cook the asparagus in the water, turning the heat down to medium, add a dash of salt. Cook until desired tenderness by taste. Drain well. Butter a baking dish. Put the asparagus in the baking dish and crack the eggs into it. Try not to break the yolks. There should be almost enough egg white to just cover the asparagus. Season with salt and pepper and dot with butter. Bake at 350 degrees for about 20 minutes, more or less.

Photo courtesy of Emily Umbarger

20

Emily Umbarger

Emily grew up with two strong women as role models, her mom, a successful businesswoman, and her grandmother, a true homemaker growing whatever she could, foraging for whatever they could find, everything made from scratch with Emily helping and learning. As a teenager she followed her grandmother to Mackinac Island, to colonial Fort Michilimackinac, an eighteenth-century fort, where she was volunteering as part of her pursuit of a master gardener certification. Emily delighted in wearing the historic clothing to reenact the 1774 era of the eighteenth-century fort, and in learning knitting, sewing, cooking, gardening, weaving, making beeswax candles, and other traditional skills. After earning her own education degree and teaching in elementary school in several different states, Emily came back to Michigan where she and her husband bought a house and created a farm around it. Chickens, goats, bees, horses, and children: Hearth and Harvest Homestead has them all.

When I spoke with Emily in 2017, she was just beginning what has become a campus-wide long-term project in sustainability for the Interlochen Center for the Arts, where she worked as an academic and college counselor. Since then the project has taken root and flourished beyond the initial greenhouse to include a community garden, several hoop houses, and a hands-on agricultural life-sciences curriculum, and is moving toward a campus-wide waste and composting initiative. Interlochen received a US Department of Education Green Ribbon Schools award, one of only fifty-three such awards in the nation. In 2019, in recognition of her leadership of what is now a strong and committed team at ICA, Emily has been appointed to a new full-time position as sustainability manager. (For a fuller description of ICA's greening, see *Edible Grande Traverse*, no. 57, pp. 28–30.)

Emily Umbarger, b. October 6, 1980
Interview: August 28, 2017
Hearth and Harvest Homestead,
1775 North Betsie River Road, Interlochen

*We were like two kids on Christmas Day when
we got to wear our first colonial outfits.*

I was born and raised in northern Michigan. The town that I grew up in was called Onaway. I was born, I think, two months before the hospital closed. It was the smallest hospital in all of Michigan. A really tiny, small kind of place. I graduated from high school with fifty-two kids. We all knew each other very well.

I had the privilege and honor and deep appreciative respect of getting to grow up next to my grandmother. She lived a quarter mile down the road from us. She had forty acres. We had forty acres. And across from both of our homes was the Pigeon River State Forest area. Hundreds and hundreds of miles of state forests.

My mom basically raised us as a single mother, although my parents were married. My father had some issues with depression and alcoholism. It was tough for her, but she built her own real estate business. She became a broker and a very successful businesswoman. But that meant she was working sometimes eighty hours a week. There's me, sixteen months later my sister, twenty months later my brother. So within the span of three and a half years there were three of us.

My grandparents really stepped in and helped raise us for a lot of our childhood, picking us up from camp, making dinner in the evenings, and I became extremely close to my grandmother and still to this day am very, very close to her. I'm fortunate that she is still alive. I count those blessings every day that she gets to be a great-grandmother to my children and to my brother's and sister's children.

During those formative years I learned from being with her to appreciate home-cooked meals, the time spent together, going mushroom hunting for morel mushrooms, picking strawberries, going out looking for blackberries and blueberries, and making jam and jelly. Anything and everything under the sun that we could forage we then made in grandma's kitchen. We were always cooking and baking cookies and Rice Krispies Treats and pizzas. Everything that Grandma could make. Nothing tasted bad. At Mom's house it was hot dogs and mac and cheese, or spaghetti or pizza. At Grandma's we were having these great meals, and we got to cook, and our hands were involved.

Over the course of years my grandmother decided that she wanted to pursue her master gardener certification. Everything that Grandma did was amazing to me. She was the coolest person. I think she would say the same thing about me but for different reasons. But we just became very close. In the course of doing her master gardener certification she had to do forty hours of volunteer work at some garden of her choosing. I was about fifteen years old, and she said, "This opportunity has come up for us to do some volunteer gardening up in Mackinac Island at the Colonial Michilimackinac," this old 1774 fort. We didn't really know anything about it, but it would be really cool if we got to dress up like those old people and work in the garden. And so she said, "Do you want to come with me?"

"Of course, I want to go with you."

So Grandma and I are going up once a week for the entire summer, and we are gardening colonial style. We were like two kids on Christmas Day when we got to wear our first colonial outfits. How cool is this! That we get to wear these amazing outfits. The woman who took us under her wing—her name was Sally Eustice; she was from Cheboygan—and she was the female lead interpreter there. She would say, "These are your assignments for today. I want you to weed out these gardens, or plant these gardens, or harvest these gardens," and Grandma and I just jumped in with enthusiasm. It was exciting to get to do this.

And then people would start to talk to us, and we would have to learn things. Fortunately, we didn't have to be first-person characters. We could be ourselves and just interpret what we were doing. Sally could see my enthusiasm for doing everything. So one day she'd say: "Well, once you finish your gardening I'll teach you how to cook. Once you finish your gardening in the afternoon I'll teach you how to make soap. Once you finish your gardening I'll teach you how to make bees-wax candles. Or I'll teach you how to dye wool. Or I'll teach you how to spin."

I became enamored with everything that was going through this process. I learned all these traditional crafts, all these traditional skills that have since gone by the wayside because we are a society of consumers.

So at fifteen, a very young, impressionable age, I worked there, and I ended up working there eight summers. I went from being this little kid volunteer to actually having Sally's job when she left the establish-ment. I became the lead interpreter teaching the new young women these skills. They were coming in, and I was teaching them how to garden. It became really special because my grandmother became a part-time employee, and so we got to spend time there gardening and doing things together. Even after she stopped being an employee she was volunteering for several years.

More importantly, it gave me the sense of deep appreciation for where your food is coming from, what your hands are doing, how you can create these things, how you can use these things for your family. In my own home, where my mom was working eighty hours a week—and, you know, she is incredibly busy and wonderfully suc-cessful, and I have all the respect in the world for what she has done—I never learned those homemaking skills. I think there's some stigma today, perhaps negativity, about women learning homemak-ing skills. In my age, and even in my mom's generation, maybe even in my grandma's generation women started moving away from that. You don't teach those things because your mom or grandma didn't know them. If they didn't teach you things like that how else would you learn those skills?

I got a really unusual and very special gift by getting to do that at the Fort. It made it even doubly good that I got to learn with my grand-mother who had already been teaching me these skills as a young child and through my teenage years. I attribute to that experience a lot of my choices to avoid many of the pitfalls that young people often fall into with drugs and alcohol and bad behaviors. I never had any inter-est in that. I just really enjoyed learning and spending time and doing cool things like that.

I went to Michigan State and graduated with a teaching degree, Elementary Ed, with majors in history and in English. I fell in love with history on account of the Fort where I was teaching history, I was living history, and I was sharing history with kids. History can be awesome if it's not just text and dates and dead white guys in a book. History really comes alive, and women have an important role in history, which is traditionally minimized or overlooked. Through working at the Fort I had a deep appreciation for how immensely difficult women's lives were. They had to keep everything going. To give birth without big hospitals. To be in the middle of the woods. To feed their entire family. To provide clothing for their family when they were in the middle of the woods.

I found my way to being a feminist through this process. When I became a teacher those lifelong skills that I had developed and cultivated earlier followed with me into the classroom. I was fortunate to have my first year teaching in Traverse City while I was an intern. It was at North Elementary. One of the units I did was on colonial history, and I brought in costumes for every kid. We spent a whole unit so it was like nine weeks planning and creating a menu and events. The kids got to march like soldiers. They loved it.

You get a handful of memories from your elementary days that you actually remember. Because I'm still in Traverse City I see these kids who are twenty-five or twenty-six now—that tells you how old I am—and they still remember me, and they say, "Do you remember that time when you taught us that lesson?" To me it is the biggest blessing and the biggest gift when they remember that. They remember me. They remember that experience because of what I was able to share with them as their teacher. That's why I always believed that it was my destiny to work in education. I still believe that it is my destiny to work through education and outreach. It's where I'm super passionate.

I spent the next several years teaching public school at the middle school level. I went from Florida to South Carolina because there were jobs there. When you are young and you don't have big bills or a mortgage or kids, or a marriage, you can go where there's work. I went around a lot. I was able to travel to Korea. I did a research grant through Michigan State in Sydney, Australia, and that took me up to Cairns, down to Fiji, and New Zealand. It permitted me to research education in other parts of the world, particularly with teachers of history.

But in the nagging back part of my mind I always had this idea that when I get settled down I want to return to my roots: living on the land, providing for my family. I enjoyed my whirlwind adventure touring around and visiting, and I still loved teaching. I had a relationship in South Carolina and had a beautiful son. The relationship didn't last for lots of reasons which I won't get into, but I ended up saying, "You know, I think at this point the universe is telling me I need to make a big change. I'm going to go work on my PhD. I think I need to go do this right now."

I came back home to Michigan, and I instantly felt like it was the right move for my son and me. I started working in the College of Ed teaching history there [Michigan State in Lansing], and on Match.com I met this awesome guy. The rest is history with that one. I said I'd never get married again. I'd never have more kids, and now I'm married and we have another kid. But I think fate knows what it's doing. You just have to hold on to the ride and trust it's the right thing.

I found this amazing man. He was unhappy with his job at the time, just paying lip service to the man in the job. He and I both said, "Let's do something radical. Let's pack up everything and move to northern Michigan." Neither of us had a job. We had two mortgages in Lansing. He had his mortgage. I had my mortgage. We didn't have a job, and he said, "What are we going to do?"

I said, "I don't know, but I feel like the universe is telling us we need to do this. We've got to make a change. We're both unhappy here. We aren't happy living in a city lifestyle." As much as I loved being at Michigan State and working on my PhD, I realized that I did not want to be a research analyst. I did not want to do tier one research. I didn't want to do peer-reviewed publications. That wasn't my cup of tea. My cup of tea was teaching. Most of my peers in graduate school were all working on the research angle. I felt like there was a disconnect from the roots of being in the classroom. I didn't want to be the supervisor or the interviewer, the researcher. I missed really connecting with the kids.

I tried finding a job in teaching up here. By that point it was really hard to find a job teaching because I was overqualified, and they could hire brand-new teachers at half the rate. That was really disheartening. I kept looking and looking, and I wasn't finding anything. Then I put in an application to the Arts Academy at Interlochen. They had a position for a college counselor, and I said, "Well, I've never been a college counselor before, but I know a lot about college because I've spent a lot of time in college. I know a lot about education and working with parents and working with students and working with faculty. I'm sure I can probably pick this up." They hired me instantly, which was awesome.

The first year was a huge learning curve, but it's been an amazing journey as a college counselor. This is my eighth year now at the Arts Academy. My husband and I, in that transition year, we ended up buying a camper. It's still in our driveway. We lived in the camper for six months. He got a job in Gaylord. I got a job here in Interlochen at the Arts Academy, and near the end of the fifth month I basically told him—we weren't married at that time—"You either get me out of this camper or someone is going to die. I need to be in a house."

So we bought a house. We settled down, and then we decided we wanted to get married. Within a year he had moved to a job in Grawn with Cherry Growers. He is a manager at their GoGo SqueeZ institution. We got married. He got a new job. We bought a house. And it was like, "Okay. All these pieces are ticking into place."

When we found this house we loved the layout. We felt connected to the family. The house was only ten years old when we decided to buy it. The people who had built this house—the woman and her husband had built it with their own two hands—they had built it as a retirement home. She was the secretary of Interlochen's president, Judy Root, and her husband suddenly and tragically passed away.

I think it was really hard for her to be here. There's a lot of driveway, a lot of yard. Every piece was her and her husband's dream. I think when that happened she was ready to go be closer to her children and her grandchildren. And I felt like it was all the stars saying, "This woman wants you to have this house." We fell in love with the property. It was all woods. We've got a huge pasture now, but that was not there when we moved in. In fact nothing was here except for the house. We have really claimed this land. My husband and I together have made a goal to homestead on this property.

I grew up raising swine in 4-H for several years in my early adolescence, and he grew up doing horse 4-H, so we both had some knowledge, not a ton, certainly not as farming or gardening or agricultural industry, nothing like that. But once we moved here our calling became obvious to us. This is how we want to raise a family. These are the values we want our sons to grow up with. We want them to understand that you can eat healthy, you can eat well. You don't have to depend on the store for everything. You should question how it's manufactured and how it's created and where it's farmed and what practices they are using in their farming techniques.

We decided to get chickens so we could gather our own eggs. We have dairy goats. We drink our own raw milk. Anybody who knows me knows that you can't bash raw milk in front of me. But I also know that I can't say "raw milk" in front of most people without them thinking I'm like a leper. I have to sort of censor myself to say, "Well, I drink raw milk," as though it's a secret. We embrace it. We're totally okay with it.

Isn't it amazing that my eleven-year-old, all his life—we've been living here six years now—he did not know that milk and eggs just don't come from your house. He thinks that all kids think that. Which is awesome. And then we got into honeybees, so we do our own honey. We do our own beeswax. We always garden, and I joke sometimes that my pantry and my basement—I think if people were to look at it they would think I'm a prepper—because we have stores of food. But we're not preppers [people preparing for the end of the world]. We're just mindful. We're mindful about what we eat, where it comes from. We take great pride in teaching our children how to do these things. Sitting down and having family meals together is important. I don't knock anybody who pops a box whether Pillsbury or whatever and puts it on the table. The point is that you are doing it together. But there's also some really cool value both nutritionally and spiritually in cooking it yourself, too, and knowing where all those ingredients come from, and how they are treated.

I grew up doing those kinds of things with my grandmother. Back then we never had to think about where our food came from. I don't even know if she did. But I know now that I can't just pretend that I don't know about genetically modified foods or pesticides or fungicides or herbicides that are really harmful. I can't pretend that I don't know that anymore. And I can't pretend for my own self that I don't know—people say: "There isn't enough research to prove it one way or another." That's just great for some people, but for me I can't pretend that I don't know that anymore. And so when I am thinking about how I'm going to feed my kids and my family, those are things that come to my mind. I find immense satisfaction from feeding them things I just picked out of my garden. It's really satisfying to see that come full cycle. To harvest it with my kids. To plant it with my kids.

My husband has taken this under his wing, too. We lease 120 acres just around the corner. We've purchased a lot of farm equipment so now we can do our own hay, and we know the practices that go into harvesting that hay. And feeding our animals which in turn feed us. We've got dairy goats, but we've also got some fiber goats. We've got Kashmir goats, which produce Kashmir fibers. We have Angora goats that produce mohair. I learned how to knit while working at the Fort, and here I am twenty years later still loving knitting. I still spin. I've got two spinning wheels upstairs.

Four years ago, two years after my husband and I had moved into the house, we decided we wanted to start a small business. We came up with the name Hearth and Harvest, the hearth being in your home—what you make in your home—and the harvest what you harvest on your land: Hearth and Harvest Homestead. Neither of us had any knowledge about running a small business. No clue of what goes into running a small business: how to market, or advertise, or keep books. But we thought, this will be a good thing, a life skill that we want to teach our kids. We want them to appreciate that not only can we create for ourselves, but we can create and educate other people as well.

The heart of the educator in me is always at work, even with my own kids. My son says, "You always know when you are an educator's kid. You never stop learning." And I said, "That's right!" But we started using our goats' milk to make goat milk soap and goat milk lotion. We were selling our surplus of honey. We were tapping our maple trees. We are surrounded by hundreds of sugar maples. Every year we tap about 300 sugar maple trees, and we've taught our boys how to make maple syrup. We sold that at the farmers market.

We also sell our surplus of eggs. My husband told me, the first year we had chickens, "You can have two." And I said, "Great. I'll get six." The second year he said, "Okay, maybe we can get six more." And I got twenty. And the third year, he said, "Why don't we just get fifty or so?" I loved how that dynamic shift happened. We had so many eggs that we were selling those at the market, too. Even over at school, at the Arts Academy, I've got my loyal customers. They come for honey and eggs and syrup and lotion and soap. They all know that they will get a really great product humanely treated and hand-made. It's not like sympathy buys. They don't buy it because they want to donate to my farm business. They buy it because it's good for them, and they like what they are receiving.

It's been an amazing adventure building a business. Starting from no knowledge at all, my husband and I. My mom is a business-woman, so this is where her role to shine has really come in. I pick up the phone and, "Mom, what do I do?" "How do I do this?" "What do you think about this?" "Is this a good business decision?" Fortunately, that is her forte. She is an amazing businessperson. While we may not always believe the same things, her advice has always been fantastic. I feel really blessed to be able to bounce ideas off her. "How do I do my books? How do I file a DBA? How do I do these things?" She has been really helpful for us.

In the course of doing a business we also created all of our own recipes. Every bottle of lotion that I sell, I have made twenty batches of experimental stuff until I got to that point where I have a product I am happy with. For every bar of soap, I take great pride in knowing that I picked every ingredient and every amount. It's been fun to teach my kids about that, too, about how there is great pride and respon-sibility for the human condition when you are putting your things out there for other people. That's been an interesting adventure, and a wonderfully rewarding one. My children have grown up as farm mar-ket rats. We are at the farmers market every Sunday. It's our family time together. It's what we do together.

My husband and I are not blessed with a ton of financial support. Everything that we do we've had to work really hard for, and then it basically turns around and goes back into the farm. We've told our sons—and as the college counselor I am always aware of how much college costs—we've told them we can't afford a college savings account, but what we can afford is every time we go to the market, out of all our profit, 10 percent goes into your bank account and 10 percent goes into your brother's bank account. So if we make $700 at the market on Sunday, you get $70 and your brother gets $70. And they are helping. They are pitching in. It's teaching them a little bit about the responsibility part, the financial aspect part, how to be a good businessperson, and what ethics and morals and values you should have as a businessperson. We try to model those for them. So we've really taken this idea of farming and homesteading and agriculture, and then we've combined it in a way that also is about our family and about a family-run business.

And then you fast forward to this year where the project of the greenhouse at Interlochen, the botanical laboratory, has sort of fallen into my lap. All the vice presidents at the school buy my honey. They are all coffee or tea drinkers, and they all buy my honey for one reason or another, and so when one of the VPs of finance, Pat Kessel, said, "We've got this idea for a greenhouse. And we've got this idea for a grant to put in a community garden. We need somebody who knows a little something about agriculture to come help us," I jumped in.

I don't have a background in agriculture other than what my husband and I have learned and cultivated on our own. I don't have a degree in science. What I do have is a lot of knowledge about curriculum and outreach and education. And enough knowledge on the agricultural side from having lived it and breathed it with my own family, and a lot of work in additional skills that help when you are managing a large project that involves nearly every department on campus.

Pat said, "We need someone to help us get this started." They roped me in. That project has been an incredible blessing. It has been so much fun. It has been wonderful to see Interlochen finally recognize the importance of sustainability on agriculture and on educational outreach. Interlochen is blessed with resources including financial resources. And connections. And all their alumni. And all this wealth of people that are well-intentioned. I think they were just waiting for a person—me—to jump on it and grab it and go wild with it and say, "I'm going to do this, and we're going to have all these pieces, and we're going to put them into motion."

The stars aligned the right way. I had enough background knowledge of the school and of farming and sustainability and all these practices that can come together if I needed to do that. We're now at a precipice in that project. We have received some grants and some funding. We've got amazing projects going on. We've got the geothermal floor going in the greenhouse. We've got solar panels that will come and power the geothermal, and then the geothermal will keep our greenhouse going all year long. We've got a hoop house. We will be producing food for our cafeteria twelve months of the year. We'll be able to have kids coming out, doing field trips and learning about sustainable practices, learning about growing your own food, learning about how they can do it at home, not just see it practiced somewhere else. For me it's always about how can we teach you so that you can do it in your own home.

Compost. My husband and I have a trash can, but we have not had or needed trash collection service in over three and a half years. Whatever we can't recycle—and we recycle 90 percent of everything—we feed to the chickens or we compost. Being mindful of our footprint is something that we can teach to kids. Out at Interlochen the last big part of our project will be putting together a composting plant where we will be able to compost 100 percent of all of our food scraps. Pre-consumer and post-consumer. That means vegetable peels before you eat it and then everything that you scrape off your plate afterward.

Our food service, our dining service crew, are outstanding. They are completely on board. They want to weigh how much food we waste, and post it for the faculty and students so they can see every day. Maybe they will do it by week and say: "This week we have wasted one ton." And then people will be aware of how much they are taking and how much they are wasting. This is a big cycle. We will eventually be able to compost 100 percent of our cardboard use, our shredded paper, all of our landscaping materials—whether it's sticks or twigs or leaves—all of that can be composted and turned back into the earth, which then feeds us again. It's a potent and beautiful cycle. I feel blessed to be able to be a part of that.

It's greatly needed. The fact that we don't compost now, the fact that we barely recycle now, the fact that we are just throwing all of our food away, the fact that nobody knows or cares how much food they are wasting and where it goes when they are done, or where their food is coming from . . . those things are important. It's urgent and it has to change. I've taken it on myself to wave a banner in this piece. It's not unrelated to what I am doing with my own family. It's on a much bigger scale because it's a whole institution, but that makes it a really exciting project to be a part of. I certainly can't claim it as mine, although I think my enthusiasm resonates to anyone because I'm so passionate about it. I want everyone else to be as passionate about it.

One of the exciting projects that we are going to be doing is creating our own Interlochen tea blend that will be 100 percent student-created, student-harvested. They will make their own solar dehydrators to dehydrate the chamomile, and the lavenders, and the bergamot. They will make their own tea blend, and then we will put those in our cafeteria and in our scholar shop. The students will create the artwork and the labels. To me, again, it all comes back to educational outreach and teaching people how to do these things.

I don't think you have to be an expert to teach. I think that we all can learn from experts. There's lots to learn from experts. Some of my best mentors are experts. But I also believe that we can all be teachers and mentors to each other and build a community of learners about all this process.

I don't feel that at any point I have been really hindered by being a woman. Fortunately, I have a husband who is the biggest feminist I know. I wish all women had a feminist husband, because we all should be feminists. We all should believe in equal rights for women. We should all believe that women must be treated fairly and with respect. I think that's a big gift for my sons, too, that they grow up seeing another strong male treating women fairly, equitably, respectfully. I think that role model is crucial.

Within our own home we have these gender roles, only because we like it. I tell our kids that I do most of the cooking—not because I'm a woman—but because I love cooking. I have my son in the kitchen helping me all the time. He's canning and cooking. My stove has all cast-iron pots and pans. He's going to grow up knowing how to cook in cast-iron pans. His kids one day will know about grandma's biscuits and gravy out of the cast-iron pan.

I love knitting, and I love sewing. I'm a quilter and a sewer and a spinner. I love those things. But I don't do these things because I'm a woman. I do them because I love them. My husband loves working on tractors. He loves plowing the field. And I love that he does that because I don't care about those things. What it does do is bring us together in a harmonious relationship where we support each other. I could see, especially running a business, where it could be difficult being a woman in a business role. I've seen it with my own mom running her real estate business. Real estate is a lot of men, especially at the broker level. I have the privilege of having strong females in my life who have paved the way for me, my grandmother and my own mother. I hope to be that strong female for my sons and for my nieces as well.

The USDA will offer loans for women, especially if you are a woman in agriculture and you are a new female in agriculture. There are loans specifically for women. And so we actually decided to make our business in my name. I am the sole proprietor. Like I said, fortunately my husband is a feminist. He didn't think twice. It's in my name. It's our business, but for our family this made the most sense. It opened up more opportunities, and that's great because it's going to benefit all of us.

There are specific loans for young people in agriculture, and there are also some loans for veterans in agriculture. My husband is a veteran. I guess we are covered on all sides. He was really into it. "You can be the sole proprietor. Go for it!" But it is a joint effort. When we go to do chores, it's not me doing chores by myself. That's our family time. We do it together. Not only does it go more quickly and more efficiently because we are dividing the labor, but we are teaching our kids that when you do things together everyone is responsible for a part. And when someone doesn't do their part, the whole team suffers. So it's a lot about teamwork. It's a lot about building that family value.

If I had to do all of this by myself it would look very different because there's only so much of you to go around. Not to mention we are also parents. We've got two kids. And we've got animals. And we have human beings. My son is in Boy Scouts, and my husband is his Boy Scout leader. It's not like we don't do anything other than the farm. People say: "Well, with the farm, you probably don't have time for anything else." No, actually, we're really crazy, but I keep a good calendar. We prioritize what needs to be done. We think about our finances and all those pieces. What has to be done? What is on fire? What is the big project? What can wait? We plan everything out really carefully. We do it together as a family. We talk together all the time.

Right now there's kind of a big strain in that because my husband recently was moved to the third shift. That's really hard when you have a solid family unit and the emphasis of your life is your family unit, and then we're just, "Where's Dad?" He leaves for work at eight o'clock in the evening, and then he works all night and comes home at 6:00 a.m. It's been a huge adjustment. He really wants to quit working out there and do farming full time. He is damn good at it. I have never seen a more hardworking man.

We are making do. It has been five months now. It's been tough. I'm only volunteering at the greenhouse while working as a college counselor. Interlochen's budget has already been set for this school year, and they don't yet have money for that position. We're hoping it will happen in October. I know that it's up for discussion as to whether they will open that up as a full-time position. Maybe a director, or something along those lines. I hope they do, because I certainly want to do that. Which is not to say that I don't love being a college counselor, because I do. I love what I do. It's win-win because I love it both ways. But I think that when anyone talks to me they know that my heart is really out here working with outreach and curriculum and kids and sustainability. That's my thing. I love all those pieces put together.

So for right now I'm undercover working at the greenhouse. I'm doing all of my projects, managing all of the projects for the greenhouse: the solar panels installed; the geothermal installed; the forest going in; the bathroom going in; the fence up together; working with my contractors while working full time as a college counselor, while going to the farmers market on Sunday, while raising my kids and putting up a farm, while my husband is working third shift.

It's not yet an official position. I'm doing it unpaid, as well as I can. We have plants growing. Seven days a week they have to be watered. Seven days a week they have to be taken care of. I go on the weekend. I take my boys with me. We go out at six thirty or seven in the morning and leave my husband still sleeping. We have some quiet time together.

We are used to picking beans and watering the garden. I choose to look at it not as an obligation but as something that I get to do with my kids. This is great time that I can spend with my boys. When you say, "How do you do it all?" it would be very easy to be bogged down in the number of things, if that's what you focus on. What I focus on is how many cool ways can I spend time with my kids today instead of: "How many things do I have to get done today?" Do it that way, and I would get really anxious. I'm not a very nice person to be around when I'm anxious. I don't hide that well. I have to put myself in the mind-set of: "What are the cool things that I can do with my kids? What are the cool things that I can do with my husband? That we can do as a family? And how is that going to enrich our life?" Instead of: "I must do X, Y, and Z." It's a 100 percent mental thing.

The heart of it all is: "How can I do this with my kids?" and fortunately they really like it. It's not like: "Oh, we have to go do this with Mom." It's something we all get excited to do together. There are always little learning things like: "Okay, when we go to the garden today, let's see how many bugs we can find on the plants. Let's see if we can find five different bugs. Or let's see if we can find three different kinds of caterpillars." I'm a huge butterfly nut so we're always looking for caterpillars.

How can we make this interesting and exciting instead of just picking weeds? It's a lot of mind over matter, and it's what you make of it. It could bog you down very easily. You could easily feel sorry for yourself. "Oh, so much work to do." I know a lot of people like that, and I don't really like them. I don't like to be around them. I don't like to talk to them. I don't like the negative. I hope to be a role model for my kids. You can have a busy life and do whatever you like. You have to be organized. You have to have a good attitude. And you have to work hard. You do those three things and you'll be okay.

Grandma's Chicken Spaghetti

EMILY UMBARGER, HEARTH AND HARVEST HOMESTEAD

Serves 4–6

3 chicken breasts, cubed, semicooked (do not overcook)

1 pound spaghetti noodles, cooked al dente

2½ cups of cheddar cheese

1 diced onion, sautéed

3 carrots, sautéed

1 cup of frozen peas

1 can of cream of mushroom soup

1 cup of sour cream

½ cup of milk

1 cup of chicken stock

1 tsp. seasoning salt

1 tsp. pepper

1 tsp. paprika

½ cup chopped parsley

Preheat oven to 350 degrees F. Mix together all ingredients in a large bowl and pour into casserole pan. Reserve ½ cup of cheese for the top. Sprinkle top with remaining cheese, paprika, and parsley. Bake until golden brown and bubbly, about 30 to 40 minutes. Can be frozen for an easy casserole dish later.

Acknowledgments

A uthors and recipients of Tony awards and Oscars have long lists of people to thank. *E pluribus unum*; it takes a village, and all the other aphorisms hold true. Writing is a solitary activity, but publishing a book takes a community.

My first debt is to the twenty amazing women in food and farming in this region of Michigan that I love so very much. Many of them did not know me before I appeared at their door wanting to interview them, but they trusted me enough to share with me the stories of their lives that I have now set out in this book.

My mother first brought me to this region when I was perhaps three or four years old. If she were still alive she would be well over 100 but still loving her corner of Michigan above any place else she ever lived. I am so very grateful to her for enriching my life by bringing me here. This book brings our history full circle.

Two librarians at the Woodmere branch of the Traverse Area District Library (TADL) encouraged me from the very start: Brice Bush (now in Lansing) and Amy Barritt (now head of the Kingsley branch). They welcomed the oral history project and agreed to give the recordings and transcripts safe harbor at TADL. More recently, Polly O'Shea provided essential assistance with some technical challenges. My thanks and admiration for these librarians and, indeed, for all librarians with their dedication to preserving our history and our histories.

I owe a huge debt to another librarian and archivist, Janet Munch, my coeditor in *Bronx Faces and Voices*, our book of oral histories from the Bronx. Whenever I turned to Janet for advice in this new project she had wisdom and experience to contribute.

Wayne State University Press saw promise in this book. I am grateful to the members of the team led by editor-in-chief Annie Martin, all of whom have worked with me to make the book the best that it could be. I am especially grateful to the meticulous copyeditor, Dawn Hall, who found errors I had overlooked and was a font of knowledge.

Anne-Marie Ooman, the outstanding Michigan author, encouraged me and brought this project to the attention of WSUP. I know only too well how excessive is the number of unsolicited manuscripts that land at the door of publishers. Thank you, Anne-Marie, for helping me to open that door.

The women in my Westchester, New York, book club encouraged me throughout the several years when I was conducting the interviews and drafting my introduction. They believed in the project. They believe in me. Several of them read individual stories. Many of them read and helped edit my introduction. They know who they are. I love them all and am grateful for their friendship and their love of books.

Other generous friends who read closely and made suggestions that improved my introduction include Marianne Evett, Paul Hohenberg, Joan Lipsitz, Virginia Calkins, Ann Ives, Kathy and Gene Garthe, and always and ever, Anne Perryman, my longtime friend and colleague who has read every word I've ever written in the past thirty years and always supported my efforts with her considerable skills as a journalist.

Last in this list but foremost in fact, I thank my daughter, Madeleine Hill Vedel. This book would not have been possible without her introduction to the food world and to some of her friends both in France and in this region of Michigan who then led me to other friends. Her knowledge, her enthusiasm, her gift for friendship were key elements in this entire project. Writer, photographer, photo historian, chef, *fromagère*, *chocolatière*, and so much more, her knowledge and her stunning portraits of most of the women in this book and her beautifully crafted image for the cover of this book have enhanced it enormously. *Grand merci*, Madeleine.

Index

About the Author

Born in Baltimore and a New Yorker since 1969, Emita Brady Hill has spent her summers in Traverse City since her childhood. Her career as a scholar of the French Enlightenment took her to France where she discovered French and North African cuisines, an interest that led to her study of the many aspects of food and farming in Michigan that are the subject of this book. A professor and administrator at Lehman College in the Bronx for twenty years, she then served as chancellor of Indiana University Kokomo and subsequently was a trustee for two international universities, AUCA in Bishkek, Kyrgyzstan, and SEEU in Tetovo, Macedonia. She published extensively in her academic field, but then turned to oral history. *Bronx Faces and Voices,* published in 2014, presents the stories of sixteen men and women who survived the years of arson and abandonment in the Bronx and helped to sustain and rebuild their borough and their community. She earned her doctorate in Romance Languages and Literatures from Harvard University, and in 2019 she was awarded an honorary doctorate in humane letters by Indiana University.

CPSIA information can be obtained
at www.ICGtesting.com
Printed in the USA
BVHW030714200420
577894BV00003B/10